# Organizational Change in Action

# Organizational Change in Action

Louise Boulter,
Thomas Calvard
and Goudarz Azar

BLOOMSBURY ACADEMIC
LONDON • NEW YORK • OXFORD • NEW DELHI • SYDNEY

BLOOMSBURY ACADEMIC

Bloomsbury Publishing Plc, 50 Bedford Square, London, WC1B 3DP, UK
Bloomsbury Publishing Inc, 1359 Broadway, New York, NY 10018, USA
Bloomsbury Publishing Ireland, 29 Earlsfort Terrace, Dublin 2, D02 AY28, Ireland

BLOOMSBURY, BLOOMSBURY ACADEMIC and the Diana logo are trademarks of Bloomsbury Publishing Plc

First published in Great Britain 2026

Copyright © Louise Boulter, Thomas Calvard and Goudarz Azar and contributors, 2026

Louise Boulter, Thomas Calvard and Goudarz Azar and contributors have asserted their right under the Copyright, Designs and Patents Act, 1988, to be identified as Authors of this work.

For legal purposes the Acknowledgements on p. xv constitute an extension of this copyright page.

Cover design: Eleanor Rose
Cover image © Andriy Onufriyenko / Getty Images

All rights reserved. No part of this publication may be: i) reproduced or transmitted in any form, electronic or mechanical, including photocopying, recording or by means of any information storage or retrieval system without prior permission in writing from the publishers; or ii) used or reproduced in any way for the training, development or operation of artificial intelligence (AI) technologies, including generative AI technologies. The rights holders expressly reserve this publication from the text and data mining exception as per Article 4(3) of the Digital Single Market Directive (EU) 2019/790.

Bloomsbury Publishing Plc does not have any control over, or responsibility for, any third-party websites referred to or in this book. All internet addresses given in this book were correct at the time of going to press. The author and publisher regret any inconvenience caused if addresses have changed or sites have ceased to exist, but can accept no responsibility for any such changes.

A catalogue record for this book is available from the British Library.

A catalog record for this book is available from the Library of Congress.

| ISBN: | HB: | 978-1-3503-3596-7 |
|---|---|---|
| | PB: | 978-1-3503-3514-1 |
| | ePDF: | 978-1-3503-3598-1 |
| | eBook: | 978-1-3503-3597-4 |

Typeset by Integra Software Services Pvt. Ltd.
Printed and bound in Great Britain by Bell and Bain Ltd, Glasgow

For product safety related questions contact productsafety@bloomsbury.com.

To find out more about our authors and books visit www.bloomsbury.com and sign up for our newsletters.

The authors are dedicating this book to the students, learners and colleagues that have lifted them to higher places than would otherwise be the case. We thank you for your enthusiasm and dedication. We can only respond to this by saying it is a privilege to be part of the transformative learning journey.

# Contents

List of Figures — viii
List of Tables — x
List of Authors — xi
List of Contributors — xii
Preface — xiii
Acknowledgements — xv
Tour of the Book — xvi

**1** Your Learning Journey: Key Concepts, the Nature of Change and Units of Analysis — 1

**2** Foundations for Incremental and Substantive Change Interventions — 25

**3** The Nature of Change in Contemporary Organizations: Strategy and Culture — 55

**4** The Human Aspects of Change — 105

**5** Intercultural Management and Effective Change — 149

**6** Understanding Power and Politics in Organizational Change and Effectively Managing Resistance — 179

**7** The Role of Change Leadership — 211

**8** The Role of Human Resource Management: Good Practices for Effective Organizational Change — 247

**9** Doing Change Ethically — 273

Index — 292

# Figures

| | | |
|---|---|---|
| Figure 1.1 | Non-exhaustive list of unfolding scenarios in the change process | 3 |
| Figure 1.2 | Lewin's planned three-step approach to organizational change | 10 |
| Figure 1.3 | A linear step-by-step process of change | 16 |
| Figure 1.4 | An iterative approach to the process of change | 16 |
| Figure 1.5 | Change at different levels of analysis | 18 |
| Figure 2.1 | Fundamental principles of TQM | 29 |
| Figure 2.2 | Balanced scorecard approach to a holistic approach to measuring | 33 |
| Figure 2.3 | Understanding process activity | 34 |
| Figure 2.4 | Block diagram for an overview of a process | 38 |
| Figure 2.5 | Process deployment flowchart | 39 |
| Figure 2.6 | Principles of lean management | 42 |
| Figure 2.7 | An organizational excellence framework: EFQM model | 48 |
| Figure 2.8 | Mean difference of percentage change in various key accounting measures one year after having won an award | 48 |
| Figure 2.9 | Mean difference of percentage change in various key accounting measures five years after having won an award | 49 |
| Figure 2.10 | Differences in share price performance between an award-winning company and comparison companies | 49 |
| Figure 2.11 | Fundamental concepts underlying excellence | 50 |
| Figure 2.12 | RADAR – diagnostic tool | 52 |
| Figure 3.1 | The 7-S framework | 61 |
| Figure 3.2 | Edgar Schein's organization culture model | 86 |
| Figure 3.3 | Competing values framework | 88 |
| Figure 3.4 | Cultural web | 90 |
| Figure 3.5 | Culture design canvas | 91 |
| Figure 4.1 | McKinsey influence model and combined conditions for personal change | 109 |
| Figure 4.2 | Kurt Lewin's concept of change as a life space | 110 |
| Figure 4.3 | Classic change curve | 111 |

| Figure 4.4 | COM-B system diagram for understanding behaviour and behaviour change | 121 |
| Figure 4.5 | Stages of group and team development | 126 |
| Figure 5.1 | Hofstede's cultural dimensions | 153 |
| Figure 5.2 | A systems model of tightness–looseness | 159 |
| Figure 5.3 | Lewis's model of cultural categories of emotional expression | 161 |
| Figure 5.4 | Creating intercultural intelligence | 164 |
| Figure 6.1 | Sources of power | 187 |
| Figure 6.2 | Affective Events Theory | 197 |
| Figure 6.3 | The Kübler-Ross Change Curve | 200 |
| Figure 6.4 | Bridges' Transition Model | 202 |
| Figure 6.5 | Methods for Managing Resistance | 206 |
| Figure 8.1 | Ulrich's roles of HR in business partnership | 249 |
| Figure 8.2 | The change communication wheel | 265 |

# Tables

| | | |
|---|---|---|
| Table 3.1 | Ambidextrous Organization Design | 68 |
| Table 4.1 | Four General Strategies for Addressing Human Aspects of Change | 108 |
| Table 4.2 | Evaluating Change and Coping Strategies | 117 |
| Table 7.1 | Leading Versus Managing Change | 216 |
| Table 7.2 | Principles of Leading Transformational Change | 224 |
| Table 7.3 | Forms of Bad Leadership | 234 |
| Table 8.1 | Categories of Change and HR's Role | 255 |

# Authors

**Louise Boulter** is Senior Lecturer at Lincoln Bishop University where is she is operational lead for the MBA and MSc programmes in Business. Louise has a breadth of experience across several universities with different student populations and learning environments. This includes the University of Leicester, where her post was funded by Rolls-Royce plc, Salford and Nottingham Trent. She has taught across undergraduate and postgraduate programmes on change over many years. She has been involved in various change programmes within organisations emphasizing effective change through strategy, people and processes. More recently, she holds an honorary position at Middlesex University Business School where formerly she was Programme Leader for the largest undergraduate programme across the university.

**Thomas Calvard** is Professor of Work and Organisation at the University of Edinburgh Business School. He has taught undergraduate and postgraduate courses on organizational change for over a decade and his research focuses on how organizations, groups and individuals make sense of shifting perspectives, limits and boundaries, with an emphasis on identity, diversity, technology, change and ethics.

**Goudarz Azar** is Professor of Strategy and International Business at Middlesex University London, where he is Head of Department of Strategy, Leadership, and Operations in the Business School. Goudarz has extensive experience in higher education, having worked at universities in Sweden and the UK. His research on organizational innovation is a key reference in the fields of International Business and Strategic Management.

# Contributors

**Jane Gilbert** is a Consultant Clinical Psychologist. The early part of Jane's career was spent as a Clinical Psychologist within Adult Mental Health Services in the UK. Subsequently she has worked as an international consultant specializing in the design and delivery of workshops/training on psychological self care, mental health issues in cross cultural contexts, counselling skills for peer support staff, and as a Staff Welfare Officer for UNHCR.

**Andrew Mayo** worked for nearly thirty years in the international corporate sector, before starting his own HR consultancy, working on change with both public and private clients, and joining academia as Professor of Human Management Capital. His special interests embraced organizational development and HR Analytics.

**Andrea Werner** is Associate Professor of Business Ethics at Middlesex University London. Prior to joining Middlesex University, she worked as a Researcher for the Institute of Business Ethics in London. Her research interests include ethics and social responsibility in small businesses, the real Living Wage, Sustainable Fashion entrepreneurship, and the link between ethics and accountability in business organizations.

# Preface

In writing this book, the authors of *Organizational Change in Action* have experienced the all-too-familiar ups and downs of research and writing. Yet the glue that has held us together, to keep writing, revising and editing this book is a shared passion of making organizational change an important subject: accessible to learners in a theoretical and applied sense, be they undergraduates, postgraduates, executive practitioners or learners. Moreover, we are propelled by a responsibility to shape learners as current and future managers and leaders to 'do' change in an empathetic, ethical and sustainable way. Not only do we focus on the scaffolding that organizations need to put in place for any type of change to be effective, we also focus on the ethical and emotional side of substantive organizational change, with a view that the greatest asset of any organization is the people.

The role of human agency in change is emphasized in several chapters from an ethical, psychological and cross-cultural perspective. The rationale behind this is that substantive change is never a linear step-by-step process: juxtaposed, the trajectory of change can be taken in a wholly different direction from that originally envisaged by a senior management team. As part of this we take the perspective that resistance to change can be perceived through a different lens so as to embrace it for optimal inclusive outcomes of significant change. We also consider how small 'p' politics, whilst having a potentially toxic side, can also be used positively to influence, guide and protect others in the change journey. We pay careful attention to the emotional journey organizational members experience as they go through cognitive processes by way of coming to terms with change. An aim is to challenge mental models that might be held by leaders to develop both emotional intelligence and affective empathy for managing change more effectively.

The authors of this book teach across a diverse set of learners and programmes. Like many colleagues, we have experienced a last minute request to teach a module, typically followed by the scramble for a meaningful core text! We very much hope that this book, accompanied by the Workout Manual, will take away some of the pain in that process. This book is not a weighty academic tome. Rather, our objective is to provide insight and make a complex, multi-layered phenomenon accessible, interesting, and above all, alive and meaningful. The theoretical paradigms throughout are illustrated with case studies and activities relevant to learners' experience, alongside a consultant in the chair feature and competency-based interview questions (CBIQ) for facilitating employability. There is a proposed slide set on the subject matter of each chapter alongside a rich set of seminar material that colleagues may wish to utilize.

A running fictitious case study features in all chapters. The case study follows Cup of Kindness, which, due to the unfortunate acronym, latterly became CUP! This case study emerged from the first author's experience of having their world rotate and change significantly from the known to the unknown. This experience is not far removed from Kubler-Ross's Change Curve. During this time, to alleviate the pain, a diary was kept to record 'small cups of kindness' experienced from colleagues, learners and people who are unknown. From the train inspector who waved me through when a credit card was forgotten, to a learner who messaged to say they were enjoying the teaching sessions, and to a patient commissioning editor whom immediately understood the value of a compact book on organizational change in action. Thanks to all of you for lifting me to a better place, until such point that the better place became my norm.

CUP concerns a fictional organization woven into each chapter to illustrate and operationalize key theoretical concepts in a coherent, joined-up way, supported by case study questions. CUP is a multi-national company founded in 1965 by two coffee enthusiasts who discovered a unique coffee bean when their campervan broke down in Brazil during a 'gap year'. It was during this time that the couple also experienced the kindness of local people who had very little but who willingly shared their resources. The entrepreneurial couple decided to name their coffee organization Cup of Kindness (CUP), and the firm has recently been acquired in a $600m takeover by a food and beverage conglomerate. Learners are presented with a scenario in each chapter that gives them the opportunity to be 'consultant in the chair', by way of providing the senior management team with good practice advice on organizational change. Learners' ability to offer advice is reinforced by the knowledge they acquire from learning and applying theory through lectures and seminar activities.

Finally, the authors acknowledge that this book is not perfect! Yet, it provides a framework that is supported by robust pedagogical practice to underpin learners' learning. Please by all means get in touch with the authors with your comments, feedback and observations, which we welcome!

Louise Boulter
Thomas Calvard
Goudarz Azar

October 2024

# Acknowledgements

The authors would like to express their appreciation to the organizations and individuals that have helped them in facilitating case studies and in giving permissions to use material. This includes the European Foundation for Quality Management (EFQM) for granting permission to include Figure 2.7, the EFQM Model; Richard D. Lewis, Richard Lewis Communications for the Lewis Cultural Categories Model of Emotions (www.crossculture.com) for permission to include Figure 5.3; and Professor Russell Salvador Cropanzano for granting permission to use Figure 6.2, the Affective Events Theory (AET) Model. We thank you all.

# Tour of the Book

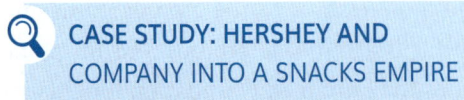

*Case studies* contextualize topics by providing real-life examples of their implementation.

*Media Link* icons indicate that you need to access material from the companion website: bloomsbury.pub/organizational-change-in-action

**ACTIVITY 7.5**

1. Imagine yourself as a leader in the workplace,

*Activities* encourage reflection and engagement to stimulate greater comprehension.

*Consultancy in the Chair* exercises provide valuable opportunities to apply your knowledge to real-world organizational challenges which are essential for developing your professional skills.

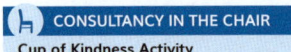

**CONSULTANCY IN THE CHAIR**
Cup of Kindness Activity
The M&A has taken its toll on many individuals within been increased absences due to illness and a negative

 **Competency-based Interview Question**

1. Can you outline an example of organizational changed too slowly, which has proved detrimental

Employability skills support is facilitated through *Competency-based Interview Questions*, which provide an opportunity to fine-tune your employability skills with scenarios that you may well have to consider during interviews.

# Your Learning Journey

## Key Concepts, the Nature of Change and Units of Analysis

> **Learning Outcomes**
>
> At the end of this chapter you will be able to:
>
> 1. Better understand key terminology that is commonly used to explain the nature of organizational change.
> 2. Appreciate the complexities and ambiguities surrounding change as a theoretical subject and its practice within organizations.
> 3. Critically evaluate different types of change.
> 4. Understand the three different levels of analysis for evaluating how change impacts organizations and key stakeholders.
> 5. Appreciate how change may impact you as an individual.

## Introduction

Your learning journey for organizational change in action starts here. In this introductory chapter we unpack organizational change in action by way of explaining different terminology, classifications, taxonomies and units of analysis that are used throughout this book. The general aim therefore is to help you construct foundational knowledge upon which the subsequent chapters are built. This foundational knowledge will enable you to better comprehend change as a theoretical subject *and*, importantly, both from a practical *and* applied perspective, appreciate that change is an aspect of organizational life that can be incredibly messy and complex, and which has implications for all stakeholders.

To that end, foundational theoretical paradigms are set out, critically evaluated, discussed and illustrated by way of case studies and applied activities. These are an important medium used throughout this book to help you appreciate some of the subtleties, complexities and ambiguities that organizations experience in the effective and ineffective management of organizational change.

In this first chapter we also set out the three distinct, yet interconnected, 'units' or 'levels' of analysis that are essential to your learning throughout this book. These are change at the following levels of analysis:

→ Organizational or macro

→ Group or meso

→ Individual or micro.

Examining and comprehending change at these three levels will provide insight into the various ways in which change has important implications for all organizational members and stakeholders. Appreciating change at these different levels or 'units' of analysis will also enable you to reflect on how change impacts you as an individual, how effective you are in managing change and how to continuously improve in this respect throughout your professional and personal life. Whilst some may not necessarily relish the prospect and implications that significant change brings, we hope that by the end of the book you will be better equipped to adjust the lens through which you view change as a way to adapt, survive and take up opportunities that you would otherwise be unable to. Likewise, if you are one of those individuals who sees change as an opportunity rather than a challenge, then we hope that you are better able to adjust the lens through which you view those who don't, understanding their perspective, and by doing so, better lead and manage change.

## A Starting Point: Understanding the Nature of Change

The words 'transform' and 'transformative' are commonly used to describe change. These words imply that change is significant and will impact all organizational stakeholders. An implication is that this type of change needs to be managed effectively to be successful. This is a theme that will feature throughout this book. However, no matter what terminology is used, central to the concept of change is *moving or shifting from one position to another*. Whilst this sounds reasonably straightforward, the reality is that for any proposed change to be effective and successful, *foresight* is required by those who initiate, manage and drive it. This is especially the case when the nature of the proposed change is transformative, in other words, involves the type of organizational change that is significant and therefore strategic, something that we will consider in some depth in Chapter 3.

The word *foresight* here relates to the idea of being conscious of the various permutations and scenarios that may occur as change unfolds. In other words, what may happen to the organization and how its various stakeholders may respond or react throughout the change process. Change is not straightforward; it does not always allow for the following of a standardized step-by-step linear process. The reality is that many organizations experience change as iterative, moving backwards and forwards and going off track as it oscillates, contracts and expands, often taking the organization and its stakeholders in totally different directions from those initially proposed and envisaged at the start of the change process. When we use the word *'foresight'* therefore, we're highlighting the importance of the senior management team being conscious of the factors that may unfold, which they should be conscious of before they propose any significant change. Some of these scenarios are outlined in the following, non-exhaustive list in Figure 1.1.

- The intended outcomes from change might not be met and revisions may be required, or outcomes might be met in a different and wholly unexpected way.
- Some organizational members may 'hijack' the change initiative and attempt successfully or unsuccessfully to take it in a wholly different direction.
- Organizational culture is so strong in maintaining the status quo, in other words, the way in which 'we do things around here', that shifting from one position to another is impossible.
- There is little support for what is being proposed by organizational members and other stakeholders, due to the ineffective way in which the change is being managed, including lack of transparency and poor communication.
- Appointment of new senior management, who have their own change agenda, as opposed to that proposed by a predecessor.
- The variables in the macro environment that have triggered the change initiative are so fluid that what was originally proposed is no longer suitable.

**Figure 1.1** Non-exhaustive list of unfolding scenarios in the change process.

Whatever the reason, prescience is required, as is the ability to adapt and manage any or indeed all of the above unfolding scenarios, and, moreover, to manage them effectively. A useful way of facilitating prescience and providing a helicopter overview of some of the potential scenarios that may arise is to frame change using the *Content-Context-Process* model of change which loosely translates as the *What? Why?* and *How?* of change. The *Content-Context-Process* model originates from the early work of Pettigrew and Whipp (1991). We use a loose interpretation of the Content-Context-Process model in this first chapter, with some additions by way of creating a contemporary framework that will aid your understanding and introduce you to both the 'hard' (structural) and 'soft' (people and cultural) elements of organizational change. Some of the key elements that make up the Content-Context-Process of change follow.

## The What of Change: Content, Nature and Types of Change

### First-order change

The content of change is focused on the *what* of change. By this we mean the subject matter of organizational change. Is this, for example, a change in a process, strategy, policy, product, service or practice? Identifying the subject matter of *what* is to be changed makes us consider the nature of the change that is being proposed and its characteristics. One of the ways in which we can understand the nature of change is by categorizing change as being either first-order or second-order change. First-order change is typically ongoing and continuous. It develops gradually over time and is a constant throughout an organization's lifecycle and, likewise, our own individual lifecycles. For organizations, this type of change happens on a daily basis and in most cases is initiated by employees at the 'coal face'. In other words, those organizational members that interface directly with everyday workplace processes, practices and customers. These organizational members experience, and are on the receiving end of, day-to-day organizational routines and practices. They are thus well-placed for initiating first-order change as not only do they have direct experience of workplace processes, they also typically interface with external customers, who, similarly to employees, are on the receiving end of an organization's processes, routines and practices.

This means that employees are an important source of valuable information, such as which aspects of the process add value to the customer experience, and which are inefficient and do little more than cost the organization in terms of taking up scarce resource and delaying the customer from getting what they want, when they want it. Inefficient and ineffective organizational workplace processes and practices are an important barometer of customer satisfaction, and employees who interact with customers and these processes will have a good understanding of small changes that can be made in order to continuously improve. We address the fundamentals for effective change in more detail throughout Chapter 2.

An example of a first-order change for a student would be to have a core text that is associated with each of their modules or units of study linked to their online learning material and thus easily accessible throughout the duration of the various subjects that make up their degree. The relevant core text would then just be one click away during lectures and seminars. In an organizational context, a first-order change might involve the steps in a customer complaint process being rationalized, with responsibility for resolution being given to one employee, facilitating a joined-up approach that reduced the time it takes for a complaint to be resolved. In this way incremental adjustments are constantly evolving and happening throughout the lifespan of an organization. These small, incremental changes occur within existing organizational structures and systems. Incremental change does not alter the fundamental characteristics of an organization, such as, for example, its culture, values, personality or the lens through which it views the world. First-order change is part of an organization's continuous improvement activities and, as we have outlined, is incremental and small in nature.

### ACTIVITY 1.1

1. With regard to first-order change (small, incremental), think of an example of small changes you have made in your day-to-day life activities, your routines and your interpersonal relationships. Write these down, reflect on them and outline how these minor changes have positively impacted the quality of your life.

2. With regard to first-order change (small, incremental), think of an example of an organization with which you are familiar (part-time job, work placement, the university that you are attending) where minor changes have been made to a process or any other aspect of an organization's day-to-day routine, behaviours and practices. Consider how these changes have positively impacted the quality of your life and/or that of a customer.

## Value of First-Order Change

Whilst first-order change is associated with incremental, continuous improvements, the collective contribution that first-order change makes towards keeping key stakeholders (such as employees and customers) satisfied should never be underestimated nor undervalued. This is illustrated in the case of Barrowford Primary School situated in Lancashire, in the UK, where a first-order small change was made to school dinners. Barrowford replaced meat with vegetarian options three days a week. This change was incremental – small steps were taken within the existing system and, according to the head teacher, this change was '… not even noticed'. This small change ended up positively contributing to the school's core sustainability values, by positively impacting society and reducing the school's carbon footprint, and thus contributing to a sustainable future for all. For a summary of this incremental change listen to the head teacher talking about this first-order change.

### ACTIVITY 1.2

1. Reflecting on the Barrowford School case study, what is the first-order change that took place?
2. Outline the key characteristics of this first-order change.
3. How did this small change impact changes in behaviour and how does it influence the children's learning?
4. In view of the learning from this case study, how important do you think first-order change is? Please explain your answer.

## Second-Order Change

The opposite of first-order change is second-order change, otherwise known as strategic change. This type of change is incredibly challenging for all organizational members as it is transformational, radical, far-reaching and, above all, disruptive. Strategic change involves a paradigmatic shift in an organization's worldview, meaning its views of the world and how it wishes to be viewed by others. Core elements of an organization's worldview include its values and norms, which are unwritten codes of conduct and strong influencers of organizational members' behaviour with which they readily identify. Organizational values and norms constitute the glue that keeps organizational members on the same page, working towards attaining goals and making a meaningful contribution towards the organization's future ambitions. Juxtaposed to this is strategic change, which goes right to the foundations of an organization, making it pivot significantly away from its historic structure, culture, systems, routines and processes. With strategic change there is a fundamental departure from the way in which an organization goes about its business, and there is no part or member of an organization, both internal and external, that it does not impact. The organization tries to radically transform the way in which it operates and either the behaviour, assumptions or perceptions of organizational members dramatically shift. Alternatively, they may decide not to adapt to the new way of doing things and consider leaving the organization. We will revisit second-order change in Chapter 3 when we address the nature of the external environment in which contemporary organizations operate.

### ACTIVITY 1.3

1. Think about and reflect upon a significant second-order change in your personal life that has been challenging.
   - What was it?
   - How did it make you feel?
   - How did you react to this change?
   - How did you manage this change in your life?
   - How well do you think you managed this significant change in your life?
2. On reflection, we can all improve how we manage significant change in our lives. How would you manage this change more effectively in hindsight?

When you have read through all of the chapters that make up this book, please revisit your response to this activity and ask yourself again: how would you manage this change more effectively in hindsight, now knowing what you know about change?

## Transition

So far in this chapter we have defined change by reference to two broad categories. There is, however, another significant aspect of organizational change that this book pays much attention to. This is transition. Whilst transition is part of any organization's second-order change, it is subtly different. It is critical to understand what transition is and how it impacts organizational members' reactions and responses to change. In doing so, change can be managed more effectively and ethically for the benefit of an organization and its stakeholder members. For the purposes of this book, we define transition as:

> *The individual inner psychological processes that people (organizational members) go through in order to come to terms with change.*

In this way, transition is about how organizational members, in particular employees, cope with the typically far-reaching implications from second-order transformational change. As we outlined previously, there is no aspect of an organization that second-order change does not impact, and there are typically far-reaching implications for all organizational members. Remember, second-order change alters structure, systems and processes in a fundamental way. Following this type of change, unwritten codes of conduct that are embedded in and govern groups and individuals' daily routines and rituals are up-ended, and organizational members find themselves experiencing an emotional roller-coaster ride as they try to come to terms with the new way of 'doing things around here'. For many this emotional roller-coaster ride is characterized by strong reactions such as shock and denial, anger, bargaining and depression as individuals try to let go of the old way of doings things whilst they attempt to engage in new patterns of behaviour. These emotions are likened to the emotional cognitive processes that people go through in trying to come to terms with death and dying (Kübler-Ross, 1989). At first, we may consider this analogy to be disrespectful towards those that are coping with death and dying. However, there is much empirical research to support this perspective. If you reflect on the last time you were subjected to significant change in either your professional or personal life, and the emotions that you were confronted by, you might decide that there is some value to be had from this analogy, and in managing change more intuitively and effectively. We return to the human aspects of change in Chapters 4, 6 and 8.

In summary then, transition is about how people come to terms with and adopt the new way of doing things, which may eventually become the norm. What is critical in all of this is for organizations to genuinely understand transition, and be mindful of the important role transition cognitive processes play in whether transformational change is effective. Consequently, it is important for the organization to provide meaningful support to help those that are impacted. We will return to individual transition processes in Chapters 4 and 6 where we respectively deal with the human aspects of change and the nature of power, politics and resistance. In general, it is critical that organizations interface with change and the individuals and groups who experience it in an ethical way. Doing change ethically is addressed in the final chapter of this book.

## The Why of Change – The Context of Change

We now turn our attention to the *'Why?'* of change. The environment in which the organization operates typically helps us answer the questions: *Why is it that change occurs? What is it that triggers change?* Whilst transformational change typically emanates from significant events in the external macro environment (such as economic booms and busts, climate change and revolutionary changes in technology such as artificial intelligence), they are also associated with notable internal events. These include, for instance, a change in the senior management team (for example, a new CEO), a change in organizational ownership or a newly formed organization following a merger and acquisition. Accordingly, new company owners and senior management teams will likely try to install new ways of 'doing things around here', to ensure the business is both efficient and effective. Typically, this means new initiatives with an objective of driving operating costs down and increasing operating income, sales, profits and share value. In the end, this leads to significant changes in strategy, structure and processes across the whole of the organization and, ultimately, to changes in employee behaviour.

Whilst we might say that, historically, second-order strategic transformative change only happened from time to time, contemporary organizations operate in increasingly unprecedented, uncertain and volatile macro and micro environments. The implication of this is that organizations and their members need to be increasingly flexible, robust and adaptive to survive. We will return to triggers of strategic change in Chapter 3.

## The How of Change – The Process of Change

In this next section we consider the 'How?' of change – in other words, the way in which organizations go about managing change. There are two juxtaposed conceptualizations that commonly depict how change is approached by organizations. These are the (1) planned, and (2) emergent, approaches to change. The planned approach was put forward by Lewin in his seminal work in 1947. This approach to change takes a central and dominant role in how organizational change is presented both theoretically and as a framework to describe how organizations approach change. The planned approach has taken centre stage in public life, as well as in articles and books on organizational change, for well over seventy years. In many respects this is due to Lewin's conceptualization of planned change being a foundational feature of a theoretical paradigm known as Organizational Development (OD), which was primarily developed during the 1960s and 1970s. For a detailed account of how OD came into being and the various theoretical strands that make up OD, see the work of Cummins and Worley (2005). Although OD came into being during the 1960s and 1970s, it still takes an important role in our understanding of organizational change. We discuss the role of OD in the human aspects of change in Chapters 4 and 8.

The planned approach to change is largely characterized by being prescriptive, deliberate, calculated and conscious. It is achieved by organizations going through a linear step-by-step process and is very much driven by the top-down; it is the senior management team's agenda. As a result, change is perceived as a linear, sequential, step-by-step process whereby organizations move through a small number of steps from one fixed state to another (see Figure 1.2). Lewin's seminal (1947) conceptualization features this approach as constituting three distinct stages, as illustrated in Figure 1.2.

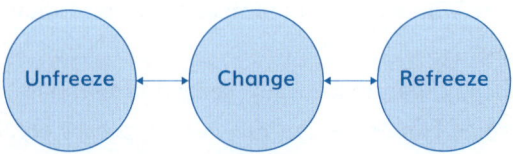

**Figure 1.2** Lewin's planned three-step approach to organizational change (Lewin, 1951).

**Step 1 – Unfreeze.** The first step is when an organization uncouples from its current position. In this respect an organization 'unfreezes', typically due to a crisis event which happens in the macro environment, for example, a global economic recession, a war, a global pandemic or a major break-through in technology. Such crisis events are a shock to the current stable organizational position. An organization is 'turned upside down' as current beliefs, values, structures and patterns of behaviour are forced out of position and thus unfreezes.

**Step 2 – Change.** During this uncertain time an organization becomes more fluid and 'unfreezes', whereby the 'old' ways of doing things are discarded during a period of instability and fluidity, which in turn creates suitable conditions for change to take place.

**Step 3 – Refreeze.** The final step in Lewin's model is 'refreezing'. Having set aside the 'old' ways of doing things, what is once thought of as 'new' behaviour, structures, systems and process are accepted. Collectively these become the organization's new reality; the way in which the company operates and how organizational members behave towards each other on a day-to-day basis and towards external stakeholders. The organization then refreezes and stabilizes. What was the new way of doing things is now the equilibrium and status quo.

Lewin's (1951) three-step model has become the classic planned approach by which to conceptualize how change occurs within organizations. There is certainly some value in this approach, which offers a helicopter overview and explanation of how change happens. Alongside Lewin's three-step model there are several similar step-by-step planned change process models. These include Beckhard's (1969, 1989) key processes and steps for attaining change:

- Envisioning a desired future state for the organization (imagining what the organization would be like after the change), and setting goals by which this can be accomplished.
- Evaluating, analysing and diagnosing the present state of the organization by reference to these goals.
- Defining what needs to be done and what resources are required to achieve the desired future state.
- Effectively managing any problems during the transition period, developing strategies and action plans.

Another step-model of planned change is that of Lippitt et al. (1958). This approach pays particular attention to the role of a *change agent*, who might be an internal stakeholder such as someone that is familiar with the process, or someone that is tasked with managing the change process, including monitoring performance and customer satisfaction. The change agent might also be someone that is external to an organization, such as a management consultant. We will cover change agents further in Chapter 8. Lippitt's steps are as follows:

1. Diagnose. What is the problem?
2. Evaluate the motivation, capability and capacity for change. This includes the organizational structure, in addition to the company's resources, including its people and finance.
3. Assess the resources and motivation of the change agent, including their commitment, their power (how much authority they have to make the change) and their resilience.
4. Identify objectives for the change and develop plans and strategies by which these objectives will be met.
5. Manage expectations. There are various roles that a change agent might take including 'cheerleader', 'facilitator' and 'expert'. Which role the change agent takes needs to be clear, understood and communicated to all stakeholders.
6. Maintain the change. For the change to 'stick' there needs to be good communication, feedback and group coordination across the organization.

**7.** Gradually withdraw from the relationship with the change agent. This is necessary once the change is integrated into the organizational culture.

(*Source*: Lippitt, Watson and Westley, 1958: 58–9).

Kotter's (1996) eight-step approach is relevant to transformational, second-order change. It is a top-down planned approach that emphasizes leadership responsibilities in the process of change management. Common criticisms associated with the model include its linear step process, which does not accurately represent organizational life. Anyone that works for an organization, whether on a full or part-time basis, understands that organizational life is sometimes messy, ambiguous and complex. The eight-step process thus may be an idealistic linear process that does not contract and expand in line with the dynamics of true organizational life. There is also little by way of explaining *how* change is to be achieved. Nonetheless, Kotter's (1996) model is one of the most well recognized in the change literature and likely constitutes the 'go to' reference for change agents and organizations. Kotter's (1996) eight-step approach is detailed below:

## Step 1 – Create, Raise and Establish a Sense of Urgency

To move away from organizational complacency and break through any fear and anger that is associated with major change, a strong sense of urgency is required. This needs to be generated by the senior management team, and is achieved through clear communication to enable important stakeholders to understand the message. However, senior management may require some leverage to do so, which can be created, for example, by external sources of information, such as a consultancy report that details the justification for radical change, or reports in the media that can be called upon to underpin the sense of urgency. Whatever and however this is done, a 'burning platform' needs to be established from which to communicate to internal and external stakeholders.

## Step 2 – Creating the Guiding Coalition

There needs to be a core body of people to lead the transformational change initiative. This body of people need to create the right timbre or tone for the change. They need to command the respect of others and have the appropriate authority, respect and credibility to implement the change.

## Step 3 – Develop a Vision and Strategy

The core body of people in step 2 then need to develop and communicate a clear vision by which key stakeholders and, very importantly, employees are compelled to buy into. This ensures everyone is thinking in a similar way. Strategy then needs to be formulated to not only achieve the vision, but also to direct organizational resources appropriately.

## Step 4 – Communicating the Change Vision

To elicit positive responses from employees and others in relation to the change vision, effective communication is critical. This increases employees' receptivity towards the proposed change and reduces uncertainty. An example of this would be having regular team meetings to communicate, discuss and involve employees in the change process.

## Step 5 – Empower Change

This step is about enabling those that have taken on board the vision to put into practice the strategy intended to achieve the proposed change. This is the part of the change process that is enabled by senior management through, for example, up-skilling employees through education and training. An important aspect of this is giving employees the freedom to take the initiative and experiment with new approaches in achieving organizational objectives. In this way, employees actively support and are engaged in achieving the change vision.

## Step 6 – Creating Short-term Wins

Long-term change is complex and difficult, and people may become demotivated because it is both hard work and emotionally challenging. It is therefore important that managers create early and easy 'wins' to encourage and motivate employees. These 'wins' need to be transparent to all and clearly linked to achieving the change vision.

## Step 7 – Keep Going

The sense of urgency should not be forgotten and all wins in the change process should be built upon so that transformation becomes a reality.

## Step 8 – Make the Change a Reality

The final step in the process is to ensure that the change 'sticks'. This is incredibly difficult given that transformational change requires a fundamental shift in the way in which people behave, alongside processes, strategies and so forth. Overall, a paradigmatic shift in culture is required.

## A Critical Lens

Lewin's planned approach has been around since 1947 and is viewed by many as foundational to the development of the theoretical paradigms underpinning organizational change. At the same time, others view Lewin's approach through a more critical lens, which is to be expected given the transformational advances in technology and the engendered interconnectedness that can foster an ongoing, turbulent environment in which organizations are forced to operate.

To this end, common criticisms include the following:

→ The concept is overly simplistic, and represents change as being linear and mechanistic.

→ A stable environment in which organizations operate is assumed and the reality is somewhat different for contemporary organizations.

→ The focus emphasizes a top-down driven approach to change, so there is little attention paid to those individuals and groups that, by default, will be on the receiving end of change.

→ The nuances of change and all of the complexities surrounding power and politics are not considered.

### ACTIVITY 1.4

Please focus your attention on the following sections of this short journal article:

1. Read '3-step model' pages 985–6.
2. Then read 'Lewin's work criticisms and responses', pages 992–5.
3. And finally dip into 'Conclusions', pages 995–8.

Once done, reflect on a change that you have experienced either in your personal or professional life. Using the grid provided below assign aspects of the change you experienced to Step 1, Step 2 and Step 3 of Lewin's planned approach to change.

| Steps | Explanation | Your Personal or Professional Change |
|---|---|---|
| Step 1 – Unfreeze | A crisis event happens which destabilizes the current position | |
| Step 2 – Change | The 'old' ways of doing things are discarded in parallel to a period of instability and fluidity, which in turn creates suitable conditions for change to take place | |
| Step 3 – Refreezes | Having set aside the 'old' ways of doing things, what was once thought of as 'new' behaviour, structures, systems and process are now accepted and become the normal way of doing things | |

Once filled out, please answer the following questions:

1. Given your application of Lewin's three-step model, do you think this is a realistic representation of how change occurs, whether in a personal or professional context?

2. Do you think that the criticisms of the planned approach to change are justified and if so, why?

For those interested in the important context on Lewin's background and an understanding of how the concept of planned change came into being, read the introductory sections.

## A More Realistic Lens Through Which to Understand the 'How' of Change

As depicted by Figure 1.2, the planned approach to change can be seen as a step-by-step process. The steps in the process are linear, fixed and predetermined, as, for example, is a lifecycle. Accordingly, step 1 progresses to step 2, from which step 3 follows, and all of these steps culminate in organizational change. This is an idealistic perspective that does not take on board interpersonal relationships between organizational members during the change process, general resistance to change or indeed any other factors such as poor articulation and communication of the change vision, resulting in groups and individuals feeling alienated and therefore resisting the proposed change. We deal with this later in this book, particularly in Chapter 6. At best this approach to change is idealistic. At worst, it may lead to sub-optimal organizational performance, as other stakeholders' views are not accounted for, which, although may be contrary to the intended direction and vison of the senior management team, may be productive in offering up a critical view that has not previously been considered.

Realistically, substantive change is oscillatory in nature. It will go through several iterations prior to being accepted, and, as a consequence, the positive impact from the change will take some time. An example situation is illustrated by Figure 1.3. In this example, step 1 in this change process was accepted, but step 2 was rejected because individuals and groups did not have sufficient skills and competencies to take on board what was being proposed.

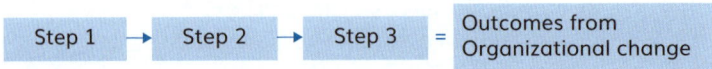

**Figure 1.3** A linear step-by-step process of change.

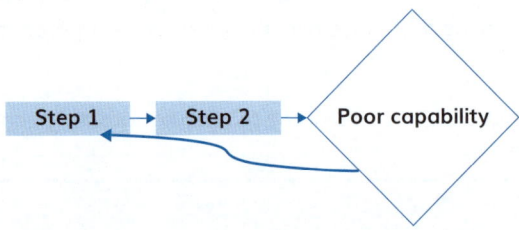

**Figure 1.4** An iterative approach to the process of change.

### ACTIVITY 1.5

1. Think of two different types of change scenario that you have experienced during your personal and or professional life that can accurately be depicted by Figures 1.3 and 1.4.
2. For both, detail the various steps in the process.
3. Which did you learn most from, and why?

## Change at the Different Levels of Analysis in an Organization

Transformational change at one level of the organization has serious implications at other levels. Unfortunately, some organizations may have no or limited understanding of this. Top-down initiatives are pushed through and onto internal stakeholders via organizational structure, processes and procedures, through which it is perceived that change will somehow 'get done'. To gain an insight and understanding of significant organizational change and how this is can be achieved in an effective, ethical and successful way, we need to unpack the levels at which change happens and, in particular, be mindful of three interrelated levels that transformational change impacts. In Figure 1.5 you will see that this is not straightforward and that these organizational levels, whilst being distinct from each other, are also entwined, interrelated and interconnected. This is why change is so incredibly complex and why organizations typically don't do it well!

An underlying aim of this book is to enable organizations, individuals and teams to do change more effectively, so we unpack change at the organizational or macro level, the team or meso level and the individual or micro level of analysis. We outline these levels below and signpost learners to chapters where these various levels are considered and discussed.

→ *Organizational or Macro Level of Change*

Transformational change is typically triggered by a significant event in either the external business and/or sector environment in which an organization operates or internally within the organization itself. This event is so far reaching that an organization radically changes its practices, processes, values, behaviour and assumptions. The key players at the macro level of change are the senior management team who may have a new vision for the organization and a strategic plan to operationalize these radical changes. A pivotal aspect at the macro level of change is organizational culture and the need to ensure that the proposed change 'sticks'. Furthermore, because this change has significant implications for all stakeholders, it needs to be carried out ethically. In this book, macro level change is considered in Chapters 2, 3, 5, 7, 8 and 9.

→ *Group or Meso Level of Change*

Macro level changes affect the whole of the organization, including groups and teams within an organization. We refer to this as the meso level of change. Groups are an important dynamic within all organizations because it is through collective efforts that strategic objectives and, ultimately, an organization's vision are achieved. The success of transformative change will depend on a group's interpretations of the change. Groups are especially loyal to norms, practices and behaviours in the fulfilment of work tasks and responsibilities. When attempting to bring about effective transformational change at the meso level, norms and other dynamics may act as a blocker. We deal with change at the meso level of analysis in Chapters 4, 5, 6, 8 and 9.

### ➔ Individual or Micro Level of Change

Just as the meso level of analysis can be an inhibitor to organizational change where not managed effectively, so too can the individual or micro level (Figure 1.5). By individual or micro level of analysis we mean how individual employees respond and react to transformative change. Some individuals might perceive change through a favourable lens, identifying opportunities for themselves. Many others will perceive radical change as bringing about unwanted uncertainties. There can be much pain in letting go of the old ways of doing things and in coming to terms with a new reality. In this book we explore the emotional relationship that individuals have with change and how perceptions of change can differ from one person to the next, alongside how managers and leaders can manage individuals more effectively in the change process. We focus on this in Chapters 4, 6, 8 and 9.

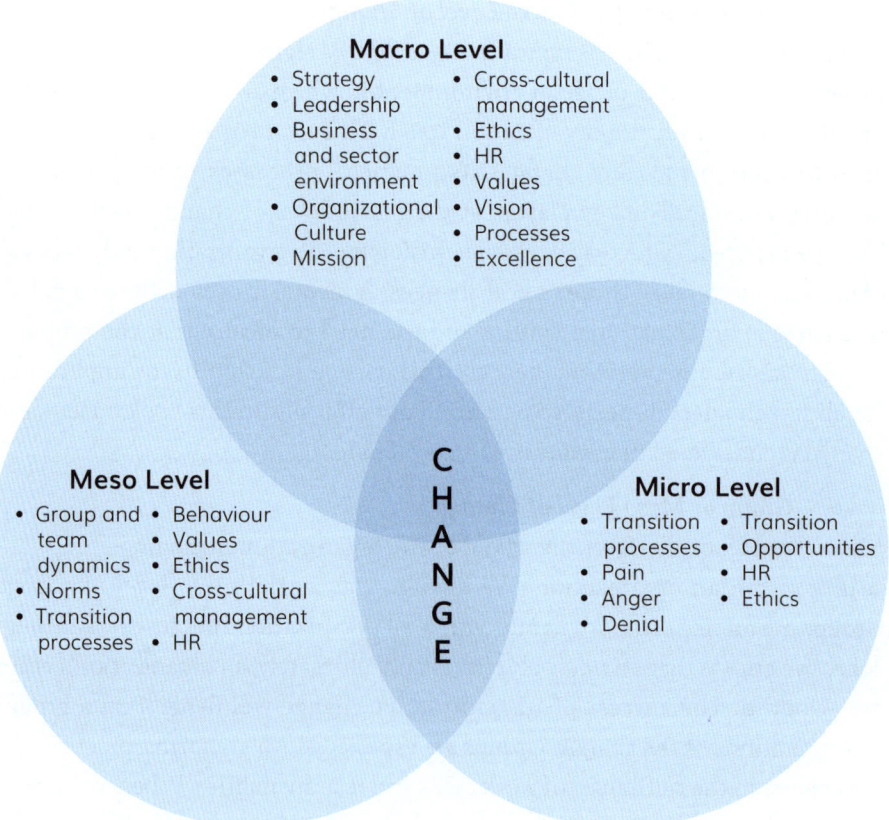

**Figure 1.5** Change at different levels of analysis.

**CASE STUDY:** ROLLS-ROYCE AERO-ENGINE
POWER AND MARINE COMPANY PLC –
A CASE STUDY OF ONGOING INCREMENTAL
AND TRANSFORMATIONAL CHANGE

* Prior to reading through this case study, you can watch a short video to familiarize yourself with both the historical development and contemporary evolution of Rolls-Royce.

Rolls-Royce plc is a significant and widely acclaimed aero-engine, marine and power company with an interesting and chequered history. Originally founded in 1906, from, it appears likely, an improbable partnership between Charles Stewart Rolls and Henry Royce (latterly Sir Henry Royce). Rolls and Royce came from contrasting backgrounds with Rolls a member of the aristocracy and the son of a Baron, whilst Royce from an early age contributed towards the family's finances when just a child by selling newspapers and later as an apprentice at the Great Northern Railway. Notwithstanding, this unlikely partnership enabled Rolls to contribute his expertise in business and sales, and Royce his expertise in engineering and design. Initially, the partnership resulted in the successful manufacture and production of elite cars such as the Rolls-Royce Sliver Ghost. When WWI started in 1914, Royce designed an aero-engine that supplied the allies' air force. It was, however, during WWII when Rolls-Royce provided the Merlin engine for the Hurricane and Spitfire that the company experienced transformative change from being a car producer to a significant producer of aero-engines.

Today, whilst the company has seen its share price perform better than ever and it is one of the most prolific suppliers of civilian engines throughout the world, the company is not without a chequered history of ups and downs. A case in point being that in 1971 the company went bankrupt due to errors associated with the costs of the RB211 engine. If it had not been for the timely intervention of the British government who took on the company's financial obligations it is likely that Rolls-Royce would have not survived. During this period of time the company was nationalized and the car division was sold to enable the focus on aero-engines. It was not until 1987 that Rolls-Royce was again privatized when it became a public company (PLC). To this day, the company continues to experience challenges in the ever-changing world in which it operates. In January 2023 a new Chief Executive Officer (CEO) was appointed taking over from Warren East. This is Tufin Erginbilgiç, who was a former CEO with considerable leadership experience at BP for twenty years before he became a CEO in Global Infrastructure Partners (GIP), a private equity firm focusing on investments in infrastructure businesses managing in the range of some $81bn for its investors.

On the appointment of Erginbilgiç as CEO of Rolls-Royce it is reported by Pfeifer (2023) that Erginbilgiç referred to Rolls-Royce as a 'burning platform'. This was part of a bleak picture Erginbilgiç painted for employees on the future of Rolls-Royce. In summary, this was a harsh assessment on the future of the company. The clear message from Erginbilgiç is that if the company does not transform the way in which it operates then it will not survive. Erginbilgiç is reported as being scathing about the way in which Rolls-Royce power-system division had been run. The power-systems division makes diesel and gas engines for ships and trains. Erginbilgiç pointed out that in this division costs had not been kept under control and referred to this as 'mismanagement'. Being a PLC, a key stakeholder for Rolls-Royce are its investors. Whilst Rolls-Royce shares rose by 22 per cent at the start of January 2023, they remain below their expected performance. Erginbilgiç is cited as stating 'Every investment we make, we destroy value … we underperform every key competitor out there' (Pfeifer, 2023). For example, Rolls-Royce profit margins are below those of General Electric (GE) in the US. In this way Erginbilgiç is laying the foundation for making radical changes with an overall brief of improving performance in a significant way. An implication is that Rolls-Royce's performance is not sustainable, this is to the extent that Erginbilgiç referred to this as being 'our last chance'. The transformation programme that Erginbilgiç is introducing at Rolls-Royce has a focus on efficiency and optimization, with an implication of job cutting. This comes on the back of successive restructures at Rolls-Royce including the loss of 9,000 jobs saving £1.3bn undertaken by the former CEO. Rolls-Royce money is generated from service contracts and the amount of hours that its engines are in the air.

To date the changes that are in process include: an overhaul of management, the appointment of a new head of power-systems, a shake up of senior management including civil and defence business heads, cuts to spending on none-core projects and the renegotiation of some of its sales and maintenance contracts with customers. There are seven areas that are identified as part of improvement as part of the transformation programme. These are:
- Improve strategy with an objective to focusing on engaging the workforce.
- Reducing Rolls-Royce working capital.
- Increasing efficiency.
- Considering synergies across the group.
- Identifying opportunities to centralize key functions.

By way of operationalizing the transformation programme, Erginbilgiç has brought in executives from his former company BP to take up posts, such as Chief Financial Officer, alongside others who will be taking the lead on the transformation programme.

*Based on Pfeifer's (2023) account of Rolls-Royce.*

## ROLLS-ROYCE CASE STUDY ACTIVITIES – ACTIVITY 1.6

1. What is happening in the case study? Who are the key stakeholders throughout its historical development to the present day?
2. Has/is Rolls-Royce undergone/undergoing first-order or second-order change? List and evaluate the incidents of first- and second-order change that have happened throughout Rolls-Royce's history in the table below.
3. What are the implications of these changes at the macro, meso and micro levels of Rolls-Royce? Please list in the table below.
4. For each of your listed first- and/or second-order changes, what do you believe is propelling that change? In other words, what is causing the change to occur? Please list in the table below.
5. What challenges has/does the CEO of Rolls-Royce face? How has the CEO responded to these challenges thus far?
6. In view of the current challenges, what do you think the implications may be for the organization and its key stakeholders?
7. What is the evidence that the new CEO's appointment is making a positive impact on the performance of Rolls-Royce, or indeed otherwise?

| Describe the Type of Change | Identify the Type of Change You Have Described (First- or Second-order) | Does this Type of Change Have Implications at the Macro, Meso and/or Micro Level? | Describe the Implications |
|---|---|---|---|
| | | | |
| | | | |
| | | | |
| | | | |
| | | | |
| | | | |
| | | | |
| | | | |
| | | | |
| | | | |

##  CONSULTANCY IN THE CHAIR

**Cup of Kindness Activity**

As the lead consultant to Cup of Kindness (CUP), you are due to have a first meeting with the CEO of the organization that has taken over CUP. Think through how and what you will need to prepare in advance of this first meeting. Prepare a set of questions for the CEO that will enable you to best advise the organization going forwards. Have ready a set of questions that you envisage the CEO will ask you.

##  Competency-based Interview Question

1. During an interview for a change consultancy position to CUP, you need to convince the CEO that you are the 'right' person for the role. The CEO asks you: 'what are your greatest strengths and what is it that you have achieved in your life so far? In summary, what are you especially proud of and which competencies in particular make you the "right" person for this role?' Prepare your answer for this question.

##  Chapter Summary

We have begun our learning journey in this chapter by reflecting on the nature of change, including both the different types of change that occur and who these changes implicate. Whilst change is traditionally depicted as linear, change in action can be far removed from the linear step-by-step process models. Transition at the meso or micro units of analysis has implications for the way in which change is managed. Substantive change is shown to be a dynamic and complex phenomenon that is not necessarily straightforward, and that has implications for the whole of the organization. The way in which this change is managed impacts the overall success of an organization.

## Bibliography

Beckhard, R. (1969), *Organization Development: Strategy and Models*. Reading, MA: Addison-Wesley.

Beckhard, R. (1989), 'A Model for the Executive Management of Transformational Change', in G. Salaman (ed), *Human Resource Strategies*. London: Sage.

Cummins, T. G. and Worley, C. G. (2005), *Organization Development and Change*. Mason, OH: Southwestern.

Kotter, J. (1996), *Leading Change*. Boston: Harvard Business School Press.

Lewin, K. (1947), 'Frontiers in Group Dynamics: Concept, Method and Reality in Social Science; Social Equilibria and Social Change'. *Human Relations (New York)*, 1(1): 5–41.

Lippitt, R., Watson, J., and Westley, B. (1958), *The Dynamics of Planned Change*. New York: Harcourt, Brace & World.

Kübler-Ross, E. (1989), *On Death and Dying*. London: Routledge.

Lewin, K. (1951), *Field Theory in Social Science*. New York: Harper & Row.

Pettigrew, A. M. and Whipp, R. (1991), *Managing Change for Competitive Success*. Oxford: Basil Blackwell.

Pfeifer, S. (2023), 'Rolls-Royce's New Chief Warns Company is a "Burning Platform"'. *Financial Times,* January.

# Foundations for Incremental and Substantive Change Interventions

**2**

## Learning Outcomes

At the end of this chapter you will be able to:

1. Critically evaluate the role of quality and processes in underpinning incremental and substantive change.
2. Understand the importance of a holistic measurement system as an indicator of the effectiveness of change.
3. Recognize the value of diagnostic tools for evaluating, understanding, measuring and changing processes.
4. Evaluate process improvement and excellence as approaches for driving substantial organizational change.
5. Gain insight to a systematic framework for driving effective change.

## Introduction

As we will see in Chapter 3, organizations that survive and flourish understand that they are connected by a permeable membrane to what happens in a fluid, unpredictable and dynamic external environment. In this way organizations are forced to respond to external opportunities and threats. This 'open systems' perspective necessitates survival through significant strategic organizational change interventions that are triggered by drivers in the macro environment such as competition, changes in stakeholder requirements, global pandemics, financial crises and artificial intelligence. Underlying the aims of such strategic change interventions is the wish to survive by bringing about significant performance improvements, which are ultimately focused on effectiveness and efficiency. This is the extent to which an organization attains its goals and objectives, and how well the organization does at acquiring and utilizing resources, which are converted by processes into services and goods for customers. However, organizations are sometimes so focused on 'doing' significant change that they overlook the internal fundamentals that need to be in place to support and underpin both long- and short-term incremental and substantive change. A crucial underpinning for all types of change is an organization-wide focus on quality, processes and excellence. Continuous improvement activities are associated with a significant impact on organizational performance through both effectiveness and efficiency, and are foundational for any significant change to be successful. This chapter considers quality, processes and excellence as part of continuous improvement activities for incremental and substantive change interventions.

## What is Quality and Does it Matter?

Quality is an ambiguous concept meaning different things to different people. For example, if you were asked to identify a quality car, you might pick one that makes efficient use of fuel and which is easy to park. For others, a quality car may be one that has the ability to go from 0 to 100 miles an hour in the space of a few seconds, and which has a sophisticated aesthetic design. In this way, the concept of quality is nebulous and imprecise. Whilst the word 'quality' is used frequently by individuals and organizations, and continues to be contemplated, it appears likely that its real meaning has somewhat been lost or at least has become confused. Garvin's (1987) eight dimensions of quality put forwards in the *Harvard Business Review* some time back continue to be a 'benchmark' by which the nature of quality as a strategic organizational approach can be understood (Fasko, 2023). This is by reference to the following eight fundamentals which are outlined below:

- → Performance: quality is functional, measurable and associated with performance. Organizations should have key performance standards that encapsulate the key operating characteristics of their services and products.
- → Features: a secondary aspect of performance are features that enhance the customer's overall perception of a product or service. These features are not necessary in terms of functionality but they do influence a customer's regard for the product or service.

- Reliability: this dimension of quality typically refers more to durable products such as cars rather than goods and services where there is a short time period by which services are bought and consumed. In this respect, reliability can be defined as the period of time from purchase to first failure.

- Conformance: products and services are designed by reference to specifications. Quality in this respect is the extent to which the product or service conforms to those specifications.

- Durability: this dimension of quality is associated with products rather than services. Durability is the life span of a product and thus the overall use a customer gets from that product prior to its replacement.

- Serviceability: this dimension of quality is focused on the responsiveness, politeness and competence of the organization's members that deal with product breakdowns.

- Aesthetics: this dimension of quality is subjective and associated with personal preferences in how products and services look. Key characteristics may include; visual appearance, how a product feels, its shape and so forth.

- Perceived quality: this dimension of quality is also subjective. It concerns the customers' inferences about the quality of a product or service based upon such things as marketing campaigns and an organization's brand.

## ACTIVITY 2.1

1. Please access and read Garvin's (1987) original article: Competing on the Eight Dimensions of Quality.

2. Having read the article please reflect on the eight dimensions of quality and apply them to a contemporary organization with which you are familiar.

3. To what extent are these eight dimensions of quality relevant to contemporary organizations? If you do not think they are relevant then please think through a list of your own dimensions for defining quality with justification.

4. Please access Fasko's (2023) reflections on Garvin's (1987) article which might help to inform your response to question 3 above.

5. Do you think that quality is still relevant as a contemporary strategic approach? Please explain.

Whilst it might be argued that the meaning of quality is ambiguous when perceived through different organizational stakeholder lenses, it is an important fundamental in planning and implementing change. To gain a better insight of this phenomenon, the next section contextualizes quality, and both *how* and *why* it needs to feature in any organizational change. We start by considering the historical development of quality.

## Evolution of Quality as a Strategic Approach

The need for for mass production and inspection were stimulated by World War I. However, during this time, quality was inspected at the end of the manufacturing line. Inspection at the end of a manufacturing line is wholly unreliable, inefficient and not cost effective as a method for quality control. As a response to this, statistical techniques for the control of products was developed. The founder of statistical process control (SPC) Walter Shewhart introduced control charts and applied statistical methods to the measurement and control of quality. With this method, quality is controlled at the point of manufacture rather than at end of the line, when the product had already been produced and when it is too late to correct a defective product. Overall, Shewhart's approach to controlling quality saw improvements in performance due to fewer non-conforming finished products, as defective products were detected earlier in the manufacturing process.

Complementing and supporting Shewhart's approach to quality, the concept of statistically-based methods of acceptance sampling was introduced by Harold Dodge. This was an efficient way of ensuring quality in products. The quality of a consignment of goods could be accurately estimated by measuring a sample of the goods, thus saving considerable resources. Statistical techniques of measuring, evaluating and controlling quality became widely accepted and used in the UK, and especially in North America during World War II. However, post-World War II the market for goods became over-subscribed. In fact, any goods would sell regardless of quality. Paradoxically, it was during this period that organizations really began to understand the concept of customer requirements in terms of the *total quality* of a product and service, which was not wholly centred on the output, but also on the way in which goods and services were delivered to the customer at all stages of the process.

The Navy Personnel Research and Development Centre are associated with the introduction of the term 'Total Quality Management' (TQM), which they used to describe their Japanese-based approach to quality improvements within organizations during the 1980s. The roots of TQM can be traced to the fundamental concepts put forward by Crosby (1979), Ishikawa (1985), Deming (2000), Juran (1988) and Feigenbaum (1991). TQM is a holistic approach to improving operational effectiveness and efficiency that involves *the whole* of the organization and focuses on the customer (Boulter et al., 2013). Whilst TQM has been defined in various ways, there is a general consensus that it involves '… strong leadership and management commitment; continuous improvement; focus on customers, employees and processes; teamwork and commitment; actions based on facts (scientific approach); emphasis on learning and innovation. Furthermore, that it involves building partnership relationships with stakeholders alongside a systematic approach to fostering a "TQM culture"' (Fonseca, 2022: 1012) (Figure 2.1). Stakeholders are defined as 'any group or individual who can affect or is affected by the achievement of the organization's objectives' (Freeman, 1984: 46).

- Continuous improvement.
- Everyone's engagement and responsibility.
- Led by senior management.
- Management commitment.
- Driven by everyone.
- Internal and external customer orientation.
- Partnership relationships with stakeholders.
- Teamwork.

**Figure 2.1** Fundamental principles of TQM.

## Quality as Part of Organizational Change

Organizational quality, as part of a change initiative, needs to be focused on the customers' requirements, and this has implications for the whole of the organization. This includes the way in which the product or service is designed, product and service performance, the interpersonal relationship with customers, communication with customers in general, marketing, the supply chain and so forth. As a consequence, change needs to involve the whole of the organization. Quality as an approach to significant organizational improvement, where properly understood, can be an essential and strategic part of an organizations' competitive advantage. The adoption of a quality approach has resulted in many organizations dramatically improving their competitive position, with a focus on meeting and exceeding customer requirements while reducing the costs of non-confirming products and services. This strategic approach is aimed at providing the best service or product through continual incremental improvement. The emphasis is on the customer in terms of their needs and expectations. Whilst it might be obvious that the customer is a key stakeholder, unfortunately, for some organizations, individual and group customers are not a priority. This is because some organizations have lost sight of the customer.

### ACTIVITY 2.2

In this article, a head teacher complains about the quality of school dinners.

1. What would you attribute the likely cause of poor quality to in this case, and why do you think that is?

2. What advice would you give to this organization on how they might go about addressing their 'quality' issue?

Given the role that artificial intelligence (AI) takes in organizations, employees can have limited or no contact with customers. Customers are removed from employees' day-to-day routines and patterns and this lack of proximity can be the source of much customer dissatisfaction. An example of this, as reported by Forbes, is evidenced in the case of Frontier Airlines, whose person-to-person call centre was replaced by an online chatbot that customers have to interface with if they wish to, for example, change their flight. Whilst the company claims this improves efficiency and is to be expected by customers, the chatbot has become the source of many customers' frustrations and overall quality-related complaints about the organization.

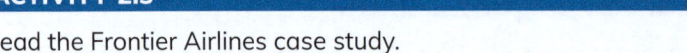

### ACTIVITY 2.3

Read the Frontier Airlines case study.

1. How do you think the introduction of chatbots affect the quality of any organization's customer service in both positive and negative ways? Please make a list of advantages and disadvantages.

2. In view of the list that you have produced, do you think that interfacing with a chatbot impacts overall customer satisfaction? Please explain.

3. Please read the statistics shared by UJET, summarized below. Does this change your view at all?

4. Think of an organization that you work for or know of. What do you think is the best way of introducing AI such as chatbots, so that it does not negatively impact customer satisfaction?

Now consider the findings shared by cloud contact centre provider UJET, which raises customer satisfaction issues associated with the use of chatbots. UJET's data suggests that:

- 78 per cent of consumers have interacted with a chatbot in the past twelve months – but 80 per cent said using chatbots increased their frustration level.
- 78 per cent of consumers were forced to connect with a human after failing to resolve their needs through an automated service channel.
- 63 per cent indicated that their interaction with a chatbot did not result in a resolution.
- 72 per cent felt that using a chatbot for customer service was a waste of time.
- More than half of consumers (54 per cent) believe that a phone call with a live agent provides the fastest resolution and best overall customer experience.

## What Should Get Measured as Part of Change?

To understand how well an organization is performing in regard to change, measurement efforts typically focus on outputs that involve key accounting measures such as share price, operating income, operating costs, capital expenditure over assets, number of employees, revenue from sales and so forth. Whilst these accounting measures are necessary and informative, on their own and in isolation, using only these methods is rather like inspecting the quality of a product or service at the end of the line, or once it has already been delivered. In this respect, the only point at which corrective and improvement action can be taken is once the product or service has left the organization. Unfortunately, at this point, change might be too late. This type of output information does not help organizations identify problems prior to or during the production process, when corrective action needs to take place.

A unified measurement system is required for all those involved, which is focused on financial and non-financial indicators. A holistic measurement system is one which, alongside key accounting measures, considers customer satisfaction, employee wellbeing, leadership, key processes, positive impacts on the community in which the organization operates, society in general, the supply chain and so forth. Such measures would need to enable the organization to anticipate problems before they occur, flag a problem to the organization during the production process and provide feedback so that an organization can manage problems after they have occurred. An important part of this is agreeing individuals' specific goals as part of their performance appraisal, alongside leaders and managers agreeing specific targets at the collective departmental level. This must be done in conjunction with the organization agreeing how the senior management team will be measured.

A unified approach to measurement across an organization can be achieved by identifying a small set of critical success factors (CSFs) that are directly linked to the organization's mission and strategy. CSFs are a small number of key performance indicators. The objective of CFSs is that satisfactory performance in the change journey can be measured. An example of a CSF for most organizations is to improve operating income, increase revenue from sales, and reduce the cost of making a sale, in addition to improvements in overall customer satisfaction. Where feedback shows that satisfactory progress is being made against specific targets, an organization is generally viewed as making satisfactory progress in its change journey.

A holistic approach to measuring organizational performance was introduced by Kaplan and Norton (1996) through the concept of a balanced scorecard, illustrated in Figure 2.2. As you can see, this particular organization, which happens to be an airline, has a balanced approach to performance that includes measures for customer satisfaction, internal business processes, learning and growth and financial results. Importantly, Kaplan and Norton (1996) identify some of these performance measures as 'lagging' indicators, whilst others are 'leading'. Financial measures are lagging because profit, assets and operational expenditure data indicate the output from an organization's past efforts. As indicated earlier in this chapter, changes around improvement activities can therefore only take place after the historical data has been understood. Juxtaposed are leading performance indicators, which in the case of the airline include learning and growth and internal business processes. Learning and growth indicators are associated with employees and their engagement in their job and with customers. This may include the organization's approach to empowering employees, enabling them to do their job in a responsive way, as well as education and training, from which the right skills are acquired to do their job. Such leading indicators are predictive of output measures. They highlight any poor practices or weaknesses, which enables corrective action to be taken in a timely manner so as to improve output measures. For example, in Figure 2.2 one leading indicator of learning and growth is employee morale. If the organization has surveyed employees and the data indicates that morale is low, the organization should take corrective action to find out why this is, before changing its approach to improving.

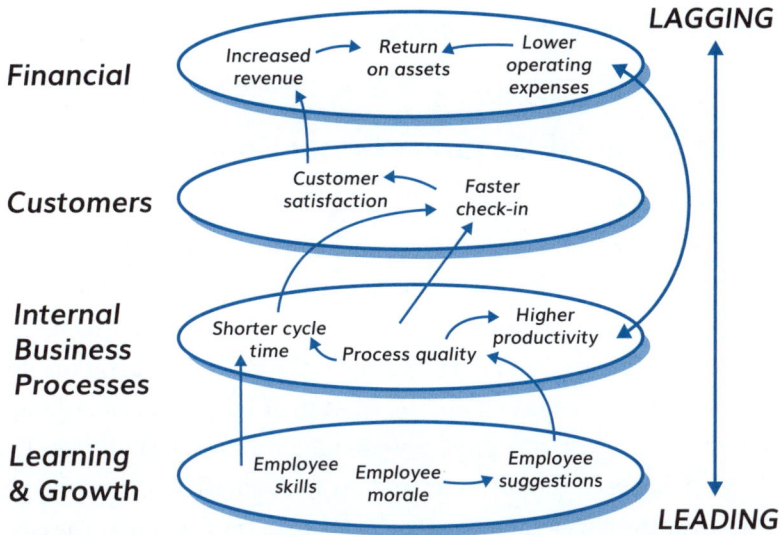

**Figure 2.2** Balanced scorecard approach to a holistic approach to measuring. Based on Kaplan and Norton (1996).

Another critical aspect of any change initiative is internal business processes, which are covered in the next section.

## The Importance of Processes for Change

Processes can be defined as a series of activities involving an external and/or internal customer, where inputs are converted into outputs. Processes are critical to all organizations because it is these processes that the customer is on the receiving end of, and is what can cause customer satisfaction or dissatisfaction. Inputs to processes typically include people, kit, equipment, facilities and knowledge, which are then converted during the process into outputs and outcomes. Figure 2.3 sums this up. One example is to think about the learning process. In this case, inputs include kit, equipment, IT, facilities, the knowledge of the individual delivering the lecture and students. All of these resources are converted during the teaching process and the output is a lecture and better-informed students. Where processes are inefficient they add cost to an organization; however, when efficient, processes add value to an organization via the resulting customer satisfaction.

There are two broad categories that organizational processes fall into. These are (1) core processes and (2) support processes, as described below.

**Figure 2.3** Understanding process activity.

## Different Types of Organizational Processes and Measures

The objective of core processes is to satisfy external customers. Core processes are frontline processes whereby customers come into direct contact with an organization. For example, when you purchase a coffee, the organization is totally exposed. You, the customer, sees how the individual server is dressed, whether the server is clean, responsive, what their interpersonal skills are like, and so forth. In this way, core processes are referred to as 'front office'; they are a 'touch point' between the customer and organization. This can be the point at which the organization's weaknesses are laid bare to the customer. The customer is on the receiving end of the organization's culture, training and responsiveness. It is also during this process that the customer will make a value judgement as to whether they are satisfied with the organization.

Support processes satisfy internal customers and are often referred to as 'back office' processes. This is because a key characteristic of back office processes is that the customer typically does not come into direct contact with them. There is little by way of proximity between back office processes and external customers. A back office process is one that helps internal customers, such as the provision of IT support. This encapsulates the concept that we are *all* customers of an organization's processes. All groups and individuals are customers and suppliers of internal business processes. The internal customer is the next individual or group in line to whom they supply work, knowledge, resources or a key bit of information so that a decision can be made. Similarly, support processes have internal supplies – people who supply what is necessary for them to carry out their work. If at any point there is a misunderstanding and breakdown in communication, then the quality of the end product or service to the external customer is impacted. To illustrate the point being made here we can use the example of IT support for teaching. The provision of IT internally is a support process because it is supplied to internal customers. In the case of a university it is a lecturer that is the internal customer of this process and IT that is the supplier. If IT support fail to ensure that the kit and equipment is fully working, this will impact the timeliness and perhaps also the quality of a learning session and, ultimately, the external customers, in this case learners. It is crucial therefore for organizations and their employees to understand that external customers will ultimately be on the receiving end of all poor support processes.

### ACTIVITY 2.4

1. Can you think of a situation as an external customer when you or anyone else has been on the receiving end of a poor quality of a service or product, due to what you assume is a faulty internal support process? Please explain.

2. What advice would you give to this organization by way of changing their approach?

## Process Outcomes: The Role of Perception

**Process outcomes** are perception-based measures that are highly subjective and incredibly difficult for organizations to measure and manage in any meaningful way. Perception-based measures can include:

- A change in attitude.
- Enabling people to realize their full potential.
- Trust in a system.
- Customer satisfaction.

Perception-based process outcomes are associated with behaviour or other strategic factors that are directly *outside* of an organization's control. Outcomes from processes are complex to manage and measure because they are perception-based and therefore subjective. They depend on the lens through which an individual is viewing the world on a particular day. For example, if someone is late for a meeting due to their mismanagement of time and the underground is running on time, but the individual is still late to their meeting, then it is likely they will be dissatisfied with the service, simply because they are viewing the world through a negative lens in general. As Tom Peters (1987) once said:

**'Customers perceive service in their own unique, idiosyncratic, emotional, irrational, end-of-the-day, and totally human terms. Perception is all there is!'**

Another example of process outcomes being perception-based and therefore difficult to measure and manage is illustrated by the following example from the public sector. Where crime rates in a residential area are high, a well-intentioned reaction might be to increase the police presence in that area during the periods of time when crimes are likely to be committed; an increased police presence may make residents feel safer. However, the reality might be that crime does not reduce in any meaningful way – it's just that residents *perceive* that the situation is improving due to them seeing a stronger police presence. Another factor that makes process outcomes so difficult for organizations to measure is that there is a time lag between an output from a process and an outcome. For example, in higher education, a university may record the number of successful students that graduate, yet the outcome of enabling students to reach their potential is only knowable some years after a student graduates.

### ACTIVITY 2.5

1. Figure 2.2 summarizes key process activities. Please select a process with which you are familiar. This could be the submission of an assessment, or a work process such as completing and submitting a claim for expenses. Use Figure 2.3's framework to identify inputs to the process, the actual conversion of inputs into outputs, alongside envisaged outcomes.

## Characteristics of Processes

Processes are critical for customer satisfaction, and have implications for effective change. Therefore, organizations need to better understand and manage their processes, and an important aspect is to consider key process dimensions: variety and volume. Variety relates to the complexity of the individual tasks that make up the process, whilst volume is the number of transactions that the process is set up to achieve. Accordingly, there are four different types of organizational processes:

- → **Capability processes** are characterized by high variety and low volume. This means that the tasks that make up the process are complex and the process is set up for only a few customers. The implications are that the price of the item being delivered to customers is high and the people in the process have specialist knowledge and skill sets.

- → **Commodity processes** are the opposite of capability processes. They are low in variety and high in volume. This means there are standard operating procedures for performing the process and the unit cost is low as the process is set up for a high volume of customers. The implications are that processes are standardized to achieve efficiency and there is little requirement for the work force to be skilled, because they are likely only

## Foundations for Change

responsible for one or two steps that make up the process. Therefore the cost of the service or product that is delivered to customers is low.

→ **Simplicity processes** have low process variety and low volume. The tasks involved in process completion are uncomplicated and there are few customers. An implication is that little by way of a complex skill set is required from employees and there are few customers.

→ **Complexity process** have high variety and high volume. This means the tasks involved in process completion are highly complex and, likewise, the process is set up for a high volume of customers.

### ACTIVITY 2.6

1. Consider the explanation of the various process types outlined above. Give an example of a different organization for each process type.
2. Take a look at the Ritz London and Travelodge's websites. Which types of processes do you think these very different organizations have?
3. If the Ritz Carlton decided to change from capability to commodity processes (i.e. run on a high volume of customers and highly standardized processes), what do you think the change implications may be?

## Diagnostic Tools for Good Practice Processes

It is important that organizations understand why and when processes go wrong: for example, when a service or product is not delivered on time to the customer, or when demand increases exponentially and the process is unable to keep up. When a process is inefficient or ineffective, time and costs are added. This is because process steps will need to be repeated and customers may respond by selecting an alternative, more reliable provider. A diagnostic tool such as process mapping or process deployment flowcharting can be used to determine what is working well in a process and what needs to be improved. A block diagram such as the one detailed in **Figure 2.4** can be used to give an overview of key steps that make up that process. Whilst this is useful in providing a helicopter overview of what the key process steps are, it does not lend insight as to what is working well and what needs to be improved. Therefore, it is more meaningful to think of processes in terms of interactions between individuals, departments and functions throughout the process journey. A good diagnostic tool needs to not only detail the process journey, but also the individual responsibilities and steps that each individual and department carry out. Process deployment flowcharts are useful in this respect. Individual steps, interfaces between departments, individuals and customers are detailed, as well as the sequence of steps.

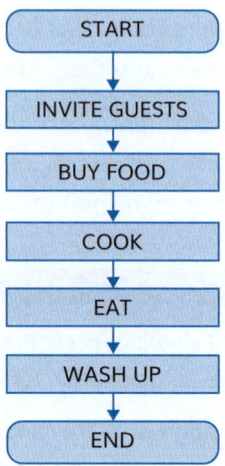

**Figure 2.4** Block diagram for an overview of a process.

Consider **Figure 2.5**. Horizontally the individuals, departments and customers involved in this process are identified as the 'cast of characters', whilst vertically the tasks that make up the process and the sequence steps are detailed. The first step is a standardized task represented by a square, which is the responsibility of Department A in liaison with Mr A. Following this, a standardized task report (represented by a baby grand piano) is issued by Department A. This is then followed by a meeting (represented by a long oval shape), which involves all of the different stakeholders in the process. Following the meeting decisions are made (a diamond shape). If the outcome of the meeting is positive, a standard task follows, no time is wasted and the process comes to an end. If the outcome of the meeting is negative, because, for example, additional information is required, or is missing, or a decision needs to be made by a more senior manager who is not at the meeting, time is wasted and earlier steps in the process must be returned to.

There is innovative software to help organizations, teams and individuals with flowcharting activities. However, a key characteristic of processes as a whole is that they interconnect individuals and groups, alongside the all-important customer, as the process makes its journey through the organization. Therefore, a good practice approach is to design and diagnose good and poor practice in processes alongside those who are involved in, or experience, the process.

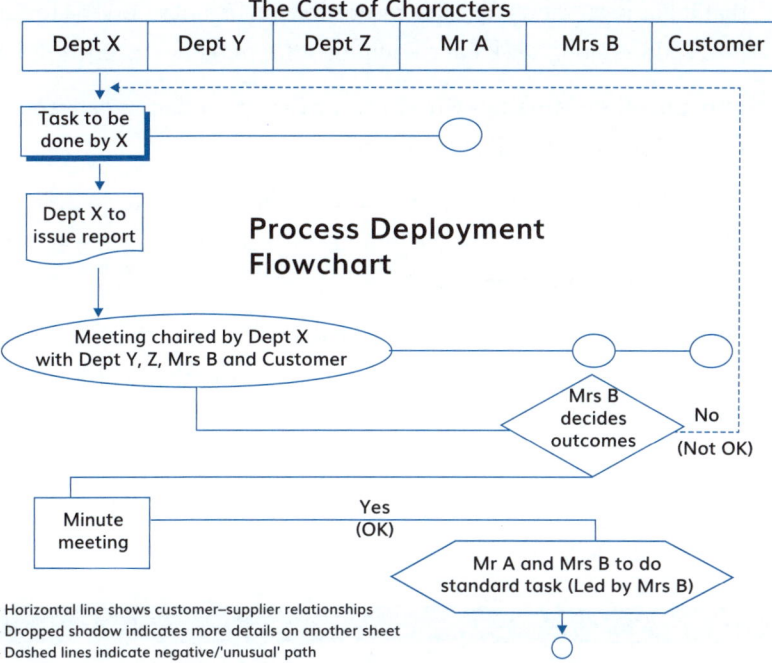

**Figure 2.5** Process deployment flowchart (based on the work of Boulter, 2024).

## Measuring Processes to Drive Change

An important aspect of managing processes for organizational change is measurement. Data from measuring processes is not only a crucial indicator of customer satisfaction, it can also be a timely reminder to take corrective action to drive change. It is important to determine whether processes are effective by reference to any differences between targets and actual results. Measuring processes also helps an organization to understand whether a change initiative is actually bringing about improved performance. A typical set of key process measures include:

→ Timeliness. Timeliness is a measure of whether products and services are being delivered within whatever predetermined timeline the organization specifies. For example, organizations usually have a specified turnaround time from customers placing an order to receiving their goods. When an order for coffee is placed, the organization will have a timeline within which they expect the servers to fulfil this order.

→ Volume. A process will have been set up for the number of products or services that are typically delivered on a day-to-day basis. However, the company must measure whether the process actually delivers the quantity that it has been set up for. This means that an organization has to consider its resources alongside kit and equipment for fulfilling customer orders.

→ Dependability. Measures whether a service or product is delivered in full and within expected delivery times.

→ Cost. Measures whether the product or service is delivered within budget. What are the total costs of the product or service, taking into account the resources used in its delivery?

→ Quality. This process measure is focused on whether the service or product meets predetermined quality standards. In other words, is it fit for purpose and free from error?

→ Flexibility. This is a measure of whether a process has the agility to adapt to significant changes in customer requirements, such as changes in demand or changes in product and service.

### ACTIVITY 2.7

Select an important process with which you are familiar and draw a block diagram depicting your key process steps. Once done, follow this up with a more detailed process deployment flowchart. For the process deployment flowchart, it will help if you firstly identify the individuals, departments and customer(s) involved, before identifying the various tasks that make up the process, and then, finally, the sequence in which the tasks occur.

1. Having completed your process deployment flowchart select a set of appropriate measures by which to understand if your process is efficient and effective.

2. If after measuring your process you found poor performance against your selected measures, what would you change to improve performance?

## Transformational Change Through Process Improvement

So far in this chapter we have considered how continuous improvement and processes support organizational change interventions. However, process improvement in itself can galvanize organizations towards change that is transformational. A strategic change intervention that can help organizations to reduce costs, attain efficiency, improve customer satisfaction and enhance and sustain continuous improvement is lean management (Naeemah and Wong, 2023; Pearce and Pons, 2017). The objective of lean management is to eliminate waste in the production process and to only focus attention on the tasks that add value to customers. This should improve customer satisfaction, as well as the quality of services and products. This approach emanates from Japanese practices post-World War II, when there were severe shortages in human resources, capital, kit and equipment. Specifically, the lean management approach to production originates from Toyota's practice, better known as the Toyota Production System (TPS). Shigeo Shingo (1984), the founding father of this approach, distinguished between the tasks in a process that add value to customers, and those that do not. Accordingly, the Toyota handbook states that the four goals of these systems are to:

1. Provide world class quality and service to the customer.
2. Develop each employee's potential, based on mutual respect, trust and cooperation.
3. Reduce cost through the elimination of waste and maximize profit.
4. Develop flexible production standards based on market demand.

Source: Toyota Production System Handbook, which can be accessed at http://artoflean.com/wp-content/uploads/2019/01/Basic_TPS_Handbook.pdf.

## Lean Principles

The five key principles (Figure 2.6) that lean management is founded upon (Womack and Jones, 2003) are outlined below. These are:

- Value – defined as any task within the production process that actually adds value to a product or service from the customer's perspective. In this way, value is specified always from the customer's perspective.

- Value Stream – refers to the activities in a process that add value to internal and external customers. Through process mapping, activities can be identified as either contributing value to the customer or not. Value Adding Activity is that which transforms, shapes or converts inputs to satisfy customer requirements. Whilst Non-Value Adding Activity (Waste) is any activity that takes time, resources or space, but does not add value. Waste should therefore be removed from the process.

- Flow – having identified the waste produced in the process and removed bottlenecks that cause delay, the organization's products and services flow to the customer as and when needed. Essential to process flow is also having a skilled, adaptive and flexible employees who work cross-functionally.

→ Pull – having removed waste and improved process flow, the timing of the delivery of the can be with customer need. Pull-based processes are focused on the customer and their requirements.

→ Perfection – an objective of lean management is to pursue organizational excellence. This means that, as part of continuous improvement, an organization needs to constantly check and re-check their processes, by reference to the preceding four key principles.

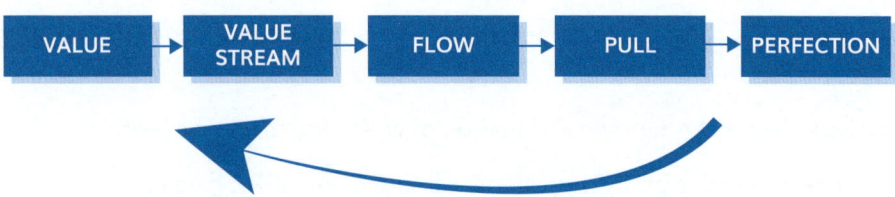

**Figure 2.6** Principles of lean management.

## Process wastes

One of the underlying objectives of lean management is to eliminate waste, 'muda', as the Japanese would identify, from a company's processes. Seven process wastes identified by Ohno (1988) are outlined below:

→ **Transportation** – any unnecessary transportation, for example, of materials, adds bottlenecks and therefore excessive time to a process.

→ **Inventory** – having excessive inventory can hide quality problems because, when things go wrong, instead of finding out the root cause of the problem the inventory is instead used. Excessive inventory can also slow down process flow and takes up valuable financial resources because it occupies expensive space.

→ **Motion** – poor workplace layout in some large organizations such as the UK's National Health Service (NHS) forces people to be in unnecessary motion, taking work packages from one department to another instead of doing valuable process work. This means that some reconfiguration will need to take place to ensure process flow.

→ **Waiting** – timeliness of processes is key for customers. Delays between steps in the process increase the time it takes for the service or product to reach the customer. Insufficient information, materials or resources all increase lead times.

# Foundations for Change    43

→ **Over production** – whilst it might feel comforting to make more than what is required by the customer, it is expensive and wasteful, because it may never be used.

→ **Over processing** – doing more than the customer is willing to pay for adds expense, as does having excessive process steps simply because that is the way the process has evolved over time.

→ **Re-work** – having to correct mistakes/faults during the production process or, worse, once the product or services has been released from the organization, can be costly in terms of an organization's reputation.

Whilst lean management started off in manufacturing, the principles and approach are now used in the service sector and, in particular, in the UK's NHS to galvanize substantial change.

## ACTIVITY 2.8

Please read the brief account of how the five key principles of lean apply to the public sector health care.

Next, listen to the WBS podcast which summarizes how lean management was able to drive significant change in Coventry and Warwick NHS Trust hospital.

Once done, answer the following questions:

1. Why do you think the NHS has used the lean approach to improve its processes? How do you think this impacts customers and people that work in the NHS?

2. What are the pros and cons of using a private sector approach in a public sector organization?

## CASE STUDY: NOTTINGHAM COUNSELLING SERVICES – HOW A PROCESS APPROACH TO CHANGE TRANSFORMS SERVICE DELIVERY

### Introduction

This case study describes how a process approach to continuous improvement, driven by a committed CEO, is returning benefits to a mental health charity's internal and external stakeholders, including clients, staff, volunteers, funders and commissioners. This is demonstrated through the charity's ongoing successful quality journey to achieving international and BSI standard certification and how the charity's holistic approach results in higher satisfaction rates among key stakeholders.

The Nottingham Counselling Service (NCS) is an independent charity and limited company formed in 1977. The aim of the charity is to improve health and relieve distress and sickness associated with emotional, personal, marital and family related problems for the benefit of adult residents within Nottingham and East Midlands. NCS believes that everyone should enjoy good mental health and wellbeing, and that access to counselling support should not be limited by circumstance or background. Their mission is to provide high-quality counselling services that are meaningful for the individual, and will also have a positive impact on the local community, wider society and economy.

The organization's counselling services are accredited by the British Association for Counselling and Psychotherapy (BACP). The BACP service accreditation is a recognized quality standard for organizations providing counselling and psychotherapy services, demonstrating that they offer an accountable, ethical, professional and responsive service to clients, staff, volunteers and stakeholders. NCS directly supports in excess of 100 clients weekly by providing face-to-face confidential counselling for individuals, couples and employees. The organization employs a diverse workforce of forty counsellors that practice a mix of theoretical approaches, all following the BACP Ethical Framework for the Counselling Professions.

## Journey Towards Process Excellence

NCS has served its local community since 1875 and today is a leading provider of therapy and support for adults living, studying and working in Nottinghamshire and the East Midlands. The service itself is founded on the needs of the client, with a focus on a humanistic people-centric approach to psychotherapy that emphasizes the quality of the relationship between a counsellor and a client based on respect, equality and authenticity. NCS's continuous journey towards excellence in service delivery is founded on their commitment to and recognition of how quality management helps put clients, staff and volunteers at the centre of everything it does, providing a robust frame for consistency of service delivery. An indicator that their quality approach works is evidenced by their client satisfaction rate for the counselling services, which currently stands at 93 per cent.

The ambition for quality recognition is a passion that the CEO, Leslie McDonald, has had since his appointment. Leslie has technical competence in quality, having been trained as an Investors in People Advisor. This enabled him to transfer good quality practice knowledge by assisting four other organizations to realize their ambitions. Whilst NCS has long subscribed to quality assurance practices, and been totally committed to enabling its staff and volunteers become their very best, it is only recently, in August 2018, that their efforts have been formally recognized through successful accreditation to ISO 9001:2015 and BS76000:2015. NCS believes the two standards are complementary and supportive, enabling them to have efficient processes for excellent service delivery and in harnessing, nurturing and developing the talents of staff and volunteers. NCS is the only Counselling Service in the East Midlands to achieve ISO 9001, BS76000 Approval and British Association for Counselling and Psychotherapy Service Accreditation at the same time.

The first author of this book was a Trustee of this charity over several years. Their view, as a former Trustee of NCS who has championed NCS's approach to quality management, is that they are an exemplar of good practice for all charities that have quality aspirations. They believe that formal accreditation benefits the charity in a number of ways that are crucial to its ongoing success, including:

- Reassuring key stakeholders including clients, staff, donors and the charities commission that the charity has excellent governance.
- Giving counsellors, clients and commissioners confidence in the charity's commitment to providing a quality service to clients.
- Putting the charity in a strong position to respond to tenders by having an internationally recognized and auditable quality system.
- Enabling the charity to manage its resources effectively.
- Having efficient and effective standard operating procedures that enable counsellors to focus on the most important thing, the clients' mental wellbeing.
- Enabling the charity to continuously improve its service by regularly reviewing key processes that impact customer satisfaction.

## Conclusion

Mental health issues in the workplace are becoming more prevalent and currently equate to a cost of some £3.6 billion. A recent NHS investigation revealed that over five million people are signed off work every year with anxiety and stress-related conditions. In view, however, of competing service priorities, juggling budgets during times of reduced resources, and a shifting sands approach to national and local policy, access to NHS mental health services is not straightforward and can be limited with protracted waiting times. This is where the provision of an excellent and quality-driven counselling service by charities such as the NCS make a meaningful contribution to key stakeholders in the local and national community. NCS's approach to continuous improvement enables them to provide mental health wellbeing that is not restricted by an individual's circumstances and background. The importance of good mental health for individuals and societal wellbeing at large is crucial. Poor mental health impacts an individual's quality of life and has an economic cost to society. In these resource-strapped times it is charities like NCS that make a much-needed contribution to the wellbeing of the local community.

## NCS's Good Practice Tips to Realize Quality Aspirations

→ It is critical to get Senior Management's commitment to driving continuous improvement throughout the whole organization.

→ Get the Board involved and have at least one Trustee who is able to champion your quality approach as part of continuous improvement in service delivery.

→ It is crucial that senior managers articulate their vision to staff, volunteers and other stakeholders as to how this approach will benefit governance and impact staff and users' satisfaction.

→ Involve staff early on. Staff have intimate process knowledge. Get them to draw out the processes as they currently are and get them to agree on how the current processes can be improved.

→ Make a formal commitment to quality in your strategic plans so that quality becomes the way of 'doing things around here'.

→ Find as much information as possible on the various quality approaches and quality standards, and be clear as to which is the right one for your charity and, importantly, why. Consider how this will ensure you focus on your priorities.

→ Don't be shy about asking and calling on other charities about their experience, gaining knowledge about their approach.

→ Choose some early easy wins so that you can point out the benefits of a quality approach to staff.

### ACTIVITY 2.9

1. Who are the various stakeholders at NCS?
2. How have the NCS's changes to their processes impacted customers' satisfaction and why?
3. What are the benefits of changes to NCS's key processes for internal customers?

## A Joined-Up Approach to Change – Excellence Models as a Holistic Framework for Managing Organizational-Wide Change

In Chapter 1 we explored various process models of change. However, a key critique made is that they do not account for the reality of how an organization's experience changes, which is multi-faceted, dynamic and complex. This is where an organizational excellence model/framework can be useful: see Figure 2.7. Organizational excellence frameworks are used across the globe including in the UK, US, Europe, Dubai, Abu Dhabi, Africa, Singapore and Japan and by a range of large and small private, public and voluntary organizations. Utilizing these excellence models as a framework for change and improving performance is proven to make a positive impact on organizational sustainability and key accounting measures, such as operating income and share value (Boulter et al., 2013). See Figures 2.8, 2.9 and 2.10, which evidence organizations that have been awarded for their implementation of excellence that results in the outperformance of other organizations in a variety of key financial variables. Furthermore, as you will see from Figures 2.9 and 2.10, this performance is sustained. Such models recognize many of the complex dimensions of change that are discussed throughout this book including culture, human aspects at an individual and group level, processes, leadership, strategy, ethics, customer satisfaction, employee wellbeing as well as measuring the effectiveness of an organization's approach to performance improvement through a balanced scorecard approach, all of which are fundamental to effective change.

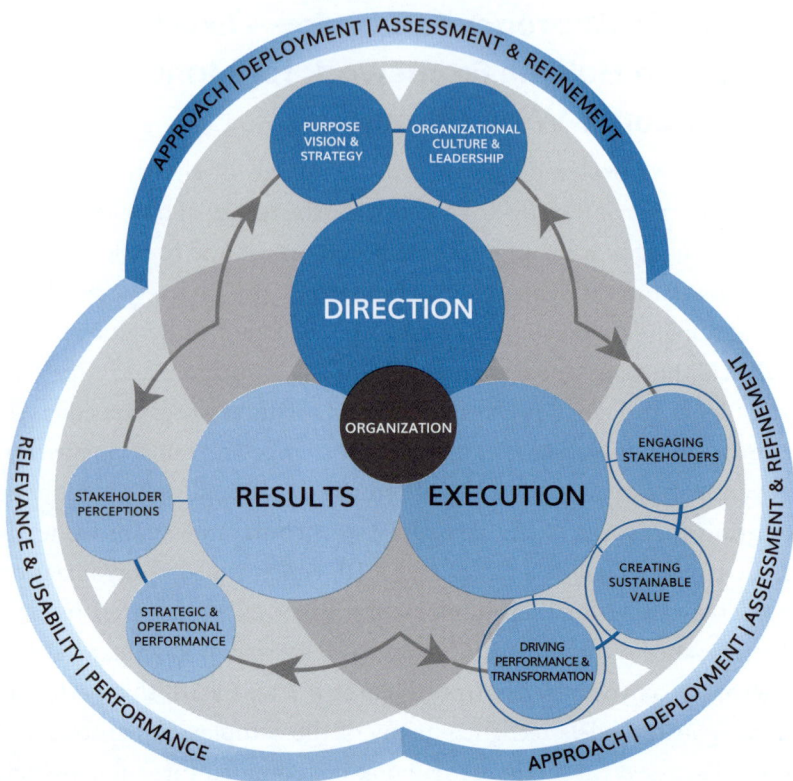

**Figure 2.7** An organizational excellence framework: EFQM model. Source and copyright: European Foundation for Quality Management.

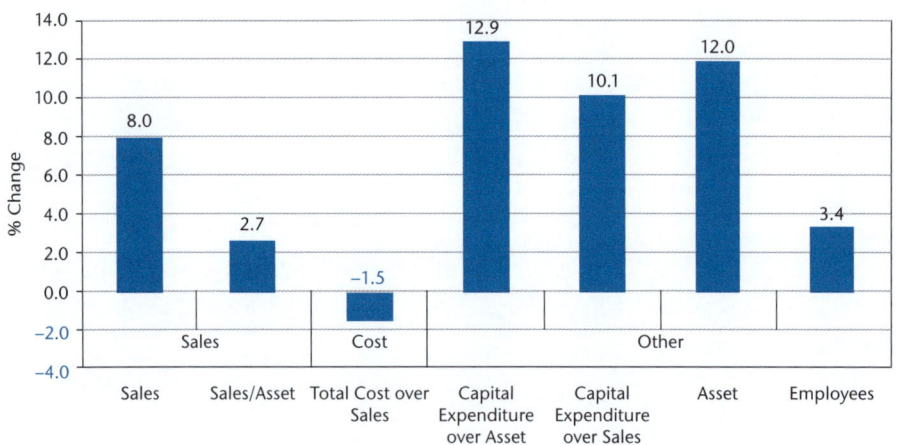

**Figure 2.8** Mean difference of percentage change in various key accounting measures one year after having won an award (Boulter et al., 2013).

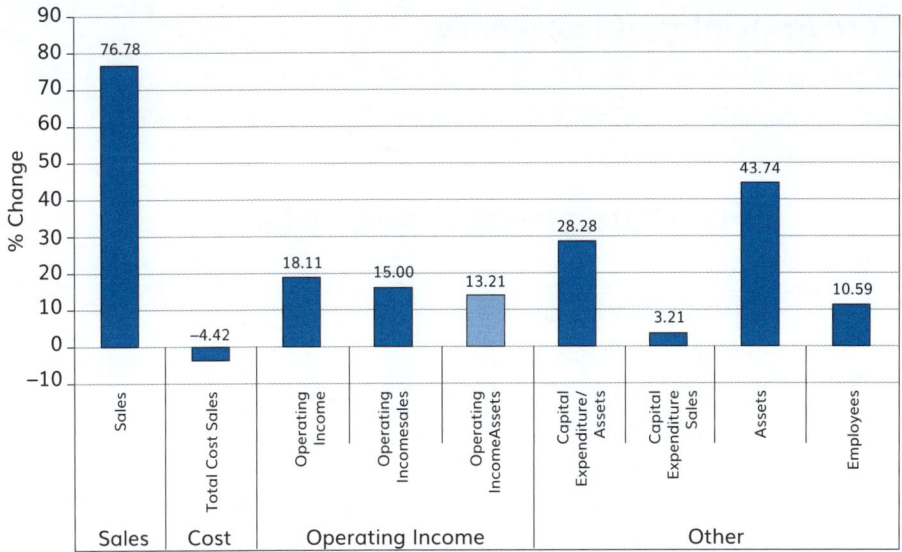

**Figure 2.9** Mean difference of percentage change in various key accounting measures five years after having won an award (Boulter et al., 2013).

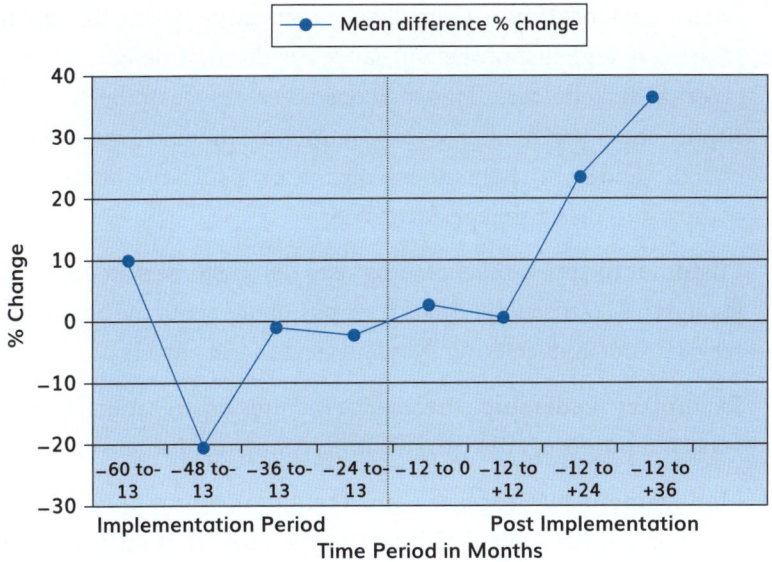

**Figure 2.10** Differences in share price performance between an award-winning company and comparison companies (Boulter et al., 2013).

## Core Principles of Excellence

Organizational excellence, upon which these frameworks are founded, encapsulate eight core principles, as set out in Figure 2.11:

### Fundamental Concepts

- Results Orientation
- Customer Focus
- Leadership and Constancy of Purpose
- Management by Processes and Facts
- People Development and Involvement
- Continuous Learning, Innovation and Improvement
- Partnership Development
- Public Responsibility

**Figure 2.11** Fundamental concepts underlying excellence.

→ **Results orientation** – an excellent organization is one that is oriented to achieve and sustain performance results that delight internal and external stakeholders. This includes investors, customers, employees, supply chain partnerships, the community in which the organization operates and so forth. In other words, the organization takes a balanced approach to measuring performance.

→ **Customer focus** – excellence recognizes that customers are key stakeholders and collects meaningful data from customers about the organization, its services and products to analyse and create a sustainable customer focus.

→ **Exemplary leadership** – excellence requires organizations to have constancy of purpose, even in a dynamic, changing business environment.

→ **Management by processes and facts** – organizational decisions are based on objective quantifiable data and feedback from key processes.

→ **Continuous learning, innovation and improvement** – the focus is upon people development and their involvement. Excellence recognizes that employees make a major contribution towards the success of an organization. They invest in training and education for employees' development to maximize the contribution made by the employees. Excellent organizations utilize learning to continuously innovate and improve services and products.

→ **Partnership development** – excellence requires organizations to have meaningful, ethical and sustainable partnership relationships with its supply chain.

→ **Public responsibility** – it is understood that excellence recognizes that decisions made by organizations have implications for local and global stakeholders and are therefore grounded in ethical standards of practice.

## Excellence Frameworks for Change

Excellence models are updated in line with what is happening in the macro environment as well as good practices of contemporary organizations and other institutions. For example, the most recent version of the European Excellence model (see Figure 2.7) has been co-created with input from over 2000 change experts and sixty leaders from diverse organizations. It also recognizes the 17 Sustainable Development Goals of the United Nations (UN), which are associated with social equity, governance and prosperity while protecting the planet, in addition to the UN's ten principles for sustainable and socially responsible business. Excellence frameworks provide a structured and holistic approach in managing organization-wide change for improving performance by asking:

→ 'Why' does this organization exist? What purpose does it fulfil? Why this particular strategy? (Direction).

→ 'How' does it intend to deliver on its purpose and its strategy? (Execution).

→ 'What' has it actually achieved to date? What does it intend to achieve tomorrow? (Results).

Organizations use the various criteria of the excellence framework to understand current performance in key areas, as well as gaps in performance, which in turn generates an action plan for change. This is facilitated by a diagnostic tool, RADAR: see Figure 2.12. This requires organizations to determine future results that it then strives to achieve as part of its strategy. To do this the organization will identify a set of approaches to attain the results, which are deployed across the whole of the organization and taken onboard by all individuals and groups. The organization will evaluate and monitor the actual results it achieves in key areas by comparison to the results that it envisaged. Following this, the organization will identify and take corrective action where achievements in performance are not being met. We might say that in this way the excellence framework is a right to left model, rather than a left to right model, which is the typical way in which many organizations approach change. Organizations commence their thinking around change based on future predicted results before thinking through which improvement activities will help them attain these results.

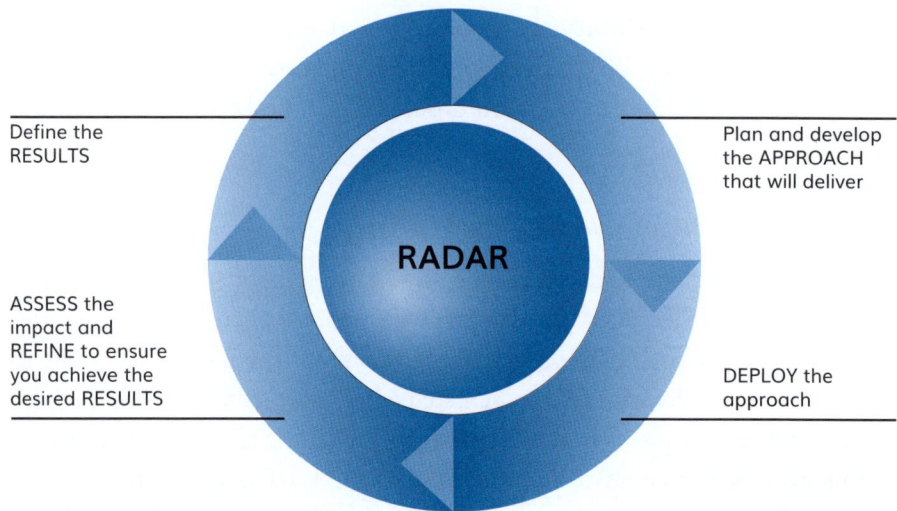

**Figure 2.12** RADAR – diagnostic tool. Copyright: European Foundation for Quality Management.

To understand how the excellence framework model has galvanized and driven change, consider the following mini case studies of the Abu Dhabi police force, the Alpenresort Shwart, and BMW.

### ACTIVITY 2.10
To understand how the excellence framework model has galvanized and driven change, consider the following mini case studies of the Abu Dhabi police force, the Alpenresort Shwart, and BMW.

###  CONSULTANCY IN THE CHAIR

#### Cup of Kindness Activity

Based on your knowledge of successful organizational change initiatives, and over many years dealing with significant and effective change projects across a wide variety of organizations, you are convinced that the EFQM framework provides a suitable framework for managing change at CUP. You are invited into a meeting with the CEO: put together a five-slide PowerPoint presentation drawing upon some of the evidence presented in this chapter that will convince the CEO of the benefits of using the EFQM as a framework for effective change at CUP.

### Competency-based Interview Question

1. Why are processes so important to all organizations? Please illustrate your answer by reference to an organization with which you are familiar.

## Chapter Summary

In summary, whilst continuous improvement, quality and process improvements constitute the fundamentals of an excellent organization, and are fundamental to change, they may well be forgotten. This is because continuous improvement activities underpin all incremental and significant change. To do well at change, organizations need to understand customer and stakeholder requirements and manage their processes accordingly because of their impact on customer satisfaction. A key part of this is ensuring that meaningful measures are in place, which will determine if change is effective or whether further corrective improvement is required. In this chapter consideration has also been given to processes as a way of driving substantial change, explicitly through the application of lean management in the public sector. Finally, we have reviewed excellence as a systematic model or framework that can be used to facilitate organizational-wide incremental and transformative change, because it takes a joined-up and comprehensive approach that encapsulates the complexities of such change.

## Useful Resources

https://www.quality.org
https://www.juse.or.jp/english
https://deming.org

## Bibliography

Boulter, L., Bendell, T. and Dahlgaard, J. J. (2013), 'Total Quality Beyond North America: A Comparative Analysis of the Performance of European Excellence Award Winners'. *International Journal of Operations and Production Management*, 33(2): 197–215.

Crosby, P. B. (1979). *Quality is Free: The Art of Making Quality Certain.* New York: McGraw-Hill.

Deming, W. E. (2000), *Out of the Crisis*. Cambridge, MA: MIT Press.

Fasko, S. A. (2023), 'Garvin's Eight Dimensions of Quality and DOD Acquisition'. *Defense Acquisition (Fort Belvoir, VA.)*, 52(6): 24.

Feigenbaum, A. V. (1991), *Total Quality Control*. New York: McGraw-Hill.

Fonseca, L. (2022), 'The EFQM 2020 Model. A Theoretical and Critical Review'. *Total Quality Management & Business Excellence*. Abingdon: Routledge, 1011–38. DOI: https://doi.org/10.1080/14783363.2021.1915121.

Freeman, R. E. (1984), *Strategic Management: A Stakeholder Approach*. Marshfield, MA: Pitman.

Freeman, R. E. (2010), *Strategic Management: A Stakeholder Approach*. Cambridge: Cambridge University Press.

Garvin, D. A. (1987), 'Competing on the Eight Dimensions of Quality'. *Harvard Business Review*, https://hbr.org/1987/11/competing-on-the-eight-dimensions-of-quality (accessed 9 April 2025).

Ishikawa, K. (1985), *'What Is Total Quality Control? The Japanese Way'*. Translated by Lu, D. J. Englewood Cliffs, NJ: Prentice-Hall.

Juran, J. (1988), *Quality Control Handbook*. New York: McGraw-Hill.

Johnston, R., Shulver, M., Slack, N. and Clark, G. (2021), *Service Operations Management: Improving Service Delivery*, fifth edition. Harlow, England: Pearson.

Kaplan, R. S. and Norton, D. P. (1996), *The Balanced Scorecard: Translating Strategy Into Action*. Boston, MA: Harvard Business School.

Naeemah, A. J. and Wong, K. Y. (2023), 'Selection Methods of Lean Management Tools: A Review'. *International Journal of Productivity and Performance Management*, 72(4): 1077–110. DOI: https://doi.org/10.1108/IJPPM-04-2021-0198.

Ohno, T. (1988), *Toyota Production System: Beyond Large-scale Production*. Boca Raton, FL: CRC Press.

Parmar, B. L., Freeman, R. E. and Harrison, J. S. (2010), 'Stakeholder Theory: The State of the Art'. *Management Faculty Publications*, 99. https://scholarship.richmond.edu/management-faculty-publications/99(accessed9April2025).

Pearce, A. D. and Pons, D. J. (2017), 'Defining Lean Change—Framing Lean Implementation in Organizational Development'. *An International Journal of Business and Management*, 12(4): 10. DOI: https://doi.org/10.5539/ijbm.v12n4p10.

Peters, T. J. (1987), *Thriving on Chaos*. London: London Guild Publishing.

Shingo, S. and Dillon, A. P. (1989), *A Study of the Toyota Production System: From an Industrial Engineering Viewpoint*. Boca Raton: FL: CRC Press.

Womack, J. P. and Jones, D. T. (2003), *Lean Thinking: Banish Waste and Create Wealth in your Corporation*, second edition. New York: The Free Press.

# The Nature of Change in Contemporary Organizations
## Strategy and Culture

**3**

### Learning Outcomes

At the end of this chapter you will be able to:

1. Understand how strategic and cultural change are related in organizations, and how they require internal transformations in response to changes in external environments.
2. Define organizational design and understand its link to strategic change.
3. Recognize the importance of redesigning organization structures to support the implementation of a new strategy.
4. Critically evaluate what strategic change can look like in specific organizational contexts, in terms of different forms of decision, setting, scenario and implementation.
5. Assess, explore and diagnose organizational cultures in terms of different levels, types, dimensions, components and values.
6. Explain how organizational cultures can be difficult to change, harm people, obstruct other changes and connect back to strategy and structure.

Please remember to dip into the reading and other resources during your learning journey throughout this chapter.

## Introduction

Strategy and culture are two crucial components in understanding the changing relationship between an organization's internal and external context. In this respect, strategy and culture are interwoven. This chapter reviews and critically reflects on how and why organizations change their strategies. This chapter also reflects on how organizations try to better understand their organizational culture in response to changing external environments. We discuss the general processes organizations follow when trying to align internal values, resources and capabilities with the changing external environment, which often results in transformational change. Strategic change is defined as how organizations transform themselves by exploring competitive, distinctive and innovative ways of doing business and generating value. Another topic covered is organizational 'redesign', focusing on how a new organizational shape and structure can support the implementation of a corresponding change in strategy. Various strategic change contexts are highlighted, such as mergers and acquisitions (M&As) and downsizings. Involvement of a top management team, improvements or declines in organizational performance, and implementation at different organizational levels are identified as common themes of strategic change. Finally, organizational culture, which impacts both strategy and its successful implementation, is discussed. Organizational culture is woven into all aspects of an organization. This includes the way in which the organization wishes to be perceived by its internal and external stakeholders. It is argued that culture can be difficult to change in any deep and meaningful way, to the extent that it may prevent strategic change from happening, and consequently may require cycles of interventions.

## Organizational Change in Response to the Changing External Environment

Changing an organization's strategy and/or culture in response to a changing external environment is arguably one of the most large-scale, ambitious, complex and daunting forms of change an organization can engage with. Often the language used to describe such change reflects this. Adjectives such as 'transformational', 'radical', 'revolutionary', 'disruptive', 'discontinuous' or 'second-order' might all be used. In part, this is because many significant drivers or triggers of organizational change come from the wider environment, such as:

→ Growth opportunities, including expansion into new markets.

→ Changes in economic conditions, such as booms and busts, competition, investment and trade.

- Technological developments, including artificial intelligence.
- New government legislation and public policy initiatives.
- The need to learn new ways of doing things, including upskilling in terms of knowledge and skills and, moreover, in terms of behaviour.

In responding to such environmental triggers or drivers of change, organizations need to look at their strategic objectives and find or create entirely new ways of doing business to accomplish them. This means making sure that internal resources, values, structures, capacity and capabilities are aligned with external changes in ways that are competitive, innovative or distinctive, for creating and capturing value in the wider economy and society.

## Strategy and Culture

Debates about the relative importance of strategy and culture have often revolved around the popular business expression that 'culture eats strategy for breakfast', sometimes attributed to management expert Peter Drucker, despite him not having ever said or wrote those exact words (Bryant, 2021). However, whatever its precise origins, the essence of the argument is that even if you have a great strategic plan and priorities for change, the change may still fail if you have not cultivated the 'right' culture to reinforce the strategy and bring it to life through norms, values and behaviours. This is not to say that one is more important than the other, but rather that both are important for driving successful organizational change, and both are necessarily part of a broader conversation about an organization's strengths and purposes (Favaro, 2014). Yet, this is challenging because it involves large-scale thinking about how different parts of the organization fit together to make a coherent and successful whole in its entirety.

One place to start could be with a few simple but profound questions about the organization (Watkins, 2007):

1. *Mission and goals:* **what** will be achieved by the organization?
2. *Value network:* with **whom** will the organization create and capture value?
3. *Vision and incentives:* **why** should people in the organization want to perform well?
4. *Strategy:* **how** should resources be allocated to fulfil the mission in the network?

The upshot of asking these questions is that the organization needs to figure out how these major components can align in terms of change to create a sense of strategic direction and action. In business strategy and strategic change, the emphasis is particularly on the *'how'* – *how to adopt and communicate a set of guiding principles that people throughout the organization can use to make decisions and allocate resources*. In a successful execution or implementation of the strategy, the organization can accomplish key objectives by generating a distinctive pattern of approaches and capabilities (Watkins, 2007).

### ACTIVITY 3.1

1. What do you think is meant by 'culture eats strategy for breakfast'?
2. Describe what you think is the interplay between strategy and culture as part of successful substantive organizational change.
3. What is the importance of organizational culture for successful change?

## Mapping and Measuring Organizational Environments

Internally, as organizations develop and grow, and become more mature and complex, they are likely to have to review their structure at crucial points to ensure it holds together, stays in alignment and remains well-designed for dealing with their external environment (Greiner, 1972; 1998). Accordingly:

→ Small organizations (e.g. start-ups) can be highly creative and dynamic but may eventually need to decide on more formal leadership arrangements.

→ As leadership sets direction but the organization gets larger, some divisions and units may need greater autonomy to adjust in their parts within the business.

→ As work becomes delegated across an even larger organization, there will be a growing need to reassert control from the centre to ensure consistency and integration.

→ As work becomes coordinated again across the organization, some control requirements from the centre may feel too bureaucratic and rigid, and therefore may need to be delegated amongst teams.

→ At the stage of a very large, complex, mature organization, further collaboration and restructuring may be required to pursue further growth and change opportunities.

In discussing these issues in relation to change, people in organizations may use terms like 'business model' to describe solving problems or fulfilling needs for their customers and stakeholders externally ('doing the right things'), and 'operating model' to describe how their processes, structures and relationships allow them to carry out the business model to a high performance standard ('doing things right'). There may be many potential connections between the internal and external environments of organizations to consider during strategic change, in terms of how they enable both innovation and growth. For companies like Apple or Amazon, their structures and capabilities become so interconnected that they are described as part of an 'ecosystem strategy'. This is because their websites, apps and platforms bring many diverse developers, buyers and sellers together as part of an integrated experience.

Externally, organizations can try to map out their environment to different forms and degrees in order to better understand and prioritize potential forces of change that they will need to manage and respond to. Sometimes the external environment is divided into two categories – a more immediate, near 'task' environment and a broader, more far-reaching 'general' environment.

## Diagnostic Tools for Mapping the Task and General Environment

For mapping the task environment, Michael Porter's five forces model remains an influential strategic management tool that focuses on changes relating to: (1) industry competitors; (2) potential new entrants to the industry; (3) the bargaining power of buyers or customers; (4) potential threats from new substitute products/services; and (5) the bargaining power of suppliers of resources to the organization (e.g. Grundy, 2006).

For mapping the much broader general environment, managers and strategists might use other tools to assess and discuss change forces, such as a PESTEL/PESTLE analysis – an acronym that systematically spells out the areas or types of factors organizations must consider: *Political, Economic, Social, Technological, Environmental* (i.e. climate) and *Legal*. Another acronym-based tool, SWOT, allows for some evaluation and mapping between an organization's internal *Strengths* and *Weaknesses*, on the one hand, and external *Opportunities* and *Threats*, on the other. Overall, there are many tools, techniques and models relating to organizational analysis and strategic change, which need to be used thoughtfully and carefully, and often in combination, to guide and focus strategic planning and discussions (Boatman, 2024).

For many corporate, market-oriented and profit-driven/private sector organizations, *competition* is typically and inevitably a major focus of strategic change. An organization needs to think about the 'factors of competition' in an industry or market (e.g. price, service and quality) and how its own strengths and capabilities compare with what its competitors are doing or offering. Understanding an organization's strategic profile of strengths and weaknesses relative to that of its competitors may prompt powerful ideas and visions of strategic change, particularly if there is an opportunity for the organization to distinguish itself by finding a new and popular way of doing business. To do so, it often helps to map the current reality 'as is', and the desired future reality 'to be'. This is because strategic change typically involves a profound shift between an 'old' and 'new' way of doing things, and further discussions about how to get there.

One influential metaphor for strategic change and competition has been the ocean. A 'red' ocean describes a market full of intense and 'bloody' competition. In this view, the aim of effective strategic change is to seek out 'blue' oceans where an organization can stand out from the competition by moving into a completely new space. For example, in the 1980s and 1990s in the short-haul US airline industry, there was a red ocean of many similar airlines competing on price, meals, seating and connections. Southwest Airlines, however, decided not to compete on these factors, but to focus all their energy on a blue ocean strategy that prioritized friendly service, speed and frequency of departures, where the only competition was perhaps travelling by car instead of by plane: 'the speed of the plane at the price of the car – whenever you need it' (Kim and Mauborgne, 2002). Like all metaphors, it can be extended and played around with to create other ways of thinking about strategy – for example, a 'purple ocean' involving simultaneous competition and innovation, or a 'green ocean' involving a pro-environmental sustainability strategy.

However, as mentioned earlier, successful strategic change typically involves paying attention to many interconnected elements in the organization, all having relatively equal importance, and all requiring focus and coordination. As a result, many influential frameworks tend to involve diagrams that reflect this as an array of interdependent elements that all need to fit and align together. One typical example of this is the McKinsey 7-S framework (Figure 3.1). First introduced in the late 1970s, it remains an enduring idea and important tool for understanding organizations, improving their performance, thinking through how best to implement a proposed strategy and examining the likely effects of ongoing and future changes on the organization (McKinsey, 2008).

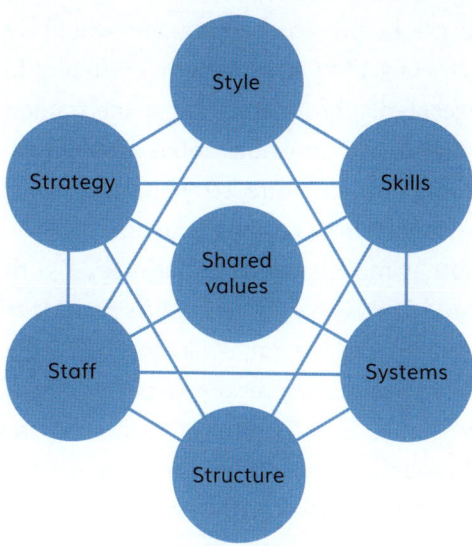

**Figure 3.1** The 7-S framework (McKinsey, 2008).

The seven 'S-word' elements of the 7-S framework can be further categorized into three 'hard' factors (strategy, structure, systems) and four 'soft' factors (shared values, skills, style and staff). The seven individual factors are as follows:

1. **Strategy:** the plan, purpose and position of the organization to achieve competitive advantage.
2. **Structure:** how people, activities, authority and reporting are organized for coordination.
3. **Systems:** procedures for measurement, resource allocation and information management.
4. **Shared Values:** a widely shared set of core values and guiding principles concerning the mission, vision and purpose of what is important for all employees.
5. **Style:** typical behaviour patterns of managers, leaders and groups, including culture.
6. **Staff:** employees' distinctive capabilities and characteristics, human resources (HR) practices.
7. **Skills:** the organization's core competencies and strengths.

Typically, organizations will hold strategic change discussions that start with shared values, and then work their way around the hard and soft elements, planning adjustments to align them and to analyse whether this alignment is working or not. This can be time-consuming, and will likely need to take place over months and cycles of activity to see whether different forces for change can be harnessed and executed appropriately. What the framework does highlight is how diagnosing and solving organizational problems for strategic change concerns understanding how structure, strategy and culture are all related and can affect each other, and be in or out of alignment.

There are many other models like the McKinsey 7-S that were developed between the 1970s and 1990s, such as *Galbraith's Star Model* (unlike 7-S, it has five points in a star shape), and the *Burke–Litwin Model* (which is made up of no less than twelve factors affecting organizational performance and change). While these models all have similar uses in terms of facilitating strategic collaboration that focuses on a thorough set of factors, they can also be criticized for their limitations. The many factors they describe can seem complex or overwhelming, and they cannot fully resolve how internal and external factors interrelate, nor what action should be taken as a result of the analysis.

> **ACTIVITY 3.2**
>
> 1. Use the 7-S framework to analyse the strategy of either a university or an organization with which you are familiar.
> 2. What does your analysis reveal about the complexities and interconnectedness between the hard and soft factors of the 7-S framework?
> 3. Which do you consider most important in regards to strategic change: hard factors or soft factors? Please explain the rationale behind your answer.

## Measuring and Feedback for Effective Strategic Change

After mapping out strategic change areas, organizations must also consider how to measure and gather feedback on the strategic change implementation actions – to check and understand whether change in the various areas is having the desired effects. Here, frameworks again stress the multidimensional and interconnected areas across the organization. One of the most influential tools in this domain is Kaplan and Norton's Balanced Scorecard, developed in the 1990s, which is a general strategic performance management tool made up of four perspectives with associated Key Performance Indicators (KPIs) or measures (e.g. Cokins, 2010):

1. *Financial:* value for shareholders through productivity and growth. Measures include cash flow, sales growth, return on investment (ROI), lower unit costs.

2. *Customer:* fulfilling what is important for customers. Measures include customer satisfaction, sales, loyalty, customer rankings.

3. *Internal Processes:* ensuring the quality and productivity of operations. Measures include cycle times, yields, relationship management, new product development, innovations, regulatory compliance.

4. *Learning and Growth:* goals relating to investment in and development of people. Measures include employee performance, team performance, leadership, culture, knowledge management, engagement in training and development programmes.

The general idea is that a carefully mapped strategic system and a corresponding scorecard system will help guide more effective strategic change execution. However, critical questions remain about using such tools in different social and technical ways. There are still difficult and varied choices for organizations to make about how responsibilities are shared, how key measures are selected, how to arrive at an overall score or conclusion, and how to reflect broader stakeholder needs rather than just financial ones.

Strategic change can be risky and uncertain, and relative success or failure difficult to predict or maintain. It is easy for organizations to make poor decisions, to try to do or be too many things at once, to lack control over multiple conditions, and for their internal environments to drift out of alignment with their external ones. Broadly, successful transformational changes tend to involve the creation of a powerful strategic identity, a process designed to build trust with important stakeholders, innovations that build up and spread through experimentation and scaling, and the preservation of valuable 'legacy' assets of the organization from the past (Kent, Lancefield and Reilly, 2018).

## Effective Strategic Change: Behaviours and Leadership

A study of top twenty-first century business transformations featuring leading global companies like Netflix, Microsoft, Tencent, Alibaba, Orsted, Siemens and Fujifilm found that such companies were building ambitious new identities relating to transforming fields of technology, climate change, healthcare and finance (Anthony, Trotter and Schwartz, 2019). The five behaviours these companies had in common were: (1) creating a higher-purpose mission; (2) not being afraid to let go of the past; (3) leveraging a core capability to enter new growth markets; (4) seizing digital opportunities for new platforms and business models; and (5) innovation that is not isolated but is widespread across departments. At the same time, strong strategic leadership typified by courage, clarity, curiosity and conviction was needed to navigate three crises that might arise during the change. These three crises were labelled: (1) *crisis of commitment* early on about seeing the change through; (2) *crisis of conflict* over how to use and share resources for new growth areas; and (3) *crisis of identity* over what the company is becoming and feelings of belonging towards it (Innosight, 2019).

There is a great deal to consider in strategic change, simply because it involves most or all of the organization, including its structure and culture. Yet reviewing successful change transformations does seem to reveal common themes within this complexity, particularly around how organizations relate their internal environments to their external environments in an ambitious, purposeful and systematic way.

It is clear that strategic change involves much recommended mapping, modelling and measuring of what the organization does and how it does it or might do it differently. Yet it is also important to bear in mind that in addition to these more planned approaches, there are likely to be unplanned elements of uncertainty, unintended consequences and sheer chance, which must be managed along the way in the implementation of strategic change. Examples of this include the death of executives (as happened at Nokia), and effects of the global financial crisis and supply chain disruptions on the automotive industry (Aspara, Lamberg, Sihvonen and Tikkanen, 2023; MacKay and Chia, 2013). Nevertheless, organizations must for the most part try to address change using what they can control. Once leaders understand their external and internal environments in relation to strategic change, they must also consider how to *redesign* the organization so that it can function effectively in relation to new realities and goals.

## Organization Design and Redesign to Support Strategic Change

In many ways, an organization's design or redesign is an extension of an organization-wide focus on strategy, structure and culture. However, as a change process, organizational design reflects a more specific or 'zoomed in' concern with changing aspects or features of workflows, procedures, structures and systems within the organization. One common analogy for organizational design is to look at it in the same way as an architect would draw up plans for a new building – how it will look, feel and be used by different people in the building. Another analogy is to say an organization's design is like the human body, where the structure is like the anatomy, the processes are like the physiology and the culture is like the psychology.

Often, organizational design will involve reviewing how to bridge a gap between the organization's current design and its desired future design, based on a change in strategy, goals or purpose. This will often be accompanied by various mapping and organizational analysis tools discussed earlier in this chapter. An organization's design has a close relationship with the organization's development, but development activities tend to come after a redesign, where further efforts are made to help people maintain and improve new ways of working within the new design (CIPD, 2023).

As a change process, organizational design may take months or even years, as many people across the organization discuss and debate potential changes to structures, processes and relationships. Four common areas of organizational design concern:

1. *Differentiation* – how different elements of work should be allocated across the organization, vertically across different levels of hierarchy, and/or horizontally across different teams and other areas of responsibility or reporting.

2. *Integration* – reducing barriers and differences in functions to ensure people coordinate and communicate more closely across tasks and roles, by working in cross-functional teams, for example.

3. *Centralization* – the extent to which power should be concentrated at the centre of the organization or top of the management hierarchy, versus empowering employees to be more proactive and take risks (de-centralization).

4. *Culture strength* – the extent to which organizational culture is formally prescribed through norms, induction and mandatory formal requirements, versus being more informal and dynamic, with discretion.

Many other areas of organizational design can be expressed in related ways, in terms of how patterns of work arrangements reflect knowledge, control and innovation. The general idea is for a design to help act as a mechanism for organizational effectiveness in response to strategy, environment, culture, technology and other changes affecting the organization over time. Indeed, organizational effectiveness may form part of the debate over what the outcome of the design should lead to, be it quality, efficiency, resilience or some other combination of effectiveness criteria. Organizational designs have evolved to reflect new challenges in the business world, such as patterns of globalization, technology adoption, social values and competition for skills and knowledge.

Most traditional organizational designs have been based around people working in *functions* (HR, marketing, finance, IT), but also in larger organizations around *divisions* (multiple functions working to serve a specific market or region).

Many organizational designs have also come to include 'matrix' characteristics, where people report both horizontally to a project team leader, and vertically to their more traditional functional or hierarchical leader. Conventional organizational designs are often based around trying to have clear hierarchies, boundaries and roles, but these can easily become too complicated, inefficient or rigid in relation to more dynamic environments. From the twentieth century and into the twenty-first, some emerging organizational designs, particularly in fast-changing technological industries, have shown a preference for flatter hierarchies, with more decentralized teams and networks, working across different boundaries and roles, to support greater adaptation and innovation (Child and McGrath, 2001).

In theory, an organization's design can be based around many different formal and informal elements or 'building blocks' making up the work arrangements. Sophisticated designs may be extensive inside and beyond the organization, with virtual working, governing boards or committees, mergers, supply chain partnerships, outsourcing arrangements, strategic alliances and flexible working practices all playing a part. However, if a major redesign is being considered as a form of organizational change, there is likely to be a lot at stake in terms of the costs and benefits of choosing between possible design options. Designs that are not simple enough or smart enough to enable effective work across an organization risk seriously disrupting staff motivation and commitment, or creating costly bureaucracy that harms organizational focus and performance.

## The Redesign Process

To guide the redesign process, Goold and Campbell (2002) proposed no less than nine tests for deciding whether changing to a new organizational structure would make for a well-designed organization:

1. *Market advantage test* – ensuring that work units match clear areas of strength or competitive market advantage.

2. *Parenting test* – ensuring that senior 'parent' or corporate-level headquarter units have ways of adding value across the units for which they are responsible.

3. *People test* – ensuring that the design places talented, motivated people in important positions where they can perform well.

4. *Feasibility test* – ensuring that constraints on implementing the design have been accounted for, such as regulatory, technological or cultural incompatibilities.

5. *Specialist cultures test* – ensuring that more specialist units can protect their distinct cultures where they need to work differently from the norm.

6. *Difficult links test* – ensuring that for units where collaboration may be more difficult or conflict more likely, there is alignment, incentives and rules for reaching agreements.

7. *Redundant hierarchy test* – ensuring that the organization only has additional 'parenting' levels and units if they are clear, distinct and improve performance.

8. *Accountability test* – ensuring that work units have efficient, motivating and relevant controls over their performance and shared responsibilities.

9. *Flexibility test* – ensuring that there is enough flexibility for people in the organization to adapt to changing circumstances and explore future opportunities for innovation.

As can be seen, this is a complex set of tests. However, they do provide a way for organizational designers to discuss and test out specific changes and then, over time, have repeated discussions around how well changes are working or affecting each other. The ninth test has special importance in terms of how organizations juggle or balance performing well and gradually improving at what they are well-designed for in the present (e.g. mature markets), while simultaneously exploring and preparing for the breakthrough innovations (e.g. emerging markets) of the future.

## An Ambidextrous Approach to Organization Design

One powerful answer has been for organizations to build this balance into the design itself – something that has been described as an *ambidextrous* organizational design (see Figure 3.1). Just as ambidexterity refers to being able to use both the left hand and the right hand equally, ambidextrous organizations can use their design to balance *exploitation* of their existing competencies with simultaneous *exploration* of new, emerging future opportunities for establishing competence in something else.

Many real-life business change successes and failures can be explained in terms of how ambidextrous an organization was. For example, Kodak exploited film photography but failed to explore digital photography. Ciba Vision managed to exploit existing glasses and optical markets, while also successfully adapting to explore new eye care treatments and contact lenses. Seiko managed to exploit existing advantages in mechanical watch markets, while also exploring opportunities in making newer, quartz watches. Some long-standing companies even manage to leverage ambidextrous qualities to go through a series of revolutionary changes across decades of change. Examples include IBM moving from mechanical office equipment to computer hardware to computer software services, or Johnson and Johnson moving between consumer products, pharmaceuticals and medical technology markets (Tushman and O'Reilly, 1996).

**Ambidextrous Leadership**
Different alignments held together through senior-team integration, common vision and values, and common senior-team rewards

| Design Element | Exploitative Work | Exploratory Work |
| --- | --- | --- |
| Strategic intent | Cost, profit | Innovation, growth |
| Critical tasks | Operations, efficiency, incremental innovation | Adaptability, new products, breakthrough innovation |
| Competencies | Operational | Entrepreneurial |
| Structure | Formal, mechanistic | Adaptive, loose |
| Controls, rewards | Margins, productivity | Milestones, growth |
| Culture | Efficiency, low risk, quality, customers | Risk taking, speed, flexibility, experimentation |
| Leadership role | Authoritative, top down | Visionary, involved |

**Table 3.1** Ambidextrous Organization Design (O'Reilly and Tushman, 2004)

Despite the engaging and influential nature of the idea, debates continue about how to define and study ambidextrous organizations, and how they might best work in practice. Most would agree it requires multiple leaders and managers with distinctive capabilities to make it work effectively, and that the tensions between exploitation and exploration might be dealt with in different ways by different individuals and organizations.

It is important to remember how challenging organization redesign can be in practice and what failure or partial success can look like when trying to change an organization's structural arrangements. In many senses, it may feel like an organization is trying to transform itself from form A to form B, becoming an entirely different type of entity; one that feels, looks and acts differently. Some researchers have described this journey as taking one of several different paths, or 'design tracks' of strategic change (Greenwood and Hinings, 1988).

Some organizations may fail to fully imagine a new design or disagree about its costs and benefits, and so remain in a state of inertia, or start to change slightly before deciding to change back and abandon the new design. Other organizations may manage the redesign, but only gradually, with some indecisive movements back and forth, or after a long delay. Finally, some organizations may be in the middle of a redesign and get stuck in limbo with the change unresolved. In this case, they may never fully achieve or balance the new design, even though they have moved away from the old. As organizations become larger, older and more complex, strategic design decisions can turn out to be too bold, risky and difficult to reverse. This could leave them trapped in vicious circles, leaving them vulnerable to further stagnation, fragmentation and decline, with recovery only possible through drastic crisis management to re-establish and revitalize them (Masuch, 1985).

At a more moderate level, organizations are likely to continue to experiment with organizational design changes as the world of work continues to change and evolve around them. Employees and managers can also express different expectations or preferences when asked to imagine the kind of organization they want to work in, or what a well-designed organization would look like to them. Organizations can abandon some aspects of organizational design that seem less effective, while retaining others. For example, the online retailer Zappos and its CEO Tony Hsieh adopted a radically flat organization design called 'holacracy' in 2013, only to bring back managers into the design some years later, while retaining some features of its more democratic 'circular hierarchy' (Groth, 2020). In general, it is rumoured that many companies may be experimenting with dynamic new models or systems. However, it seems that managers, employees and customers still want a more traditional degree of structure and stability. In general, managing links between the centre and the edges of an organization, or between the top, middle and bottom, remains one of the most fundamental areas of design to consider.

Organizations usually need to maintain a mixture of stability and change in their designs, or of structure and flexibility, as part of a 'semi-structured' approach that allows them to maintain some core strengths and processes while acting as a platform for more dynamic units and projects to explore ideas for change. Design is also often described as going far beyond having a formal organizational chart with fixed and static lines and boxes. Organizations need to be prepared to focus on informal mindsets and networks and can benefit from insights where staff are crossing and shaking up internal and external boundaries to discuss or spread change.

## Key Characteristics of Good Organizational Design

Ultimately, the 'best' organization designs are those that align with a great strategy. One further useful concept for linking the two together is for organizations to have 'simple rules' to help solve problems and set boundaries around strategic design and change decisions in different circumstances. The rules should be simple but flexible so that organizations can leave them open to feedback and adjustment as needed, while also agreeing with the underlying principle or priority. The simple rules concept was developed by Eisenhardt and Sull (2001), and they proposed five main types:

1. *How-to rules:* specifying how to execute a process in a unique way. For example, customer service rules that require technical product experts to be on service teams, research staff to rotate through customer service, and for staff to answer all customers' questions in response to their initial queries.

2. *Boundary rules:* specify how managers should focus on pursuing some opportunities but not others. For example, only seeking to acquire other companies that are below a certain size, and with over a certain percentage of qualified engineers in the workforce.

3. *Priority rules:* rules that help managers rank or sort through acceptable opportunities. For example, deciding how much manufacturing capacity to allocate to different products based on a product's gross margin.

4. *Timing rules:* specify how managers should try to synchronize their actions with the pace of emerging opportunities and other parts of the organization. For example, project teams having to know when a product needs delivering to a leading customer by to ensure competitive advantage, and limiting product development time to under eighteen months.

5. *Exit rules:* rules that help managers decide when to pull out of old or failing projects and ideas. For example, a rule that specifies that a project under development should be cancelled if any team member chooses to leave it and join another project in the organization instead.

## Strategic Organizational Change in Context

While strategic organizational change involves changes to plans, purposes, policies, objectives, structures and business models, in practice and in context it can also involve a dramatic variety and range of specific decisions, settings, scenarios and implementation experiences. Strategic change can look very different in organizations of different sizes and sectors.

Often the aims are growth, survival or sustained competitive advantage, but the plans, processes and paths for achieving it may involve very different circumstances and approaches, with elements of more gradual, incremental or evolutionary change unfolding in conjunction with more sudden, radical or revolutionary change. Shorter implementation timescales tend to range from a few months up to less than a year, whereas longer strategic change timescales may involve five to ten years or more, subject to industry and economic cycles or other institutional norms. Objectives may be financial, social, environmental or some combination of the three.

In context, there are also many specific types of strategic transformation that can take place involving, for instance, changes to markets served, value propositions for customers, supply chain operations, global or international expansions, digital technologies adopted, innovations coming from R&D, IT infrastructure, partnerships or alliances, and more (Hemerling, Dosik and Rizvi, 2015). Furthermore, some common types of strategic change scenarios are important enough to have specific names and involve specific approaches and processes, such as:

- *Downsizing:* a strategic restructuring that involves reducing an organization's workers and divisions to cut costs and address poor performance or economic conditions.

- *Mergers and acquisitions:* a strategic financial transaction or deal between companies where assets are acquired, consolidated and integrated into a new entity.

- *Rebranding:* a strategic change in the identity and image of an organization achieved by changing its name, logo and other symbols or stories reflecting its values.

- *Public sector:* large-scale, planned changes to local, regional and national administration of services in response to public policy agendas and political leadership.

→ *Ownership:* strategic changes in who owns and governs an organization be it founders, families, nationalization (public sector ownership), privatization (private sector ownership) or investors (IPO – initial public offering of shares).

→ *Crisis:* strategic crisis management changes to address an organization's failing performance and help it recover, perhaps because of a scandal, disaster or other disruption.

These strategic change contexts can often overlap and occur in combination – for example, in a merger of two companies in which some people in each company perform similar jobs or functions, there may be decisions about how to downsize in these areas. Or a crisis of mismanagement by a large private sector company may lead to it being nationalized so the public sector and the state can bring it under control for the sake of citizens and taxpayers. Strategic change contexts and decisions can also be subject to serious criticisms over their desirability, effectiveness or risk of failure – such as whether a merger will really result in 'synergies' that make the organizations stronger together, or if a downsizing will reduce costs in the short-term but damage the organization's profitability and growth in the long-term.

### ACTIVITY 3.3

The five examples set out below of specific organizational cases of strategic change may seem very diverse, but there may be similar stories, concepts and circumstances that we can analyse to better understand success and failure factors in more context-specific terms. Read the five examples below before answering the subsequent questions.

1. IBM and ambidextrous transformations: a multinational technology company over 100 years old, IBM has been strategically transformed multiple times, particularly under the leadership of Lou Gerstner in the 1990s, who developed the company in such a way that enabled it to deliver many new services. Strategic change at IBM has been enabled by an ambidextrous structure, where cross-functional teams work in parallel to existing business units, assessing trends and proposing change programs with top management support, allowing for regular review and swift resource allocation and realignment when a need for change is established (Gerstner, 2002).

2. LEGO and rebranding journeys: the Danish toy company and global brand faced a changing 1990s world of digital toys and new fashions and franchises aimed at children. In response, LEGO became too diversified and fragmented, and its brand risked losing consistency and coherence. Across the turn of the

twenty-first century, LEGO embarked on a strategic rebranding journey, setting up new task forces and stakeholder partnerships (e.g. with customers and universities) to co-create company values and review them in annual cycles, redesigning websites and retail outlets accordingly (Schultz and Hatch, 2003).

3. Adidas and rediscovering heritage: the German sportswear organization faced new competitive pressures in the 1970s and 1980s, not least with the rise of its rival Nike, leaving it unfocused on pursuing growth and resulting in losses. Subsequently, two senior managers with outsider respect for its authenticity joined Adidas from Nike and spent years in the 1990s and 2000s reconnecting the organization with strategic knowledge of what had made it great in the past. Their actions restored Adidas to growth by establishing an archive of products and capabilities, and new, more stringent product standards inspired by the company's founder, German cobbler, inventor and entrepreneur, Adi Dassler (Ind, Iglesias and Schultz, 2015).

4. Apple's 'quantum' strategy: over a fifteen-year period, American technology company Apple revolutionized personal electronics, telecom, computer and media industries through a string of blockbuster products offering unique, designer, integrated customer experiences. Key to navigating these strategic changes has been its rare ability to balance high operational efficiency with high-quality product design – seemingly being able to be in two places at the same time, like a 'quantum' particle. As Chief Operations Officer, Tim Cook streamlined Apple's manufacturing processes, supply chain and distribution operations for efficiency, carefully targeting smaller tech companies for acquisitions, while the late Steve Jobs established exceptional design processes allowing premium pricing for distinctive, innovative products (Heracleous, 2013).

5. Strategic misalignment at WorldCom and Nortel: WorldCom was a US telecommunications company, Nortel a Canadian one. Both organizations ultimately went bankrupt after a series of extremely risky strategic change actions, which were not executed carefully. The company CEOs pursued strategies of aggressive growth and diversification through numerous acquisitions to dominate networks and technologies, but the complexity of integrating these changes was not adequately addressed. This resulted in a host of problems, with the organizations and leadership lacking alignment/a common mindset. Following economic decline and collapse of the telecom boom after 2000, WorldCom initiated fraudulent accounting activities and Nortel initiated a radical downsizing programme – with the share price of both going into terminal decline (Heracleous and Werres, 2016).

Questions

1. Consider these five examples involving global companies. Describe their strategic transformation by reference to one of the common types of strategic change scenarios outlined above.

2. What, if anything, do all the strategic change scenarios have in common?

Given the many different types of strategic change and change contexts, it might be reasonable to ask what, if anything, all strategic changes have in common. One study looking at a group of ten Spanish companies from a variety of sectors across an eight-year period sought to investigate general patterns and components of strategic change (Dominguez, Galán-González and Barroso, 2015). The findings emphasize the general importance of the 'strategic apex' at the top of the organization, involving the CEO, board of directors and shareholders, as well as reorganizations of the top management team (TMT). In general terms, strategic changes tended to be associated with changes in CEO, and responses to changes in the organization's prior performance in the period leading up to the change. Yet, even at this very general level, strategic change could involve different patterns of more gradual or continuous adjustments versus more proactive, radical or urgent transformations.

## Balancing Top-down and Bottom-up Influences in Strategic Change

From a top-down perspective, a new top leader or CEO represents a powerful signal and window of opportunity for launching strategic change ambitions. An executive may spend crucial '100-day periods' planning, preparing, launching and building momentum with major change programmes, to fulfil the hopes of establishing growth, sustained performance improvements, efficient restructuring or resource reallocations and the building of dynamic new capabilities (Bürkner, Fæste and Hemerling, 2015).

In different sector and industry contexts, however, this may involve thinking in very different ways about what strategy means – the factors of technology, regulation and competition, and the timeframes associated with developing different products or securing different assets. For instance, strategic change in the pharmaceutical sector is intimately related to healthcare costs in different countries, and strategic change in the sports industry is intimately related to fan culture, merchandising, sponsorship and media rights. Industries like oil and aviation may involve large organizations with stable cores that take longer to change because changing strategy is costly and threatens existing assets and operations. By contrast, strategic change in the technology sector is likely to involve much more dynamic investments and partnerships, sometimes between established competitors and start-ups with bold, new, innovative ideas. Finally, there are distinct ways that entirely new industries can emerge and develop, such as wind energy or nanotechnology, where years of funding and research are needed to generate resources for growth and develop regulatory standards before more mature markets and competitive positions are established (Gustafsson, Jääskeläinen, Maula and Uotila, 2016). Overall, knowing what strategy and strategic change means in a particular industry involves investigating specific potential challenges and opportunities, including sources of disruption and transformation, which can have both short-term and long-term implications.

At the same time, strategic change in context is also about aligning the workforce – and top management may often need to consider shaping and adapting their plans or programmes by engaging with bottom-up 'platforms' representing the rest of the organization. For example, the British National Health Service has held 'Change Days' where thousands of employees pledge to take concrete change actions to improve healthcare objectives, while building materials company Cemex encourages self-defined communities and networks of specialist employees to generate and implement thousands of change initiatives each year (Hamel and Zanini, 2014).

## Good Practice in Managing Effective, Transformational Strategic Change

Most transformational strategic change will involve balancing top-down and bottom-up forces in the organization over a period of at least eighteen months. The top-down elements of planning, vision and rationale are likely to take place in the earlier months, but will also closely overlap and interweave with months of design and dialogue as the rest of the organization offers feedback, launches initiatives and translates general plans into more specific plans for implementation. This will then be reflected in action plans, evaluations, further monitoring and adjustments, which are carried out in efforts to sustain the change as part of a 'new normal' way of working (Couto, Plansky and Caglar, 2017). This is the 'final phase' of the change process, to the extent that strategic change has a 'final phase'. One UK report studied these types of transformational change in four case organizations:

1. *BBC Worldwide:* a television programme distributor seeking to increase its profit generation through a 2012–15 change programme focused on restructuring, culture change and more dynamic ways of working.
2. *HMRC:* a UK government department (responsible for collecting tax and administrating state support) ran change initiatives over 2013–15, involving the restructuring of teams to deliver digitized services, workforce consultation and new guidance and processes in personal tax operations.
3. *News UK:* a media and newspaper subsidiary of the global media business, News Corp, and its Newsroom 360, ran a change programme between 2011–15, seeking to capitalize on increasing digital news consumption. In a related move, they also relocated to a prominent new office building in London.
4. *Zurich UK Life:* a business unit within a leading global insurance group that sought to improve its expense management processes and customer experiences through a 2012–15 change programme named PACE (Passion, Agility, Collaboration, External Focus).

The report on these four cases presents them as successful examples, in part due to the variety of leaders and facilitators being involved (e.g. HR, organization development, organization design, learning and development). Across these cases, seven areas are proposed as important for understanding how to manage strategic transformational change successfully, converting knowledge into action (CIPD, 2015):

1. *A long-term approach:* quick fixes are unlikely to work, so leaders and managers need to prepare to expend sustained effort and investment over time.
2. *Sequencing:* the importance of carrying out initial cuts and restructuring to address short-term financial issues first, with longer-term culture change and transformation coming in later change phases.
3. *Leading by example:* CEOs and leaders need to 'walk the talk' and set an example for how the context is changing.
4. *Investment in softer interventions:* changes to 'harder' structures and control systems play a relatively minor role. Much more investment in terms of communication, training and culture is likely to be needed.
5. *Pushing strategies down to the front line:* helping those in customer-facing roles understand how to deliver the change in their work to ensure performance and advantage.

**6.** *Translating rhetoric into tangibles:* translating the change message from the top of the organization into more tangible involvement and implications for day-to-day work occurring lower down in the organization.

**7.** *Transparency and proximity:* bringing the tops and bottoms of organizations together to emphasize the significance of the change for the entire organization.

Many of these general points are related in terms of how strategic transformational changes require working on systematic connections and end-to-end implementation across organizational levels and over time.

### ACTIVITY 3.4

1. With regard to effective strategic change at an organization with which you are familiar, please prioritize and rank the seven good practices outlined above in order of importance (1 being most important and 7 being the least important) for effective strategic change. Please explain the rationale behind your ranking.

2. Are there any other factors that are not on the list but which you feel are important for effective strategic change?

3. Why do you think these other factors are important?

## Mergers and Downsizings and Strategic Change

As mentioned earlier in this chapter, more specific strategic change situations like *mergers* and *downsizings* have their own versions of systematic approaches to change management and implementation, and much has been written about their stages, designs and success and failure factors (e.g. Cooper, Pandey and Quick, 2012; King, Bauer and Schriber, 2018). Indeed, mergers and downsizings remain perhaps two of the most influential and prevalent strategic change scenarios in organizations around the world, although they can take many different forms. They are also often criticized for failing to deliver value, where alternative ways of managing change may in fact have been more beneficial for stakeholders.

For example, mergers remain an attractive way for organizations to grow and remain competitive by acquiring and integrating other organizations. However, to succeed, they require very careful *due diligence* when researching how the organizations might be combined, and very thorough post-merger integration (PMI) planning and design to ensure proper blending, as well as maintenance of the two organizations' respective strengths and resources (DiGeorgio, 2002). Too often mergers fail to achieve anticipated benefits because executives are unrealistic and overpay for an acquisition due to high expectations of a deal with great 'synergies' between the two organizations. This results in insufficient attention being paid to potential culture clashes and lost talent. It also leads to inadequate attention being paid to ensuring skilful integration and communication between the two organizations (Schuler and Jackson, 2001).

Similarly, downsizings remain an attractive way for organizations to cut their workforce and other costs during a period of challenging economic conditions. However, like mergers, to succeed in restructuring and refocusing the organization for recovery, growth and profitability, downsizings need to be carefully analysed and planned to avoid losing valuable workers in reckless rounds of layoffs or doing lasting damage to the organization's culture and reputation. This means considering how to legally and fairly support 'victims' of job losses, 'survivors' worried about their future at the company and the change agents who must communicate the bad news and absorb the negative emotional reactions. In the end, many downsizings fail to improve organizational recovery and profitability in the longer-term, can discriminate against workers, and can prove very costly in terms of the reparation of trust and employment relations (Cameron, 1994). In many contexts, careful HR decision-making procedures should be followed in line with employment law (Campion, Guerrero and Posthuma, 2011). Furthermore, it may be more prudent and responsible to exhaust many alternative cost-cutting measures first – such as recruitment or pay freezes and furloughs – because they are easier to reverse and less destructive than large-scale redundancies, which are perhaps best treated as a last resort (Cascio, 2002).

## Implementing Strategic Change in Practice

However clever, careful and thorough plans for strategic change may be, they are unlikely to be effective if there are not suitable ways to realize them in practice. As we have seen earlier in this chapter, there is a need to try to influence and mediate a balance between top-down and bottom-up forces in strategic organizational change. These dynamics and tensions might involve resistance or reactions to change agents, unintended consequences, process problems and other learnings or improvisations related to executing or carrying out the change. These issues might be best summed up as *implementation* activities associated with strategic change.

This is also important because the reality in many organizations is that strategies are made up of broad *programmes* of change, which in turn are made up of many specific *projects* of change, running in parallel and overlapping ways across the organization. Ideally, this means there should be some systematic way of keeping track of how these changes are being implemented. One way to think about this is in terms of implementation through layers or levels of change agents and/or recipients:

→ *Senior strategic change agents:* leaders, consultants, planners and advisors. These agents will be held accountable for ensuring that the change results in a smooth overall transition, with transparency, formality and integration. They also act as 'sponsors', providing time and resources to other parts of the organization. They may have various sources of expertise in organization development, design, HR and programme management.

→ *Project teams:* teams of more specialized leaders and change agents each working on specific parts of a wider strategic programme or portfolio of projects.

→ *Middle managers:* potentially both change agents and recipients at the same time, which may result in tension. They are agents in the sense that they can bridge, connect, translate, resist and adjust influences from project teams and more senior agents in relation to the rest of the workforce. They are recipients in that they are also subject to implementing formal, planned elements of strategic change that they may not have been directly involved in deciding.

→ *Workforce/frontline:* change recipients at lower levels of the organization not designated as formal change agents or on project teams. Here, the 'macro' strategic plans and projects will be related to in more 'micro' terms – employees engaged with how changes will affect their routines, relationships, identities and everyday working environments (e.g. Bruskin, 2024).

Relationships between these levels are likely to be two-way. For example, although overall strategic direction may trickle down from the top, agents, managers and employees at lower levels may nevertheless actively shape the change through local experiments, initiatives, improvisations and ideas, which initially start out informally, but later become formalized into strategic change.

In this way, strategic portfolios of multiple change projects can be tracked and managed, forcing cross-organizational conversations about the success levels associated with their implementation. Nevertheless, it should be acknowledged that, in practice, implementation can involve considerable challenges associated with politics and resistance. For example, one study of an insurance company implementing strategic changes to its claims-handling processes found that some middle managers formed an informal group ('The Gang of Four') that sought to take control of some of the information and decisions coming from senior management and the formal project team (Hope, 2010). However, it should be noted that some of the middle managers' responses were constructive and helpful, pointing out alternatives to more time-consuming or expensive change proposals. In the end, one of 'The Gang of Four' ended up joining the formal change project team, which helped smooth the implementation (Hope, 2010).

In general, it is important to bear in mind that middle managers can interpret strategic change in ambiguous ways during its implementation. At lower organizational levels, there may be less big-picture information or data about a change, and different views on whether things are getting better, worse or staying the same (e.g. Sonenshein, 2010). Over a period of years, employees with values more congruent with wider changes may prove more committed to seeing a transition through, whereas others may only conform more superficially (Amis, Slack and Hinings, 2002). Ultimately, radical strategic change is not necessarily rapid or widespread, with some elements having more impact and momentum than others and change unfolding in a messy way across different parts of the organization, at different speeds and in different directions (Amis, Slack and Hinings, 2004).

## DICE: A Strategic Implementation System

Based on significant research and experiences with transformational change programmes at many companies, one team of consultants has called the strategic change implementation system the 'hard side' of change management. They suggest it can be represented as four measurable factors associated with success or failure, in the acronym DICE (Sirkin, Keenan and Jackson, 2005):

- → **D**: *Duration* – changes involve regular project reviews every two months or less.

- → **I**: *Integrity of performance* – changes involve highly capable project members and leaders with strong skills and motivations. At least 50 per cent of their time should be assigned to effective project completion.

- → **C**: *Commitment* (two components) – the senior management team (C1) has clearly communicated the need for change and devoted actions and resources to it. The employees most affected by the change locally (C2) understand the need for it and are enthusiastic about taking it on.

→ **E**: *Effort* – changes do not impose too much additional demand on top of employees' existing workloads (e.g. the percentage of extra work required should not be too high).

This approach involves organizations attempting to calculate a total DICE score by rating each factor on a 1–4 scale, where lower scores are more positive and the I and C1 components are weighted double and multiplied by two. These scores tend to correlate well with the success outcomes of strategic change projects, while allowing low-scoring projects to be classified as 'wins', medium-scoring as 'worries', and high-scoring as 'woes' with a high risk of failure (Sirkin, Keenan and Jackson, 2005).

## CASE STUDY: HERSHEY AND TURNING A CANDY COMPANY INTO A SNACKS EMPIRE

The Hershey Company, commonly referred to as Hershey or Hershey's, is an American multinational company known for its various confectionery products including chocolates, cookies, cakes and beverages. Its strategy has been closely linked to chocolate for over 128 years. In the past it has spent decades focused on providing generations of consumers with chocolate and sweet treats, innovating with different brands, flavours, sizes, packaging and products, and growing its international business by taking them to key regions around the world (Buck, 2022).

However, in March 2017 Michele Buck (the first female CEO at Hershey) outlined her vision of the organization as something more than a candy-maker. As a result, the organization embarked on an ambitious journey of strategic change. This strategy aimed at expanding into savoury and 'better-for-you' product categories, and involved streamlining global operations, bolstering the organization's core competencies, developing a more courageous culture and executing a series of diversifying acquisitions. In doing so the organization learned to be more entrepreneurial, adaptable and agile, as well as more willing to embrace disruption as an opportunity for growth. As a result, the company more than doubled its market capitalization, approaching $10 billion in sales (Buck, 2022).

Drawing on and revisiting its history has helped the organization define its most long-standing, core strategic capabilities more clearly. These include a deep understanding of consumer snacking needs; taste science, product development and packaging expertise; effective and extensive marketing; and ubiquitous distribution in chosen markets. Michele Buck joined in 2005, and over a decade worked to boost performance at plants, streamline business units through divestiture and build brands via advertising investment. In this time she occupied the roles of Chief Marketing Officer, Chief Growth Officer, Head of North American operations, and Chief Operating Officer roles in North, Central and South America. She took over as CEO as successor to John Bilbrey when he decided to retire.

Michele Buck explained her strategic change vision and plan to every stakeholder – for the organization to reimagine itself as an innovative snacking powerhouse. There was some resistance both inside and outside of the company from those who noted previous failures at expanding beyond sweets. Drawing on her decade of Hershey's experience, Buck brought them onboard by using other leaders that she knew embodied the newer, more entrepreneurial culture as influencers, sometimes pairing them with outstanding executors who could bring the strategic plan to scale. In the existing US confectionery businesses, growth was driven through creative changes to marketing, packaging and pricing, such as identifying 'snacking occasions' like family movie nights, re-sealable bags, single-serving sizes and targeted social media promotions (Buck, 2022).

To expand further into snacking, but not diversify out of confectionery, they looked to make 'smart' acquisitions of savoury and better-for-you organizations and brands with high sales growth and strong consumer interest that would fit well within their operating model. Acquisitions included fast-growing makers of popcorn, tortilla chips, low-sugar/high-protein bars and pretzels. Hershey managed the strategic change process of these M&As by developing a strong and repeatable process, with robust due diligence research for the companies and leaders to get to know each other better. Careful relationship-building and negotiation with acquisition targets helped explain how they could grow well as they integrated into Hershey's portfolio.

As an additional benefit, while implementing its strategy, Hershey was also able to adapt to challenges created by the COVID-19 pandemic and world events, learning from customers about demand for products in safe outdoor settings and for larger household packages when shopping trips became less frequent during lockdowns.

Overall, Hershey made significant progress in transforming itself from an iconic confectionery company into a leading snacking powerhouse. As of 2022, it owns three of the six fastest-growing US snack brands; savoury and better-for-you products have grown from making up 1 per cent to 10 per cent of the company's portfolio; and both old and new business units are growing by double digits each year, significantly driving further overall growth. Michele Buck summarizes how this strategic change was accomplished: by setting out a bold vision; using key influencers to develop a more agile and entrepreneurial culture; bolstering successful areas of core and international business while streamlining operations;

and branching out into new and popular snack product categories with acquisitions of well-vetted up-and-coming brands (Buck, 2022).

### ACTIVITY 3.5

1. Given what you have learned so far in this chapter, which factors to you think account for the successful transformation of Hershey?

In the next section of this chapter we consider organizational culture as a complex and interrelated aspect of successful strategic change.

## Defining and Classifying Organizational Cultures

Organizational culture relates to an organization's identity (how it is perceived inside), its image (how it is perceived outside) and its relationship with national or societal cultures more generally. Organizational cultures and culture change have been the subject of much independent interest, in both the worlds of research and practice, for over forty years. Organizational culture is not easy to define because it has many components; it is somewhat like a toolkit of different elements. However, typical definitions of organizational culture tend to emphasize an organization's shared values, purposes, priorities, stories, symbols, categories, behaviours and assumptions (e.g., Giorgi, Lockwood and Glynn, 2015). A shorter, sharper definition of organizational culture is often simply **'the way we do things around here'** (also 'the way we think around here' or 'what matters around here').

Culture tends to affect how employees think and feel about their work in a deep and meaningful way. It therefore plays a significant role in the success or failure of strategic change. Culture is often closely linked to a company's founder and history, having accumulated and persisted over time. It may exist at different levels of awareness or consciousness, with some features very visible and easy to put into words (e.g. on a company website), while others may be difficult to explain or simply assumed as natural or normal, without question (e.g. rivalries between old and new departments).

Organizational culture became of increasing interest in many US organizations during the 1970s and 1980s, partly due to influential, best-selling books like *In Search of Excellence* (Peters and Waterman, 1982). Along with wider societal changes, such as increased forms of globalization and increases in forms of knowledge and service work, there was a sense that top global American brands could distinguish themselves and perform at the highest levels by having 'excellent' cultures, where employees were especially active, focused and values-driven in their work.

In the twenty-first century, this view may be seen as dated, simplistic and idealistic, but the idea that a strong and positive culture can improve organizational performance through processes of competitive advantage, cooperation, conflict reduction and control still exists. Organizations may seek diverse and talented employees that 'fit' their culture. They may also try to shape the culture through policies, practices and procedures that signal to employees what is expected, supported, rewarded and punished. Perceptions of these more observable signals by employees has been termed the organizational 'climate' (Schneider, Ehrhart and Macey, 2013). One of the most obvious ways culture manifests is in organizations' prominent and familiar value statements, which define their organizational culture and brand identity. For example, Virgin's commitment to keep its staff happy to allow them to better serve other stakeholders; Disney defining entertainment as hope, aspiration and positive resolutions; or Vodafone's 'passion' for customers, 'our' people, results, and the world around 'us' (Smollan and Sayers, 2009).

## Organizational Cultures That Underpin Strategic Change

An excellent, great or inspirational organizational culture might seem difficult for an average organization to aspire to, but the search to define or imagine what it might look like remains a powerful ideal. One study found the 'best' workplaces have cultures that try to make work as engaging, productive and rewarding as possible (Goffee and Jones, 2013). They're places where people can be themselves (authenticity, inclusion), are given information about what is really going on (transparency), have their strengths magnified (growth, development), stand for more than just shareholder value (ethics, wellbeing), are shown how their daily work makes sense (purpose) and are able to believe in workplace rules (simplicity, efficiency, legitimacy).

These cultures are difficult to achieve for many organizations and may even seem conflicting or confusing when put into practice. Nevertheless, there are other ways to improve a culture, by understanding how best to define, classify and keep it in balance. Organizations can consider how strong or weak their cultures are, for example, and how best to keep these elements in balance, in terms of the extent to which employees agree on values, exhibit behaviours consistently and role model the culture with belief and intensity. If an organization's culture is too strong it might benefit from coordination, influence and commitment but lack capacity for adaptability, diversity and change. Conversely, if an organization's culture is too weak it might be more inclusive and adaptive but lack competitive distinctiveness or a compelling identity. Furthermore, organizations are likely to have multiple *subcultures* that vary within the wider culture, based on other identities, such as people's professional or occupational group, the time or location of their work and the nature of the jobs they undertake.

In these regards, culture must be balanced between competing imperatives. At the heart of many of these issues are likely to be different views about values – beliefs and principles concerning what is important about ways of working within the organization. Values can vary greatly, and be physical (e.g. a clean or safe workplace), organizational (e.g. cooperation, discipline), or psychological (e.g. loyalty, creativity, happiness). In the public or third sectors, certain private sector values around profit or market competition are likely to be given much less emphasis. Public service culture, for example, is more likely to be based around the prides and pressures of providing essential services efficiently to citizens and communities in need. Cultures may also be based around how an organization engages in *knowledge production* and *learning*. For example, Google's culture is characterized by learning from web search data to generate knowledge for advertising, whereas Greenpeace learns about environmental risks and harms to generate knowledge with which to guide pro-environmental campaigns and activism (Kilduff, Mehra and Dunn, 2011).

## Models and Tools for Diagnosing Organizational Culture

However, defining and classifying culture may require more thorough investigation in an attempt to uncover more unofficial, informal aspects of the company's culture that only insiders know about and tell each other. These levels of culture are more likely to be conveyed through stories and imagery, concerning people that have been admired or ridiculed as heroes, villains or fools through their actions, for example (Hawkins, 1997).

Early attempts to define and classify organizational cultures that remain influential have tended to focus on several main types or levels. For example, Charles Handy proposed four types of organizational culture based on how centralized and formalized the organizational structure was. These are: (1) *role* cultures based on hierarchies and divisions; (2) *task* cultures based on a matrix of teams and projects; (3) *power* cultures based on high-status individuals or groups at the top or in the centre; and (4) *atomistic* cultures based on professional individuals working mostly independently of one another (Handy, 1985).

Another four types of organizational culture were proposed by Deal and Kennedy (1983), which are based on the degree of risk an organization has to deal with, and the speed of feedback an organization can expect from its environment. Combinations of these conditions led to distinct culture types labelled *bet your company* (high risk, slow feedback); *work hard, play hard* (low risk, fast feedback); *tough guy, macho* (high risk, fast feedback); and *process* (low risk, slow feedback).

The classic model of organizational culture as levels, rather than types, was developed by Edgar Schein (1985). It is made up of three distinct levels, often represented as a triangle indicating shallower, more visible elements toward the top and deeper, less visible factors toward the bottom (Figure 3.2). However, while artefacts are very tangible and easy to observe, they may still be difficult to interpret. Values tend to be understood through interview, documentary and survey data relating to the organization. The underlying assumptions are deepest and most invisible, but they are powerful and may only be fully understood by people deeply accustomed to how the organization works.

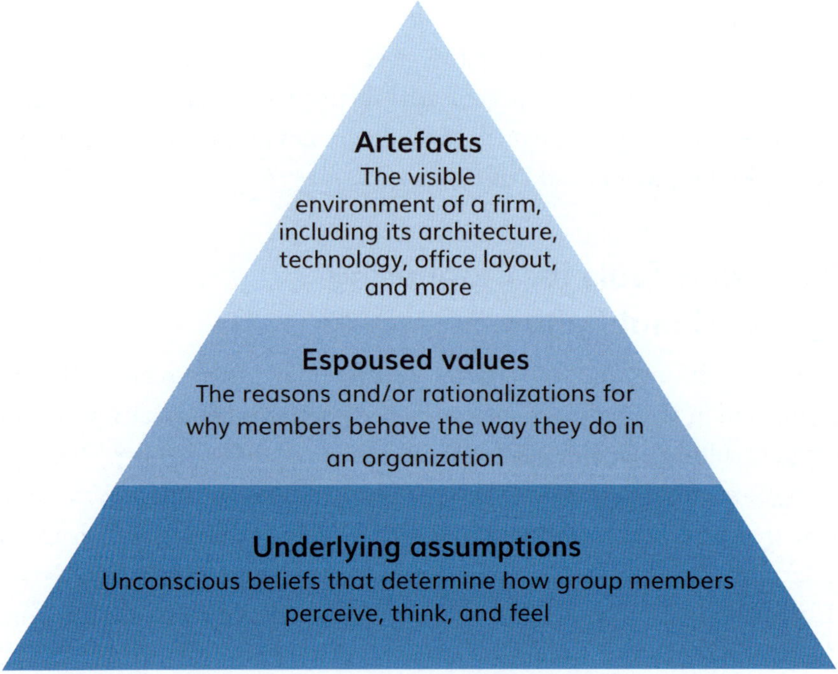

**Artefacts**
The visible environment of a firm, including its architecture, technology, office layout, and more

**Espoused values**
The reasons and/or rationalizations for why members behave the way they do in an organization

**Underlying assumptions**
Unconscious beliefs that determine how group members perceive, think, and feel

**Figure 3.2** Edgar Schein's organization culture model (Somers, 2023).

The implications of these culture models for organizational change are that changing culture at deeper levels, or from one type to another, may take longer than other types of change. It may also require cycles of different multifaceted leadership and management activities. David Logan has likened organizational cultures to 'tribes', or groups of 20 to 150 people known to each other in a shared situation or network. There are five distinct types or stages of tribe culture, and leaders must work to upgrade an organizational culture gradually from its current stage to the next, through leadership and communication that appeals to higher, more inspiring values within the wider group (Logan, King and Fischer-Wright, 2008):

1. **'Life sucks'** – a culture of despair, hostility and violent or illegal behaviour you might find in prisons or gangs (estimated 2 per cent of population, most organizations skip this stage).

2. **'MY life sucks'** – a culture of sarcasm, resistance, passive-aggressiveness, frustration, boredom and ineffectiveness (estimated 25 per cent of population).

3. **'I'm great (and you're not)'** – a culture of confidence and competence, but also competitiveness, individualism, independence and holding on to knowledge (estimated 49 per cent of population).

4. **'We're great'** – a culture where people are excited to work together for the benefit of the entire organization, but are still not engaged with wider groups (estimated 22 per cent of population).

5. **'Life is great'** – a culture where diverse people work together on significant innovations with positive global impact and inspiring social change (estimated 2 per cent of population).

### ACTIVITY 3.6

1. Reflect on Logan et al.'s (2008) five cultural types. Identify separate organizations that you think illustrate each distinct cultural type.

2. Explain your thinking behind each of the five organizations.

## Culture Surveys and Other Frameworks

Organizations may also use culture surveys and other frameworks to try to better define and understand their culture's profiles. This is in terms of combinations of values that they emphasize to different degrees as part of an overall profile. One model that embodies this approach is the Competing Values Framework or CVF (Quinn and Rohrbaugh, 1981). It is similar to models of organizational culture types but suggests that cultures lean toward dominant values along particular dimensions. The model has two dimensions and four quadrants (Figure 3.3).

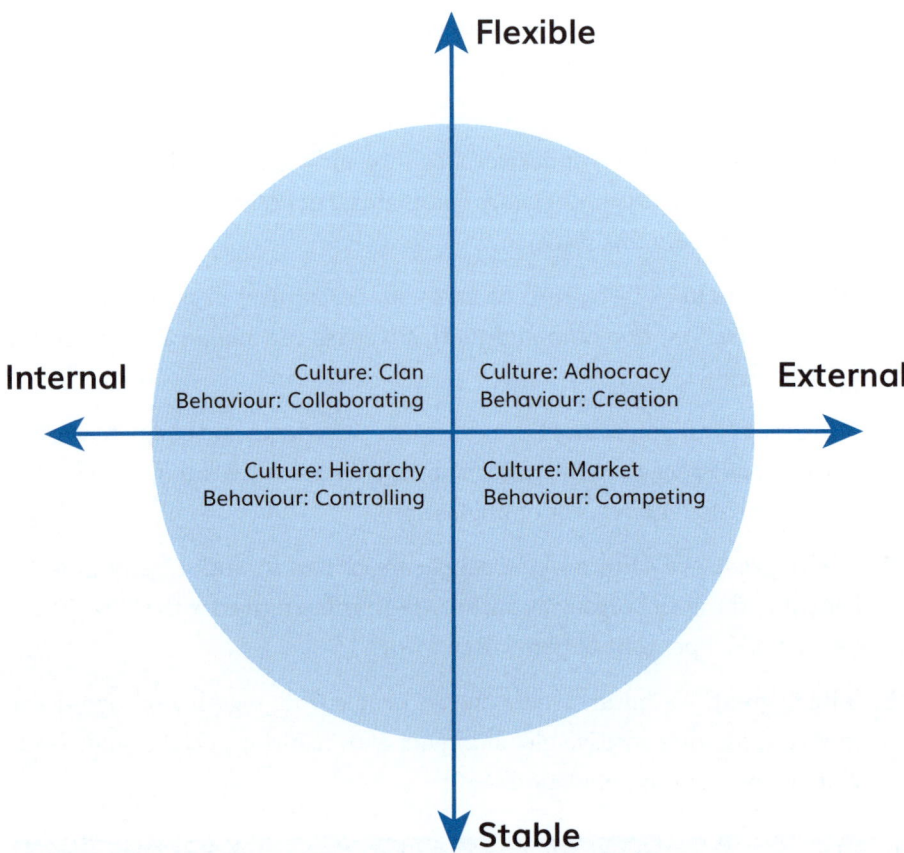

Figure 3.3 Competing values framework (MindTools, 2024).

The CVF can be put to a wide range of uses, but the general idea is that organizations can analyse how their organization, leaders and activities are positioned for effectiveness. There is not necessarily a 'best' or 'worst' quadrant, but the CVF can be used to diagnose, plan and change cultural shifts. There are variations of this model, and the axes and positions could be labelled slightly differently, but key distinctions revolve around how outward or inward a company's focus tends to be (e.g. toward customers or employees), and how flexible or stable its focus tends to be (e.g. dynamic and creative vs safe and reliable). Various positions plotted across axes in cultural space could be captured by discussing different value words – distinctive company cultures that are oriented toward authority, order, safety, caring, purpose, learning or enjoyment, for instance (Groysberg, Lee, Price and Cheng, 2018).

During a strategic change like a merger and acquisition, two organizations might use a tool like the CVF to think about how to blend or accommodate the different cultural dynamics between them. In the end, balancing these types of values will affect what is measured in the organization, what leaders pay attention to, how employees are treated, and affect other reactions and resourcing decisions (Schein, 1985).

## Changing the Organizational Culture

Changing an organizational culture in a deep and lasting way is likely to happen gradually and take a significant amount of time. This is because, beyond defining and classifying cultural levels, values and dimensions in general, changing organizational culture still requires actively mapping and redefining what the culture is and what it might be in more detail. This means breaking culture down and building it back up again to make sure it is constituted of clear, consistent and comprehensive practices that align with the values and behaviours the organization is seeking to embody. The changes may also involve some people from the 'old' culture leaving the organization over time, while new employees join and recompose the workforce, being selected and inducted in ways that reinforce the new culture.

One popular tool for breaking culture down into seven interrelated elements for change is Johnson's *cultural web* (e.g. Johnson, 1992). At the centre of the web is the 'paradigm', or the core assumptions about how an organization sees itself in its environment – this could be anything from playing a world-class game of football at a sports organization, to providing professional and reliable service at a retail bank. Surrounding the paradigm are six other elements which help to provide a specific sense of where and how a culture might need to be changed (Figure 3.4). These are *stories* (about important people and events); *rituals and routines* (committees, procedures, relationships); *symbols* (buildings, logos, dress codes); *organizational structure* (hierarchies, functions); *control systems* (rulebooks, budgets, rewards); and *power structures* (executives, directors, influencers).

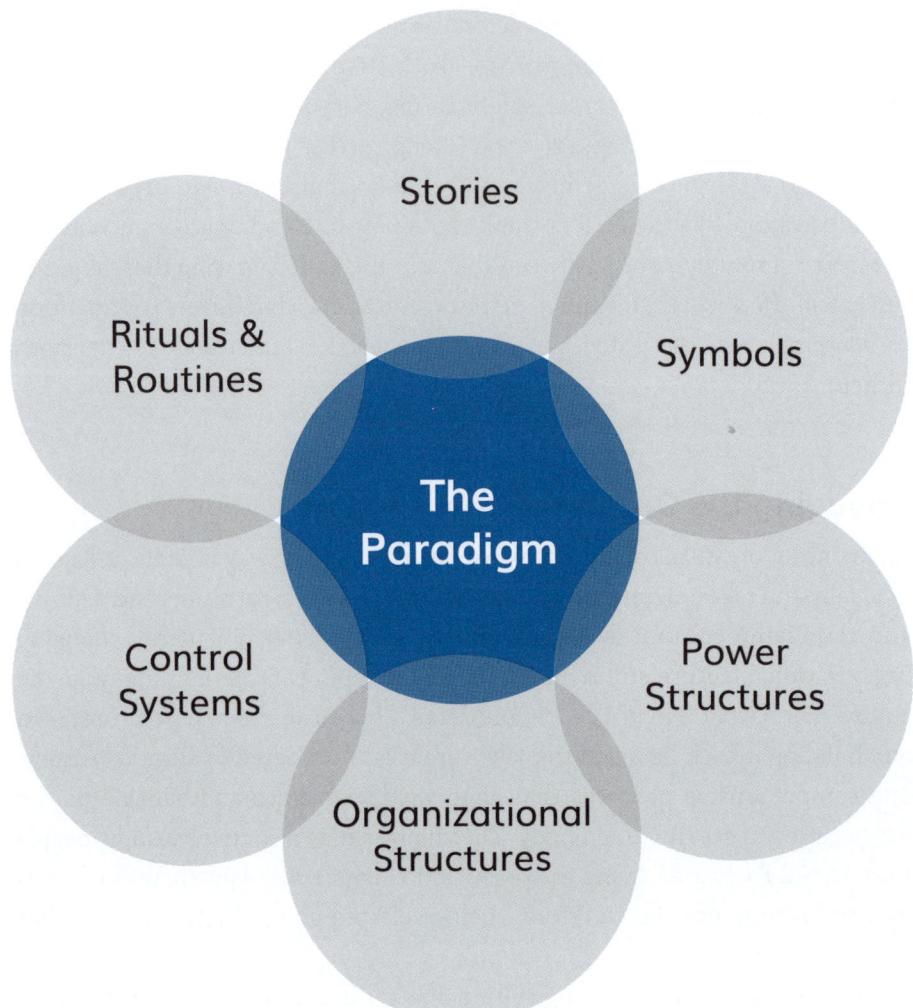

**Figure 3.4** Cultural web (Johnson, 1992).

The cultural web can provide an in-depth analysis of what an organization's culture looks like in the present, but can also guide a re-mapping of the culture as people want it to be, along with differences between the two. Discussions of these changes should help establish priorities and plans for change in relation to the specific elements. A similar tool for mapping culture change, but with some slightly different additional elements, is a *culture design canvas* (Figure 3.5).

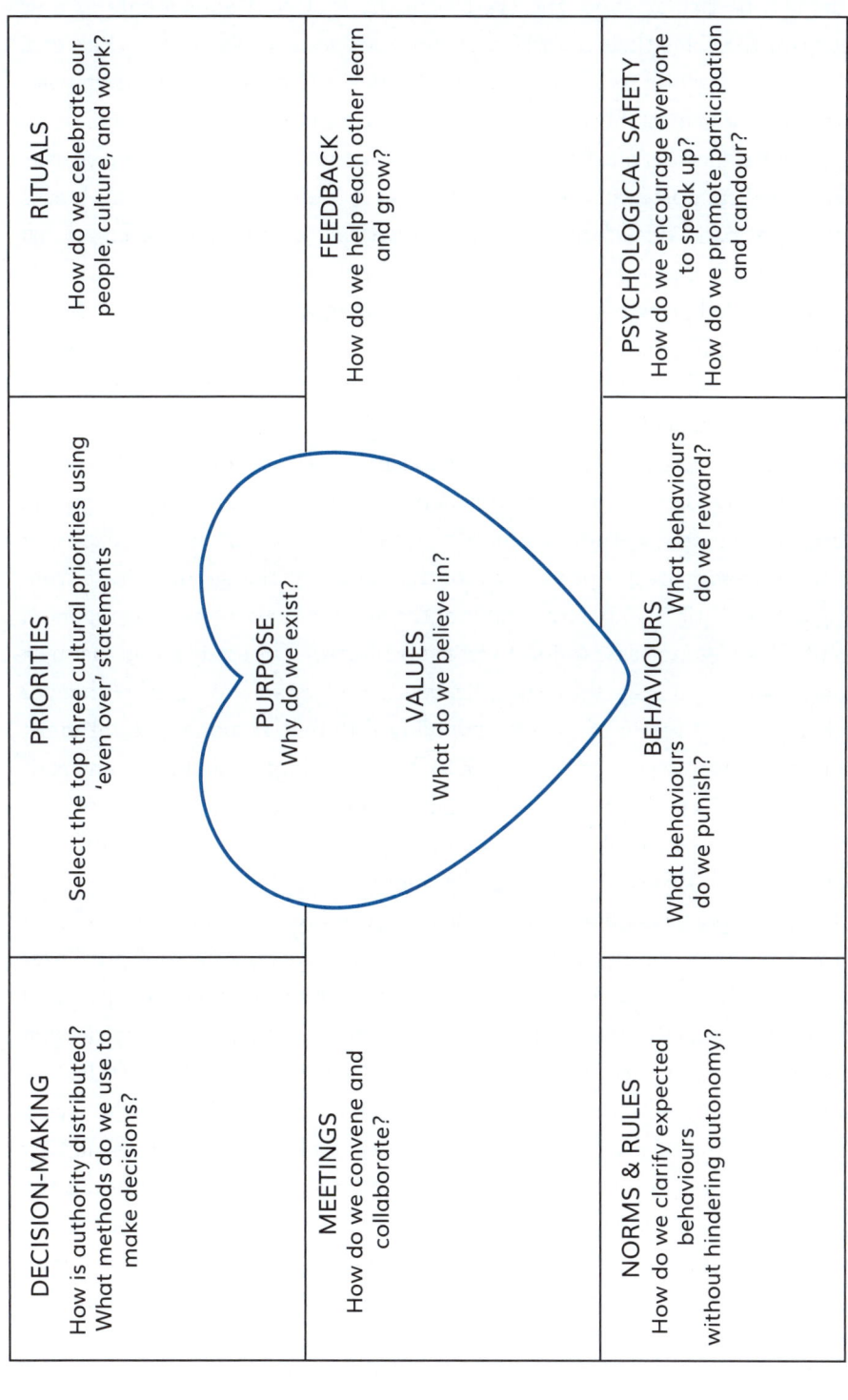

**Figure 3.5** Culture design canvas (Razzetti, 2019). Gustavo Razzetti: https://fearlessculture.design/canvas.

By using a culture design canvas, organizations can avoid limiting themselves to being a particular 'type' and start with the four central elements of how they want to evolve their priorities, purpose, values and behaviours (Razzetti, 2019). An interesting tool for mapping priorities is to come up with 'even over' statements, which establish how an organization can make difficult choices by putting what matters most first, such as 'product reliability even over elegance' or 'employee support even over customer service'. Next, the three building blocks on the right-hand side of the canvas can be worked on as to how the emotional culture helps people feel safe, open, celebrated, connected and feedback-friendly for learning and growth. Finally, the three elements on the left-hand side can be covered, which map how the organization can best make decisions, share information, collaborate and follow sets of clear, sensible rules as part of a healthy functional culture.

While these mapping tools are very specific, practical and accessible, they may still involve significant rounds of change discussions with stakeholders and leaders over company strategy, identity and initiatives. One study looked at a top US university over a period of months, trying to change its culture from being paternalistic (hierarchical, stable authority, top-down) toward being more decentralized (empowered units, diverse subcultures). The study found that new leaders trying to manage the change needed to understand how culture changes gradually over a series of stages, involving different responses to different change initiatives in context (Latta, 2009). New buildings, programmes and staff needed to be related back to the old cultural profile, demonstrating how the previous culture was evolving into something new, with leaders monitoring for implementation issues, impacts and alignments.

Another report looked at a variety of European organizations from different sectors working to develop culture change. This change typically took place over a period of three years or more, with efforts to translate environmental and strategic changes into cultural drives for improving customer focus, partnership working, peak staff performance and business development (CIPD, 2011). The findings tended to emphasize culture change as an ongoing journey, involving a whole host of new roles, initiatives, structures and communications, all part of an effort to relate changing behaviours and activities back to the values the organizations were trying to change. Honest evaluations of the process also show that culture change is not without setbacks or downsides, such as not all employees feeling equally passionate or consistently informed, as well as concerns about the impact of other changes in the environment happening at the same time. This relates back to the many different elements of culture to be mapped and explored, and how difficult it is to manage or account for everything in a short space of time. A helpful seven-point checklist for cultural change derived from this research was as follows (CIPD, 2011):

1. *Planning* – a clear plan for culture change to stick to, which is public and widely 'owned' by the organization, while being open to external events along the way.

2. *Involvement* – open, honest and appropriate messages about who will be involved in culture change, when and to what extent, including HR and key stakeholders.

3. *Leadership* – active, visible forms of leadership among leaders and managers at different levels, acting as part of diverse but effective teams for representing the culture change.

4. *Employees' buy-in* – helping and encouraging employees to emotionally engage with the 'new' cultural values, and how to promote and bring them to life on a consistent basis.

5. *Enabling infrastructure* – understanding how the organizational structure is helping or hindering culture change and looking across subcultures and systems for visible signs of resistance or progress.

6. *Developing capabilities* – developing and integrating new skills and behaviours into the culture change, with regards to HR processes, line managers' work and limited resources.

7. *Measuring impact* – efforts to continuously collect the right data from a variety of sources and measures to evaluate change progress and communicate it to staff.

Driving culture change has also been described as requiring a mixture of 'hard' and 'soft' strategies. For example, leaders inspire the organization to go along with change, and at the same time management will require information, structure and tools to embed the culture. There will also be elements of 'force' and power to ensure compliance with changed values and behaviours (Denning, 2011).

## ACTIVITY 3.7

1. Given what you now know about the interplay between organizational culture and change, revisit your answer to Activity 3.1 and respond to the following: Why is it that culture strongly influences strategic organizational change?

In context, culture change will always link back to strategic and structural considerations, whether it is downsizing or growth, international operations, societal crises or various other management concerns over quality, efficiency and innovation. Mergers and acquisitions are again an insightful example here, because they involve addressing change in terms of two organizational cultures, rather than just one. Here, managing culture change is often done with the help of HR professionals, to facilitate constructive criticism, assessment and learning between the culture of the acquiring company on the one hand (the buyer), and the company being acquired, on the other (the seller). Merging two cultures together can be managed in different ways to achieve different 'cultural end-states' (Marks and Mirvis, 2011):

- **'Best of both'** – the two companies both share, exchange and integrate strengths of both cultures.
- **'Absorption'** – the acquired company conforms and assimilates its culture to the culture of the acquirer, often the case if the acquirer is a larger with a more influential brand.
- **'Preservation'** – the acquired company retains independence and autonomy from the acquirer, to keep its culture the same, often preserving its distinct name and brand.
- **'Transformation'** – both companies find new ways to operate together, and the merger transforms them into a new, third type of cultural entity.
- **'Reverse merger'** – the relatively unusual case of an acquired company leading the acquirer to change its culture, despite the fact it is the one being acquired.

## Critical Perspectives on Culture and Organizational Change

Often organizational culture and culture change are described in positive terms. However, it is possible to ask why and reflect critically on this topic. One reason for this is because it is not clear whether culture can or should be changed towards someone's version of an ideal. Culture, after all, is about people's values and behaviours, which may extend deeply into their private and family lives, being very psychological in nature. Sometimes culture is described as a 'variable' – something that organizations have, and can change and control through skills, tools and levers. However, culture can also be described by using a 'root' metaphor – as something that organizations just 'are', made up of people and constantly evolving, which cannot be readily controlled.

We might also think about why, if it is so obvious what an excellent culture is, many organizations still seem to have 'toxic' or harmful cultures characterized by bullying, harassment, abuse, long working hours and other forms of unhealthy values and behaviours. Furthermore, although we might hope that culture change would be *conciliative* and based on supportive discussions of what everyone agrees upon, it can also be *aggressive* and controlling, *corrosive* and unplanned, or *indoctrinative* and more like brainwashing, depending on the context (Hawkins, 1997).

It is probably simplistic and inappropriate to always assume that culture change is the answer to many of an organization's problems. For example, between the 1980s and up to 1996, British Airways reversed its fortunes as one of the worst performing airlines in Europe to one of the best, a change often described in inspiring terms as a culture change 'fairy tale' of a CEO bringing new training and supportive HR practices to put employees first (Grugulis and Wilkinson, 2002). However, this neglects the role of more complicated structural, strategic and political factors affecting British Airway's changing circumstances. Rather than the culture change programme itself, much of the change in the organization's performance could also be explained in terms of its control over competitive slots at Heathrow airport, its flight network and its competitive status, and its international agreements relating to other airlines. A positive cultural change story also ignores the fact that staff were affected by fear of redundancies, and, as a consequence, strikes and employee absence issues followed in 1997 (Grugulis and Wilkinson, 2002).

Although culture change may be described in terms of very positive values and ideals on the surface, among employees the reality may be very uneven, with some people holding much more mixed or negative reactions about how the culture is reflected in their daily work experiences. There may be cynicism about how the rhetoric of the culture is superficial and hypocritical, not matching the experienced, yet less visible, reality. Similarly, when asked to change themselves as part of a culture change, not all employees may be ready or on board with doing so. In fact, some employees may never be. The existing culture itself may be the impediment or barrier to other organizational change efforts, something employees are trying to preserve or protect, and something neither employees nor managers have full control over.

Certain ideas of culture can therefore be constraining or misleading. Organizations like Disney become known for their extremely powerful and positive brand in global and popular culture, but the organization's culture and history can be viewed as a more complex mixture of positive and negative stories, perspectives and events (Boje, 1995). A study of the American network marketing organization, Amway, found that its culture of passionate sales and distribution could be experienced by sales representatives as quite intense, exerting a strong effect over their identities and sense of self, which taken to extremes could be compared to the tightly controlled, enclosed dynamics of a cult (Pratt, 2000).

None of these lines of argument necessarily mean that organizational cultures cannot be positive or open to improvement, but they are useful for drawing our attention to the dangers of overemphasizing the benefits and possibilities of culture change in isolation. Critical thinking here can help us to be more accepting of the limits and ethics of cultural change actioned via control, and more questioning of how values are formed and expressed in organizations in relation to different people, structures and practices.

### CASE STUDY: RIO TINTO AND CHANGING TOXIC CULTURE IN THE MINING INDUSTRY

Rio Tinto, the British-Australian mining multinational, commissioned an external, independent review of its organizational culture in 2021, conducted by former Australian Sex Discrimination Commissioner Elizabeth Broderick. The purpose of this review was to better understand, prevent and respond to harmful behaviours across its global operations. The findings, based on surveys and testimony from interviews and focus groups, released in February 2022, were disturbing, with many minority employees reporting experiencing bullying, sexual harassment, assault and racism in recent years. In a positive step to face up to the problem of a toxic culture, and to be transparent with its stakeholders, the company published the report on its website, along with an apology from the CEO who took over in early 2021, Jakob Stausholm (Rio Tinto, 2024).

The report and the transparency about its findings seemed to build some increased trust and confidence among employees that Rio could make meaningful change in stamping out toxic behaviour in its culture. However, the report itself came out of specific circumstances, such as the damage to Rio Tinto's reputation in 2020, when it destroyed Juukan Gorge, a mining site in Western Australia whose ancient rock shelters were sacred to indigenous people. This cost the previous CEO their job and further reinforced the need for culture change (*The Economist*, 2022). In general, the mining industry has workforces composed mainly of men (about 80 per cent), and can involve work at remote, isolated mining sites, which was where some of the worst employee behaviours were reported to have taken place. However, high rates of abusive behaviour were also reported in Rio Tinto's more corporate offices, such as in its strategy, sustainability and development group.

Interviewees traced cultural problems back to issues such as suspicion of internal reporting mechanisms and a fear of speaking out in a 'culture of silence', while bullies were rewarded at the company for high performance levels, regardless of their other behaviours.

In following and implementing the recommendations of its culture report, Rio Tinto has established new specialist units and working relationships across the business to make improvements in areas such as responding with care to complaints and whistleblowing. They also changed leadership behaviours and began managing facilities with a risk and safety emphasis (Rio Tinto, 2024). The CEO, Stausholm, has a positively regarded leadership style for engaging with data and reports and trying to change Rio's culture so that it becomes less hierarchical and more open-minded about making decisions (Hume and Fildes, 2022). Parallels have been drawn between Rio's successful pivot towards a safety culture with reduced worker fatalities in earlier decades, and the current need to realize that supporting diversity, inclusion, work-life balance and psychological wellbeing is crucial for a healthy business (Thomas, 2022).

Rio Tinto's problems are extreme in some respects but far from unique, and collecting and disclosing such extensive data on their corporate culture is an important step for change that many other organizations could learn from (*The Economist*, 2022). Culture may be hard to measure precisely, but stakeholders such as investors, customers and employees are increasingly concerned about problems with toxic cultures and behaviours, particularly in the wake of social movements in the wider culture, such as #MeToo and Black Lives Matter. Organizations need change proposals to address toxic or 'hypermasculine' cultures, or they risk serious threats relating to employee wellbeing, turnover and damaged reputations.

## ACTIVITY 3.8

1. Have you ever worked in a toxic workplace environment? If yes, please outline the key characteristics that made it toxic. If not, please reflect on the toxic workplace environment in the case study and detail the key characteristics that make it toxic.

2. How do the issues that you have identified fit with the theory of culture that has been discussed in this chapter?

3. Given what you have learned about good practices and strategic change and culture, how would you go about improving the toxic workplace environment you worked in, or in the case study outlined above?

**CONSULTANCY IN THE CHAIR**

**Cup of Kindness Activity**

As a consultant to CUP you are now part of the steering committee at board level that is responsible for formulating new strategy. Other board members look to your expertise, and during a meeting one of the senior management team calls on you to explain what they overheard when an employee was cracking a joke with a colleague. Apparently, this employee said to another colleague 'this organization's culture will eat the proposed new strategy for breakfast'.

Please explain and come up with a solution or solutions as to how best to tackle the view expressed by the employee, which is no doubt representative of a general feeling within the organization.

 **Competency-based Interview Question**

1. Can you outline an example of organizational strategy that you think has changed too slowly, which has proved detrimental to an organization?

 **Chapter Summary**

This chapter has covered several important areas relating to managing strategic change and culture change in organizations. To briefly recap, these included:

→ Various ways to map out change across organizations' external and internal environments that link strategy, structure and culture together.

→ The importance of organizational design in strategic change for ensuring structures and ways of working properly reflect and help execute strategy.

→ The importance of understanding specific forms of strategic change in context, such as M&As and downsizings, which often involve distinct motivations, options and effects.

→ How to understand strategic change in terms of a balance between top-down and bottom-up forces, which helps organizations think through the implementation of strategic change carefully.

- How to understand and change organizational cultures by defining them, classifying them and mapping them across different types, levels and components relating to values and behaviours, including national as well as corporate cultures.

- How to think critically about culture change to better understand how culture is linked to other strategic and environmental conditions, and how cultures can involve harmful behaviours and it may not always be straightforward or desirable to change too directly or forcefully.

## Useful Resources

- Boatman, A. (2024). Organizational Analysis 101: Your Comprehensive Guide for 2024. Academy to Innovate HR (AIHR). https://www.aihr.com/blog/organizational-analysis (accessed 10 April 2025).

- Innosight (2019). The Transformation 20: The Top Global Companies Leading Strategic Transformations. September. https://www.innosight.com/insight/the-transformation-20 (accessed 10 April 2025).

- Razzetti, G. (2019). How to use the Culture Design Canvas – A Culture Mapping Tool. Fearless Culture. November 20. https://www.fearless-culture.design/blog-posts/the-culture-design-canvas (accessed 10 April 2025).

## Bibliography

Amis, J., Slack, T. and Hinings, C. R. (2002), 'Values and Organizational Change'. *The Journal of Applied Behavioral Science*, 38(4): 436–65.

Amis, J., Slack, T. and Hinings, C. R. (2004), 'The Pace, Sequence, and Linearity of Radical Change'. *Academy of Management Journal*, 47(1): 15–39.

Anthony, S. D., Trotter, A. and Schwartz, E. I. (2019), 'The Top 20 Business Transformations of the Last Decade'. *Harvard Business Review*. September 24. https://hbr.org/2019/09/the-top-20-business-transformations-of-the-last-decade (accessed 10 April 2025).

Aspara, J., Lamberg, J. A., Sihvonen, A. and Tikkanen, H. (2023), 'Chance, Strategy, and Change: The Structure of Contingency in the Evolution of the Nokia Corporation, 1986–2015'. *Academy of Management Discoveries*, 9(4): 469–96.

Boje, D. M. (1995), 'Stories of the Storytelling Organization: A Postmodern Analysis of Disney as "Tamara-Land"'. *Academy of Management Journal*, 38(4): 997–1035.

Bruskin, S. (2024), 'Why Micro Changes Can Be HR's Secret Recipe for Success'. *People Management*. January 30. https://www.peoplemanagement.co.uk/article/1859229/why-micro-changes-hrs-secret-recipe-success (accessed 10 April 2025).

Bryant, A. (2021), 'Does Culture *Really* Eat Strategy for Breakfast?' *Strategy + business*. May 27. https://www.strategy-business.com/blog/Does-culture-really-eat-strategy-for-breakfast (accessed 10 April 2025).

Buck, M. (2022), 'The CEO of Hershey on Turning a Candy Company into a Snacks Empire'. *Harvard Business Review*. November–December. https://hbr.org/2022/11/the-ceo-of-hershey-on-turning-a-candy-company-into-a-snacks-empire (accessed 10 April 2025).

Bürkner, H. P., Fæste, L. and Hemerling, J. (2015), 'The New CEO's Guide to Transformation: Turning Ambition Into Sustainable Results'. BCG. May 15. https://www.bcg.com/publications/2015/transformation-change-management-new-ceo-guide-transformation (accessed 10 April 2025).

Cameron, K. S. (1994), 'Strategies for Successful Organizational Downsizing'. *Human Resource Management*, 33(2): 189–211.

Campion, M. A., Guerrero, L. and Posthuma, R. (2011), 'Reasonable Human Resource Practices for Making Employee Downsizing Decisions'. *Organizational Dynamics*, 40(3): 174–80.

Cascio, W. F. (2002), *Responsible Restructuring: Creative and Profitable Alternatives to Layoffs*. San Francisco: Berrett-Koehler Publishers.

Child, J. and McGrath, R. G. (2001), 'Organizations Unfettered: Organizational Form in an Information-intensive Economy'. *Academy of Management Journal*, 44(6): 1135–48.

CIPD (2011), 'Developing Organisation Culture: Six Case Studies'. June 15. https://www.cipd.org/globalassets/media/knowledge/knowledge-hub/reports/developing-organisation-culture_2011-six-case-studies_tcm18-10885.pdf (accessed 9 May 2025).

CIPD (2023), 'Organisation Design'. Factsheet. Chartered Institute of Personnel and Development. February 14. https://www.cipd.org/uk/knowledge/factsheets/organisational-development-design-factsheet (accessed 10 April 2025).

Cokins, G. (2010), 'The Promise and Perils of the Balanced Scorecard'. *Journal of Corporate Accounting & Finance*, 21(3): 19–28.

Cooper, C. L., Pandey, A. and Quick, J. C. (eds), (2012), *Downsizing: Is Less Still More?* Cambridge: Cambridge University Press.

Couto, V., Plansky, J. and Caglar, D. (2017), *Fit for Growth: A Guide to Strategic Cost Cutting, Restructuring, and Renewal*. Hoboken, NJ: John Wiley & Sons.

Deal, T. E. and Kennedy, A. A. (1983), 'Culture: A New Look Through Old Lenses'. *The Journal of Applied Behavioral Science*, 19(4): 498–505.

Denning, S. (2011), 'How do you Change an Organizational Culture?' *Forbes*. July 23. https://www.forbes.com/sites/stevedenning/2011/07/23/how-do-you-change-an-organizational-culture (accessed 10 April 2025).

DiGeorgio, R. (2002), 'Making Mergers and Acquisitions: What We Know and Don't Know–Part I'. *Journal of Change Management*, 3(2): 134–48.

Dominguez CC, M., Galán-González, J. L. and Barroso, C. (2015), 'Patterns of Strategic Change'. *Journal of Organizational Change Management*, 28(3): 411–31.

Eisenhardt, K. M. and Sull, D. N. (2001), 'Strategy as Simple Rules'. *Harvard Business Review*, 79(1): 106–16.

Favaro, K. (2014), 'Strategy or Culture: Which is More Important?' *Strategy + business*. May 22. https://www.strategy-business.com/blog/Strategy-or-Culture-Which-Is-More-Important (accessed 10 April 2025).

Gerstner, L. V. (2002). *Who Says Elephants Can't Dance? Inside IBM's Historic Turnaround*. New York: HarperCollins Publishers.

Giorgi, S., Lockwood, C. and Glynn, M. A. (2015), 'The Many Faces of Culture: Making Sense of 30 Years of Research on Culture in Organization Studies'. *The Academy of Management Annals*, 9(1): 1–54.

Goffee, R. and Jones, G. (2013), 'Creating the Best Workplace on Earth'. *Harvard Business Review*, 91(5): 98–106.

Goold, M. and Campbell, A. (2002), 'Do You Have a Well-Designed Organization?' *Harvard Business Review*, 80(3): 117–24.

Greenwood, R. and Hinings, C. R. (1988), 'Organizational Design Types, Tracks and the Dynamics of Strategic Change'. *Organization Studies*, 9(3): 293–316.

Greiner, L. E. (1998), 'Evolution and Revolution as Organizations Grow'. *Harvard Business Review*, 76(3): 55–64. (Original work published 1972.)

Groth, A. (2020), 'Zappos has Quietly Backed Away From Holacracy'. Quartz. January 29. https://qz.com/work/1776841/zappos-has-quietly-backed-away-from-holacracy (accessed 10 April 2025).

Groysberg, B., Lee, J., Price, J. and Cheng, J. (2018), 'The Leader's Guide to Corporate Culture'. *Harvard Business Review*, 96(1): 44–52.

Grugulis, I. and Wilkinson, A. (2002), 'Managing Culture at British Airways: Hype, Hope and Reality'. *Long Range Planning*, 35(2): 179–94.

Grundy, T. (2006), 'Rethinking and Reinventing Michael Porter's Five Forces Model'. *Strategic Change*, 15(5): 213–29.

Gustafsson, R., Jääskeläinen, M., Maula, M. and Uotila, J. (2016), 'Emergence of Industries: A Review and Future Directions'. *International Journal of Management Reviews*, 18(1): 28–50.

Hamel, G. and Zanini, N. (2014), 'Build a Change Platform, not a Change Program'. McKinsey. October 1. https://www.mckinsey.com/capabilities/people-and-organizational-performance/our-insights/build-a-change-platform-not-a-change-program (accessed 10 April 2025).

Handy, C. B. (1985). *Understanding Organizations*, fourth edition. New York: Facts on File Publications.

Hawkins, P. (1997), 'Organizational Culture: Sailing Between Evangelism and Complexity'. *Human Relations*, 50(4): 417–40.

Hemerling, J., Dosik, D. and Rizvi, S. (2015), 'A Leader's Guide to "Always-on" Transformation'. BCG. November 9. https://www.bcg.com/publications/2015/people-organization-leaders-guide-to-always-on-transformation (accessed 10 April 2025).

Heracleous, L. (2013), 'Quantum Strategy at Apple Inc'. *Organizational Dynamics*, 42(2): 92–9.

Heracleous, L. and Werres, K. (2016), 'On the Road to Disaster: Strategic Misalignments and Corporate Failure'. *Long Range Planning*, 49(4): 491–506.

Hope, O. L. E. (2010), 'The Politics of Middle Management Sensemaking and Sensegiving'. *Journal of Change Management*, 10(2): 195–215.

Hume, N. and Fildes, N. (2022), 'Rio Tinto Seeks Redemption After Laying Bare Workplace Failings'. *Financial Times*. February 7. https://www.ft.com/content/fdaa9764-3969-4ed3-a0cf-b3ef77e9f60e (accessed 10 April 2025).

Ind, N., Iglesias, O. and Schultz, M. (2015), 'How Adidas Found its Second Wind'. *Strategy + business*. August 24. https://www.strategy-business.com/article/00352 (accessed 10 April 2025).

Johnson, G. (1992), 'Managing Strategic Change—Strategy, Culture and Action'. *Long Range Planning*, 25(1): 28–36.

Kent, A., Lancefield, D. and Reilly, K. (2018), 'The Four Building Blocks of Transformation'. *Strategy + business*. October 22. https://www.strategy-business.com/article/The-Four-Building-Blocks-of-Transformation (accessed 10 April 2025).

Kilduff, M., Mehra, A. and Dunn, M. B. (2011), 'From Blue Sky Research to Problem Solving: A Philosophy of Science Theory of New Knowledge Production'. *Academy of Management Review*, 36(2): 297–317.

Kim, W. C. and Mauborgne, R. (2002), 'Charting Your Company's Future'. *Harvard Business Review*, 80(6): 76–85.

King, D. R., Bauer, F. and Schriber, S. (2018), *Mergers and Acquisitions: A Research Overview*. London: Routledge.

Latta, G. F. (2009), 'A Process Model of Organizational Change in Cultural Context (OC3 Model). The Impact of Organizational Culture on Leading Change'. *Journal of Leadership & Organizational Studies*, 16(1): 19–37.

Logan, D., King, J. and Fischer-Wright, H. (2008), *Tribal Leadership: How Successful Groups Form Great Organizations*. New York: HarperCollins.

MacKay, R. B. and Chia, R. (2013), 'Choice, Chance, and Unintended Consequences in Strategic Change: A Process Understanding of the Rise and Fall of NorthCo Automotive'. *Academy of Management Journal*, 56(1): 208–30.

McKinsey (2008), 'Enduring Ideas: The 7-S Framework'. *McKinsey Quarterly*. March 1. https://www.mckinsey.com/capabilities/strategy-and-corporate-finance/our-insights/enduring-ideas-the-7-s-framework (accessed 10 April 2025).

Marks, M. L. and Mirvis, P. H. (2011), 'A Framework for the Human Resources Role in Managing Culture in Mergers and Acquisitions'. *Human Resource Management*, 50(6): 859–77.

Masuch, M. (1985), 'Vicious Circles in Organizations'. *Administrative Science Quarterly*, 30(1): 14–33.

MindTools (2024), 'The Competing Values Framework'. https://www.mindtools.com/aydu02k/the-competing-values-framework (accessed 10 April 2025).

O'Reilly, C. A. and Tushman, M. L. (2004), 'The Ambidextrous Organization'. *Harvard Business Review*, 82(4): 74–83.

Peters, T. J. and Waterman, R. H. (1982), *In Search of Excellence: Lessons from America's Best-Run Companies*. New York: Warner Books.

Pratt, M. G. (2000), 'The Good, the Bad, and the Ambivalent: Managing Identification Among Amway Distributors'. *Administrative Science Quarterly*, 45(3): 456–93.

Quinn, R. E. and Rohrbaugh, J. (1981), 'A Competing Values Approach to Organizational Effectiveness'. *Public Productivity Review*, 5(2): 122–40.

Rio Tinto (2024), 'Everyday Respect Report'. https://www.riotinto.com/en/sustainability/talent-diversity-inclusion/everyday-respect (accessed 10 April 2025).

Schein, E. (1985), *Organizational Culture and Leadership*. San Francisco: Jossey-Bass.

Schneider, B., Ehrhart, M. G. and Macey, W. H. (2013), 'Organizational Climate and Culture'. *Annual Review of Psychology*, 64: 361–88.

Schuler, R. and Jackson, S. (2001), 'HR Issues and Activities in Mergers and Acquisitions'. *European Management Journal*, 19(3): 239–53.

Schultz, M. and Hatch, M. J. (2003), 'The Cycles of Corporate Branding: The Case of the LEGO Company'. *California Management Review*, 46(1): 6–26.

Sirkin, H. L., Keenan, P. and Jackson, A. (2005), 'The Hard Side of Change Management'. *Harvard Business Review*, 83(10): 108–18.

Smollan, R. K. and Sayers, J. G. (2009), 'Organizational Culture, Change and Emotions: A Qualitative Study'. *Journal of Change Management*, 9(4): 435–57.

Somers, M. (2023), 'Five Enduring Management Ideas from MIT Sloan's Edgar Schein'. MIT Management Sloan School. February 9. https://mitsloan.mit.edu/ideas-made-to-matter/5-enduring-management-ideas-mit-sloans-edgar-schein (accessed 10 April 2025).

Sonenshein, S. (2010), 'We're Changing—Or Are We? Untangling the Role of Progressive, Regressive, and Stability Narratives During Strategic Change Implementation'. *Academy of Management Journal*, 53(3): 477–512.

*The Economist* (2022), 'Rio Tinto and the Problem of Toxic Culture'. February 12. https://www.economist.com/business/rio-tinto-and-the-problem-of-toxic-culture/21807599 (accessed 10 April 2025).

Thomas, H. (2022), 'Rio Tinto's Toxic Culture Should be a Wake-Up Call for Business'. *Financial Times*. February 4. https://www.ft.com/content/7a4b0437-ce29-44fb-a959-da414ef99884 (accessed 10 April 2025).

Tushman, M. L. and O'Reilly III, C. A. (1996), 'Ambidextrous Organizations: Managing Evolutionary and Revolutionary Change'. *California Management Review*, 38(4): 8–29.

Watkins, M. D. (2007), 'Demystifying Strategy: The What, Who, How, and Why'. *Harvard Business Review*. September 10. https://hbr.org/2007/09/demystifying-strategy-the-what (accessed 10 April 2025).

# The Human Aspects of Change

**4**

> **Learning Outcomes**
>
> At the end of this chapter you will be able to:
> 1. Explain and evaluate the importance of understanding the human aspects of organizational change.
> 2. Deploy models and frameworks showing how individuals and groups experience and adjust to organizational change as a transition.
> 3. Define and assess types of individual and team characteristics relevant to managing organizational change.
> 4. Understand and explain critical limitations and challenges with managing human aspects of organizational change.
> 5. Understand how to manage the people side of change in an integrated way through organization development and soft systems approaches.

## Introduction

This chapter reviews and critically reflects on approaches to understanding and managing the psychological aspects of organizational change as experienced at both the individual and group level of analysis. Models and frameworks that summarize how human beings experience change as a transition are described, with an emphasis on outlining the cognitive and social processes individuals and groups go through in adjusting to organizational change. It is argued that human-centred tools and models can be used to diagnose and understand distinctive issues within change processes. Individual differences are discussed including, importantly, personality characteristics and emotional skills, which have implications for how different people respond to change. Team and group types, team development and team diversity are also discussed for managing groups through change. Finally, some limitations and challenges regarding the human aspects of change are acknowledged, and organization development (OD) and soft systems approaches are explored as ways to integrate people management and organizational change across levels of the organization.

## People and Organizational Change

It is hard to overstate the general importance of the human aspects of experiencing and responding to organizational change in shaping its overall success. People populate organizations and their environments – both as individuals and as parts of groups or teams. These human aspects of change can be seen as a fundamental level of organizational change – with people representing crucial 'building blocks' necessary to the acceptance and implementation of the change. Without the understanding, motivation, support and cooperation of people, organizational change and its effective management are likely to fail to make progress.

As we have seen so far in Chapters 2 and 3, the 'harder' aspects of change management tend to be concerned with controlling the economic strategies and resources of the organization from the top. In contrast, the 'softer' human aspects of change management concern the capabilities, opportunities, emotions, attitudes, motivations and behaviours of people affected by the change emerging from the bottom up. The human side of change can involve people working at various levels in an organizational hierarchy, not just leaders or senior managers, but middle managers, frontline workers and people working in various arrangements, such as project teams or functional departments. Such people might see themselves as active agents helping manage the change, more passive recipients told to accept the changes proposed or a mixture of both. Beyond employees, we might also consider the human side of organizational change experienced by other stakeholders, such as customers or members of communities.

The human side of change is local and intimate, but no less complex than the bigger organizational picture at the macro level. People will relate the overall situation of the organizational change to their individual and diverse circumstances in many different ways ('what does this change mean for me?'). For example, if the change involves organizational restructuring, then people will be wondering how this will affect their jobs, and if they might be laid off at some stage. Similarly, if the change is significant, such as a merger between organizations, one organization acquiring another, a change in CEO or some other mixture of changes, people might try to guess what this will mean for the organizational culture and their work relationships.

Many organizations and leaders may be tempted to focus only on the external economic and strategic environment – namely, having a plan for the 'hard' side of change and ensuring an organization's financial survival. However, ignoring or neglecting the human aspects inside the organization severely risks the longer-term health of the organization, and may contribute to change failure for a variety of reasons, especially if employees are not sufficiently aware, ready or informed about change, and are therefore likely to resist. We consider this in more detail during your learning journey in Chapter 6.

## Historical Development and Contemporary Perspective

The human side of change management has a history in the Western world going back at least to the 1940s, with the founding of research institutes on both sides of the Atlantic concerned with applying social and behavioural psychology to how humans train, learn and develop in changing societies. For example, German-American psychologist Kurt Lewin founded the National Training Laboratories Institute for Applied Behavioral Science (NTL) in America in 1947. Similarly, in the same year in the UK, the founding of The Tavistock Institute of Human Relations occurred, arising from the Tavistock Clinic and social and psychological research projects carried out during World War II. Both institutes' approaches emphasized the importance of working democratically with people affected by change, including the human relationships and activities embedded in groups and wider social systems, such as organizations. These approaches have influenced many organizational change consultants ever since, although they have continued to require further development to deal with changing organizational demands and environments across the late twentieth and into the twenty-first century (Neumann, Holvino and Braxton, 2004).

Today there are many different approaches and names for human-centred approaches to organizational change, grounded in human relations and organizational behaviour (OB) traditions of management, as well as organizational development and other forms of psychological and behavioural science. To understand the human aspects of organizational change as fully as possible, it is important to critically consider these interdisciplinary influences in combination, along with any models and evidence put forward to support them. An underlying aim of this chapter is therefore to offer guidance on this challenging task.

Bearing in mind the saying that 'there is no one best way to manage change'; rather than making general prescriptions, it is important to consider the choices open to organizations in terms of what they are trying to change about people (if anything), and how they are trying to do so (Burnes, 1996). One early and influential human relations model (Chin and Benne, 1969) outlined three general strategies for changing human systems, which Quinn and Sonenshein (2008) later updated, adding a fourth and working from an OD perspective:

### ACTIVITY 4.1

1. Consider the four approaches put forward in Table 4.1. Which type of strategy do you think would be most effective in successfully managing people through change, and why?

| Strategy | Emphasis and Perspective |
| --- | --- |
| (1) Forcing | - Emphasis on power, politics, internal structure and control.<br>- A minority of more powerful people can use legitimate authority and leverage (e.g. rewards and punishments) to impose change on a majority of less powerful people and ensure their compliance. |
| (2) Telling | - Emphasis on logic, technical expertise, external data, structure and control.<br>- People can use analysis, facts and rational argument to justify a change as in the best interest of the other, persuading them to accept and engage with it. |
| (3) Participating | - Emphasis on trust, possibilities, values, skills and relationships in the organization.<br>- People can include others in open communication exchanges, supportive dialogues and democratic decision-making to discuss conflicting positions and emerging possibilities about change. |
| (4) Transcending | - Emphasis on vision, potential, purpose and external uncertainty.<br>- People can inspire others to move forward together by appealing to a common good or higher moral purpose with the potential to transform themselves, the organization and its environment. |

**Table 4.1** Four General Strategies for Addressing Human Aspects of Change

These four approaches offer very different perspectives on how to manage people in change, and we might critically reflect on and discuss how suitable, feasible or acceptable they seem according to our own views and the specific change situation. Ethics, politics, leadership, culture, strategy, structure and technology might all influence how we see the wider system surrounding people affected by change, and thus our decisions and choices about how to treat them as part of that system.

Contemporary views of human change and influence developed by consultants draw further insights from psychology and behavioural science. Changing people's mindsets and behaviours as part of a large-scale transformation can be challenging for a variety of reasons, and some strategies may not have the desired effect on people or be as effective with as many people as initially hoped. As a result, twenty-first-century models of human change need to integrate multiple, reinforcing means of changing people's attitudes and behaviours (or 'winning their hearts and minds'). Creating a deep, lasting change in people requires a systematic understanding of the complexity of human nature, beyond limited solutions that may not sufficiently motivate or influence people.

The McKinsey influence model (e.g., 2003, 2016, 2020) is a good example of how to address this, because it brings together four interrelated, evidence-based building blocks for changing people's minds and behaviours, which suggest a combination of reinforcing practices and complementary courses of action (see Figure 4.1).

| Role Modelling | | Understanding and Conviction |
|---|---|---|
| Seeing and mimicking other people behaving consistently in a different way, in person or online, e.g. colleagues, leaders, influencers. | | Personalized communications that are clear, frequent and inspire people through meaningful stories that show how their beliefs and actions fit into the change. |
| | **Effective Personal Change of Mindsets and Behaviours** | |
| **Confidence and Skill Building** | | **Reinforcement with Formal Mechanisms** |
| Personalized coaching and learning that addresses people's individual needs, with opportunities to practise and celebrate change skills and behaviours, in person or online. | | Structures, processes and systems that remove barriers and offer motivating rewards and personal recognition for changing behaviour and performance. |

**Figure 4.1** McKinsey Influence Model and Combined Conditions for Personal Change.

Having explained the overall importance of understanding the human aspects of organizational change and outlined a couple of general models proposing ways of addressing it, the remainder of the chapter looks more deeply into how individuals and groups adjust to change, affect change and make up a wider organizational system requiring appropriate interventions and development.

## Individuals Adjusting to Change

In general, there are many ways of describing and understanding human processes of individual adjustment to change both in and around organizations. This is because forms of personal adjustment and transformation depend on an enormous variety of personal and situational factors, as well as the different forms of human attitudes and behaviours associated with different objects and ideas of change. At the same time, however, there are many common frameworks and ideas about how individuals tend to experience change in similar underlying ways – at least to some extent.

From Kurt Lewin's early psychological theories of behaviour change is the idea of individuals and groups within a 'field', where the environment contains a 'gestalt', or an organized pattern of forces. Some of these forces will be more likely to drive us in the direction of change, while others will be more likely to restrain us and hold us back. It is the overall interplay of these forces that will determine the strength, direction and distance of change (Burnes and Cooke, 2013). For example, if we are trying to achieve the change of losing weight, observing fit role models and caring about our health might drive us toward more change, while bad dietary habits, genetic factors and lack of time to exercise might restrain and limit more change. Taken further, Lewin also proposed that we could think of people's wider fields of change as a 'life space', or a type of mapped out environment that they experience moving through, between different positions at different times, and in different directions relative to the position of a change goal (Burnes and Cooke, 2013) (Figure 4.2).

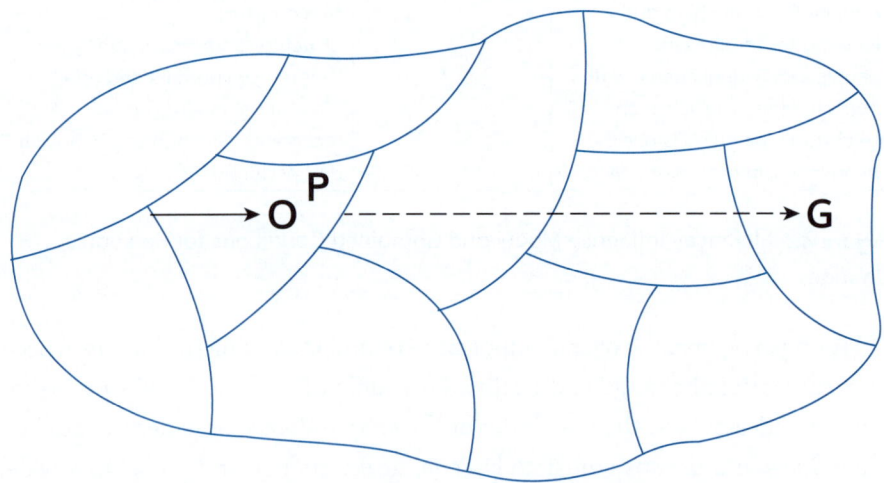

**Figure 4.2** Kurt Lewin's concept of change as a life space – person (P), current starting situation or behaviour (O), and goal (G) (Burnes and Cooke, 2013).

## Individual Transition: Change Curves and Stages

Most models of individual or group change adjustment have tended to represent it as a curve, a series of phases or stages, or a mixture of both. Kurt Lewin's (1952) three-phase model of change (*unfreeze-move-refreeze*) and Swiss-American psychiatrist Elisabeth Kübler-Ross's (1969) five-phase model for coping with the changes associated with death, trauma and serious illness (*denial-anger-bargaining-depression-acceptance*) are two early and influential examples of this.

In their review of such models of the human response to change and transition, from the 1950s through to the 1990s, Elrod and Tippett (2002) found a majority consensus where nearly all such models involve a difficult disruptive period in the middle, which they label quite negatively as a 'death valley'. Specifically, in the middle of a change, people experience a degradation or dip in their capabilities before they can redefine normality, fully adjust to a change and progress through it to greater stability and achievement.

For employees, changes could take an enormous variety of shared or personal forms – to their physical environment, work relationships, equipment and/or tasks – with a variety of effects. For managers and leaders guiding people through organizational changes, an effective process is likely to involve efforts to manage expectations, minimize disruptions and offer necessary support and encouragement along the way. This guidance has the potential to make the change curve smoother in its progression, the dip in the middle shallower and the overall experience less disruptive and more positive. One helpful visualization of this is that of Schneider and Goldwasser (1998), with their 'classic change curve' (Figure 4.3).

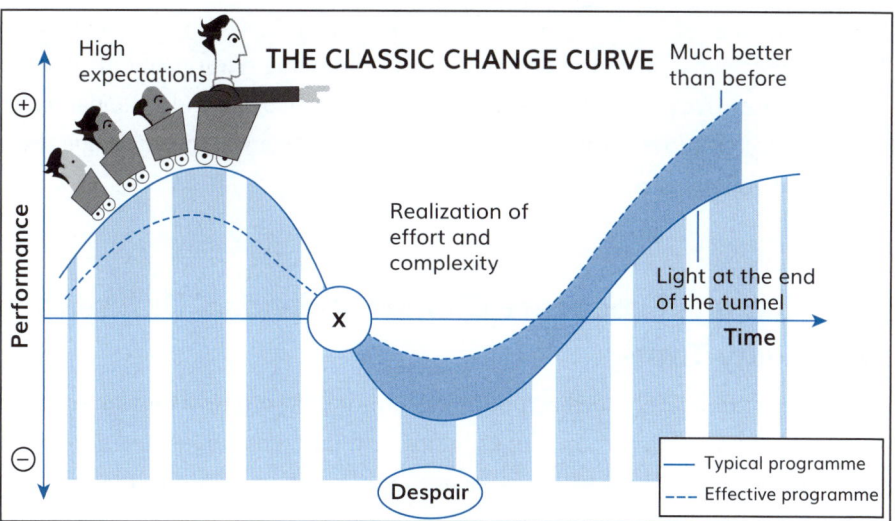

**Figure 4.3** Classic change curve (Schneider and Goldwasser, 1998).

Over time, change consultants and organizations have continued to develop and adopt versions of these models for guiding people appropriately through stages of change. Another widely used example in recent decades has been the 'ADKAR' model, developed by Jeff Hiatt, founder of Prosci, a US change management research institute and consultancy (e.g. Hiatt, 2006). ADKAR shows how leaders and teams can manage change effectively by guiding individuals in a structured way towards being able to implement it, first by enabling them to deal with change and then by keeping them engaged with it. The five letters of the ADKAR acronym indicate five major change goals and suggest distinct ways of implementing them:

1. *Awareness* of the need to change. Enabling awareness involves two-way communications and explanations sharing information about the reasons for the change and proposed solutions.

2. *Desire* to participate and support the change. Enabling desire involves gauging employees' positive and negative reactions to the change, highlighting personal benefits and addressing personal concerns.

3. *Knowledge* of how to change and what the change looks like. Enabling knowledge involves providing employees with training, coaching and other forms of educational and informational resources (e.g. role models, examples) to address skill gaps and reference change progress and behaviours.

4. *Ability* to implement required change skills and behaviours on a day-to-day basis. Enabling ability involves scheduling practice runs for employees to practice new skills, processes and tools, while monitoring and adjusting performance with goal-setting and feedback.

5. *Reinforcement* to keep the change in place. Enabling reinforcement involves using incentives, rewards, celebrations, positive feedback and personal recognition for employees fulfilling desired change outcomes, to encourage them to keep following new processes.

## How Humans Experience Change: Individual Differences, Personality Traits

However, while it is somewhat possible to understand human experiences of change in terms of common stages, goals and patterns, *individual differences* and *personality traits* are likely to explain further differences in human aspects of change within and across such experiences. For example, one study of hundreds of individuals going through several organizational changes (structural reorganization, workplace relocation and technological change) found that while 77 per cent showed different levels of discomfort from one change to the next, 23 per cent showed identical and stable reactions to all changes (Bareil, Savoie and Meunier, 2007). This suggests that people have personality traits that sometimes give rise to quite strong general and stable reactions to change based on longstanding psychological habits and tendencies in their behaviours (Allport, 1927).

The psychology of personality traits and types remains influential in understanding and responding to individual differences in organizational behaviour. We need to make sure we carefully assess personality tools when using them in managing change, in terms of how much evidence there is for their reliability and validity in explaining and predicting workplace attitudes and behaviours. Some models of personality, such as the 'Big Five' personality traits – *neuroticism, extraversion, openness to experience, agreeableness* and *conscientiousness* – have been highly influential across many research studies and settings, including showing relationships with employees' attitudes toward organizational change (Vakola, Tsaousis and Nikolaou, 2004).

Yet the most popular and famous personality test in the world is the *Myers-Briggs Type Indicator (MBTI)*, first created in 1943, but revised and republished many times since. Based loosely on the psychological theories of Carl Jung, the test has four main dimensions: *Introversion–Extraversion, Sensation–Intuition, Thinking–Feeling* and *Judging–Perceiving*. Test scores on the four dimensions classify people into one of sixteen possible personality 'types', according to which end of each bipolar dimension they score more highly on, and as indicated by a four-letter combination (e.g., ENTJ, ISFP). There have been heated debates and critiques about the quality, purpose/design and interpretation of the MBTI, and we should carefully consider its strengths and weaknesses for ensuring responsible use in each organizational context (Furnham, 2020).

Many people place great value on the MBTI for fostering a positive sense of self-awareness and self-acceptance, for helping people to understand the individual complexities of themselves and others, and its general clarity and usefulness for driving personality descriptions, discussions and applications (Furnham, 2020). At the same time, the MBTI can be seen as reductive, encouraging simplistic or inappropriate interpretations of personality types. Consequently, conflicting assumptions about the theory it is based on and the limits of its usefulness remain. The MBTI remains popular in practice for a variety of training and teamwork purposes, but is much less used in academic research. One study of its use during a culture change programme in an Australian manufacturing organization found that employees reacted to it in many different ways, with mixed results (Garrety, 2007). As with any change tool or intervention, it is important to bear in mind that employee reactions can be complex and varied. Ironically, some employees may be more enthusiastic *about personality tools* than others, as well as the possibilities for putting personality insights into practice.

### ACTIVITY 4.2

1. How effective do you think you are in managing change?

2. Complete the online Myers-Briggs personality test. Does your personality type offer you any insight into how effectively you're able to manage change in your professional and personal life? Is this different from what you expected? Please explain.

## Individuals Coping With and Adjusting to Change Throughout Their Lives

In and around organizations, individuals experience changes *similarly* according to certain stages and processes, and *differently* according to different personality traits and abilities. Another way of looking at the human side of organizational change is in terms of *what* happens to people across the course of their lives – the *events* or the *contents* of the changes – and how they cope, develop and transform as a result.

One example from the fields of social psychiatry, stress research and occupational medicine that remains influential is the Social Readjustment Rating Scale (SRRS), developed in 1967 by two US psychiatrists, Thomas Holmes and Richard Rahe (Holmes and Rahe, 1967). The SRSS tool is a checklist of forty-three *life events*, commonly reported as stressful, which can contribute to and predict mental and physical illness in the months following the events. Users of the tool are typically asked to check off all applicable events they have experienced in the previous six months or year of their life. Crucially, these events all relate to life *changes*, and are weighted, scored and summed with larger or smaller values assigned according to the degree of 'change required in a person's life as a function of life events' (Scully, Tosi and Banning, 2000: 866).

Of the forty-three life events in the SRRS checklist, two of the top ten with the highest scores for stressful life change are related to organizational life ('dismissal from work' and 'retirement'), while many others can happen to people in parallel with changes at work, such as family changes, financial circumstances and/or lifestyle changes (Holmes and Rahe, 1967). While the significance and stress associated with changes experienced as life events is likely to vary across cultures, generations and individuals, such tools remain relevant, consistent and useful because of their *environmental* and *preventative* emphasis on seeking to protect people's wellbeing and mental health. These tools are also humane and inclusive for detecting shifting inequalities in diverse people's lives. In change management terms, employees exposed to too much challenging life change over a short period of time face significant health risks unless provided with enough social, economic and community support to counteract the stress associated with these experiences (Smith, 2020).

More frequently, people experience stressful changes in the form of *daily hassles*. Daily hassles can be any changes in a person's environment that they experience as harmful or threatening to their wellbeing (e.g. anything from being late in a traffic jam to worrying about job security), whereas *uplifts* are experiences or conditions viewed as positive and favourable (e.g. anything from relaxation time to relating to a friend). Importantly, the general frequency and intensity of these daily events can be more predictive of people's general health and wellbeing than other life event changes, and of their job performance and absenteeism (Ivancevich, 1986). As with life events, there are survey scale and checklist tools available for organizations to use to better assess and understand a range of specific employee concerns and hassles across work and life domains (e.g. Holm and Holroyd, 1992) to aid in better managing them through change. One three-year study of organizational change in the New Zealand customs service, a public sector organization, found that daily events, such as receiving thanks from the public, showed robust associations with job satisfaction over time, as set against a wider backdrop of changing employment conditions and interventions (Mansell, Brough and Cole, 2006).

## Different Coping Strategies for Change

Perspectives on the impact of life events and daily experiences can help those in positions of seniority to better understand stress and support people during organizational change, which may be directly or indirectly related to other changes people are experiencing.

One final useful element, from a stress perspective, is that of *coping psychology* and *coping styles* (Lazarus and Folkman, 1984). Whether a small change or a large change, coping psychology suggests that individual people react differently to changes in their environments based on their appraisal of the situation and their confidence in finding ways to deal with it. For example, one person's minor inconvenience can be another person's ruined day. Appraisals come in two main forms:

1. *Primary appraisal* – how relevant is this event to my wellbeing, and if relevant, will it have a positive effect or a stressful effect on me?
2. *Secondary appraisal* – do I have the control, resources and ways of coping for dealing with the situation, and what will I do about it?

After the appraisals, which are cognitive understandings of the situation, people engage in coping actions to manage or resolve the event. At this point, there are two main ways of coping with a stressful event:

1. *Problem-focused* – Strategies aimed at directly managing the problem or the source of the stress, such as time management, delegation, analysis for solutions, confrontation, cooperation and so on.
2. *Emotion-focused* – Strategies aimed at managing the emotions arising because of a stressful event or encounter, such as wishful thinking, emphasizing the positive, avoiding or distancing, but also self-blame, anger and frustration.

### ACTIVITY 4.3

1. Think of two historic and/or recent significant change situations that have involved coping and adjusting to changes in your life.
2. Use Table 4.2 to outline each situation and, following on from this, select the appraisal type that accurately describes how you evaluated the situation – either primary or secondary. Then select one of the two coping strategies, either problem- or emotion-focused, to accurately describe the way in which you coped with the situation.
3. What does this tell you about how you as an individual handle significant change in your life?
4. What could you do to improve the way in which you cope with change?

| Significant Change | Please put a tick in the appropriate box | | | |
|---|---|---|---|---|
| | Primary Appraisal | Secondary Appraisal | Problem-Focused | Emotion-Focused |
| Situation 1 Please explain | | | | |
| | | | | |
| | | | | |
| | Primary Appraisal | Secondary Appraisal | Problem-Focused | Emotion-Focused |
| Situation 2. Please explain | | | | |

**Table 4.2** Evaluating Change and Coping Strategies

While this distinction is useful for broad discussions of coping with change, it is important to reflect that there are many different coping strategies, and that the use of each strategy is partly affected by the situation. Strategies can be classified in different ways, and no strategies are inherently more or less effective, but are likely to form part of a complex process of understanding and adaptation (Biggs, Brough and Drummond, 2017). Nevertheless, if people are encouraged to discuss change situations and ways of coping with them, they may be able to identify what it is about the environment and people's interpretations and behaviours that are most likely to affect the success of the change. Supporting people to engage in more adaptive or effective coping strategies may be a case of providing them with better management relationships, resources, training, coaching, counselling and other interventions as part of the organizational change.

## Psychodynamic, Psychosocial and Developmental Perspectives

Different from life change and stress perspectives of change, but still related to them, are *psychodynamic, psychosocial* and *developmental* perspectives. These perspectives focus on human change in terms of how people's identities evolve and grow over time and over the course of their lives and careers, in ways that are highly meaningful to them and their relationships with significant others and their communities. Addressing these processes of change may involve people having to confront deep-seated tensions that they may not always be fully aware of, and that can be difficult to resolve without further reflection, growth and support. For organizations and change management, this might mean arranging for additional coaching, counselling, learning, rewards/benefits and open discussions tailored to people's age, career and personal circumstances, alongside a wider programme of organizational change.

For example, the German-American psychoanalyst Erik Erikson, who coined the term 'identity crisis', developed a model of psychosocial development with *eight stages*, ranging from when we are born through to old age (after sixty-five years of life) (Erikson, 1959). Each stage features a crisis or conflict for our personality and identity, where we must try to cope with tensions between opposing values to develop a healthy personality and virtuous character. The first four stages concern childhood up to the age of eleven and mastering a fundamental sense of trust, independence, initiative and confidence in our abilities. The fifth is adolescence through to the age of eighteen, which involves a struggle with change around trying out different adult identities and roles. The final three stages cover the bulk of our adult and working lives (aged 19 to 65+). Here, the changes people are struggling with concern establishing intimate, loving relationships with others; making meaningful contributions to family, community and society; and looking back on our life's overall accomplishments with wisdom and satisfaction.

American psychologist Robert Kegan, who conceives of changes in adult development (Kegan, 1998), put a similar but more modern example forward. Kegan argues that as we evolve to adjust to the everyday demands of modern life, we need support to master the complexity of the different tasks and expectations placed on us across our roles and relationships in a variety of domains. These domains include working in organizations, but also families, friendships, health and wellbeing and education. In order not to feel overwhelmed, we need to be helped and supported to gradually develop a more complex understanding of ourselves in relation to the complex modern world around us. Successful adult development is therefore a series of profound transformational changes along these lines. Although not everyone will develop at the same pace and to the same degree, with age-related maturation and the right forms of meaningful reflection and empathic experience, people can positively develop to more successfully navigate relationships, conflicts and tasks concerning themselves and others. Kegan (1998) describes these changes in terms of five 'orders of consciousness' and, like Erikson, sees them as progressing from early childhood to mature adulthood, representing a way for us to build self-awareness, adaptability and management of our life's categories through storytelling and reflections on the meanings of our changing roles and identities (e.g. team member, spouse, parent, trainer, leader, mentor).

Admittedly, these sorts of personal transformations can feel unclear and involve very difficult periods of adjustment in people's lives. They can also offer rich rewards if people are able to gain insights into themselves and discover more positive forms of growth and contribution to society. Furthermore, for organizations, there are implications for sustaining the wellbeing and competence of employees wrestling with the personal ramifications of changes to their work, jobs, careers and lives.

Relevant research here by Toubiana and colleagues (2022) involved hundreds of interviews with people who had gone through major life changes, both positive and negative, to better understand how, despite feeling like their identities were 'stuck' or paralysed, they nevertheless found ways to overcome these feelings and move forward with growth into a new role or situation. Examples of these journeys of personal transformation included nuns leaving the Catholic Church; immigrants having to radically change jobs in a new host country; people changing jobs due to injury; women leaving sex work; and former prisoners. The researchers found five main strategies helped people navigate such change processes:

1. *Marking a clear break with the past* (e.g. recognizing a particular moment or milestone as the end of the past).

2. *Crafting a story to tie past and present together* (e.g. recognizing that the past was necessary in leading the way toward a more positive present).

3. *Acknowledging and working through challenging emotions* (e.g. accepting the causes of feelings of fear, shame or anger about a situation and refocusing on positive feelings like forgiveness or pride).

4. *Focusing on meaningful, non-work identities* (e.g. defining oneself more in terms of family relationships, community or volunteering roles or activism).

5. *Imagining and fantasizing about ideal futures* (e.g. seeing current circumstances as stepping stones to ambitious plans and alternative futures).

## ACTIVITY 4.4

1. Think of a situation in your own life (be that in a work or personal context) that has involved significant change. Apply the five key strategies for coping to craft a narrative around your significant change.

2. On reflection, how helpful do you think these strategies are in helping you or others come to terms with significant change, and why?

What is striking about this research is that, while it is important for organizations to support individuals through change, its findings are a reminder that people nevertheless play very active roles in how they make change meaningful as it happens to them. We can further develop this idea in terms of individuals 'making their own change happen'; for example, in situations where they are entrepreneurial, inventive, proactive, compassionate and participative in coming up with new stories, perspectives, supports, innovations and initiatives.

At the same time, individuals are limited in how much they can reinvent themselves or their jobs without some wider structural resources and support, and organizations and management should not try to avoid responsibility for this. Simply asking or telling someone to participate in change or to make it work by themselves is unlikely to have a positive effect if what they are being asked to do does not match their motivation, training, workload, knowledge, experience, networks or background (Pasmore and Fagans, 1992). Nevertheless, if many of the conditions are conducive to change and growth, and an entrepreneurial person finds themselves successfully pursuing a series of highly meaningful changes across their career, their 'quest' for change can give rise to far-reaching business ventures and drive large-scale strategic change. One example of this is twenty-five years of the career of the world-leading Spanish chef, Ferran Adrià. Adrià pursued visionary changes across 1983–2008 that led him from being a restaurant employee to an owner-manager, and from there to an entrepreneur and leader of an entire business model, establishing cookery schools, laboratories, menus, books and other influential changes linking philosophies of cooking and creativity to valuable forms of innovation (Svejenova, Planellas and Vives, 2010).

## Behavioural and Brain Sciences

A final area for explaining how individuals adjust and respond to changes, and one that is increasingly influential, concerns interdisciplinary approaches associated with behavioural and brain sciences. Here, different subjects like psychology and behavioural economics can be drawn upon to understand how to observe and experiment with people's actions, and how and when they change their behaviours. For example, it might involve experimenting to see people's responses with changing incentives, decisions, comparisons and presentations of information. Some would argue that behaviour change can be seen as a 'gold standard' of human change, in the sense that it represents strong observable evidence that an individual has achieved a desired change. In healthcare policy, examples include how to reliably help people change their behaviours to lose weight or give up smoking.

In reviewing a great deal of behavioural change evidence and frameworks, Michie and colleagues (2011) have proposed the 'COM-B system' (Figure 4.4). In this acronym, the B stands for behaviour, and COM stands for the three interactive and essential components of capability (e.g. knowledge and skills), opportunity (e.g. environmental factors that help or prompt behaviours) and motivation (e.g. goals, decisions, brain processes).

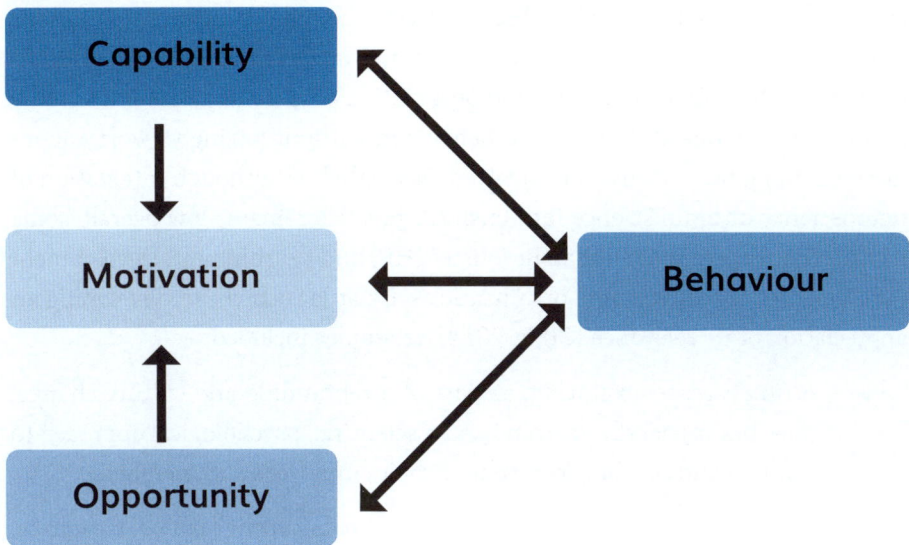

**Figure 4.4** COM-B system diagram for understanding behaviour and behaviour change (Michie, Van Stralen and West, 2011).

The COM-B model can be used to identify which barriers are preventing successful behavioural change in more detail – whether they are conscious or unconscious, psychological or physical. Then, several appropriate *interventions* can be selected, such as training for capability, incentives for motivation and adjustments to physical or social environments for opportunity. The final part of this approach concerns having the appropriate *policies* in place – actions by responsible authorities that consistently support the interventions. For example, policies might include things like marketing communications, guideline documentation, regulations, financing, laws and other forms of planning and support (Michie, Van Stralen and West, 2011). There are many other detailed choices around specific tools and techniques, but COM-B provides a useful general overview of how the main components governing human behaviour fit together, and a way to ensure none of them are missed out. It is flexible enough for use in various workplace applications, but also comprehensive and based on large amounts of experimental and observational evidence.

## How Our Brains Respond to Change

How our brains respond to change is less clearly understood, and workplace 'neuro' techniques may lack firm evidence or explanations. They therefore need to be treated with caution, and critical reflection must be undertaken before using them. Research attempting to find clues for successful change management interventions based on people's brain activity changes in different situations remains expensive, imprecise, inconsistent and unclear on practical solutions (Horvath, 2022). Questionnaires and observations can be far quicker and more cost-effective, while still relating to behaviour, without having to worry about understanding how the brain is involved. Nevertheless, although integration of neuroscience or brain science into business practice remains low overall, some research has shown that Human Resources (HR) and Learning and Development (L&D) professionals in some organizations are at least open to developing an appreciation of its relevance (CIPD, 2014). Examples included:

- A *fitness centre* exploring, as part of a rebranding and culture change, how 'brain-friendly' learning and a scientific, psychological approach to training and coaching can benefit their employees and members.
- An *ambulance service* exploring potential relationships between exercise, movement and brain functionality as related to changes in meetings, coaching, communication, work breaks and the introduction of mindfulness programmes.
- An *international law firm* considering how employees' changing views of their careers might relate to threat or reward brain responses, and designing learning programmes that encourage staff to be more active in reflecting on their habits and how they practise and apply skills.
- A *telecommunications firm* seeking to change leadership style across its business, and using neuroscientific insights on threat, habits, reinforcement and social connection in its leadership development programmes.
- A *vehicle manufacturer* using brain-friendly learning principles to redesign some of its employee classroom training towards more engaging and efficient videos and flexible access to context-relevant content to support day-to-day and instant 'just-in-time' learning.

We may question to what degree such change initiatives are really about neuroscience and the human brain, or if they are instead based on more general discussions about psychology, behaviours and learning. However, provided those involved in organizational changes are careful about how they source their psychological evidence, theories and assumptions, and are evaluating the implications of their decisions in terms of resources and employee feedback, a general emphasis on better supporting human experiences through psychological insights should be welcomed. Such approaches should also complement, but not distract from, changes to wider organizational contexts and systems.

## Relating Groups and Teams to Organizational Change

As mentioned earlier in this chapter, in the second half of the twentieth century, approaches to management based on human relations and organizational behaviour became more popular and influential. A major part of this shift involved recognizing how much employees' motivations and behaviours were influenced by group dynamics, and how ignoring or suppressing these more social aspects of work was likely to harm performance, impede organizational change efforts and reflect a less effective management approach. Late in the twentieth and well into the twenty-first century, people working in groups or teams has become extremely popular and widespread, perhaps even taken for granted. Often 'group' and 'team' are used interchangeably; however, groups can refer to looser and more informal arrangements, whereas teams tend to have more specific shared purposes and responsibilities for outcomes (Katzenbach and Smith, 2005).

Although teams are widely discussed in management and OB in general, they are not always linked more specifically and explicitly to organizational change or change management. Here, given that our focus is on organizational change, it seems worth clarifying how teams might relate to change in at least three main ways:

1. *Teams themselves can change* – over time, people working together as teams can go through cycles of development and achievement; involving changing structures, goals, members, working processes and even disbanding and reforming.

2. *Teamworking can be a change intervention* – managers can decide to put individual employees into more formal teams or types of teams with the aim of improving performance and innovation.

3. *Teams can be part of implementing other changes* – for example, two companies merging might use a special purpose 'integration team', with members from both companies, to help ensure the wider change is implemented successfully.

In practice, these three links between teams and organizational change are likely to overlap and could occur at the same time. However, it seems important to distinguish that while pre-existing teams are going through continuous changes, new team structures could be introduced as a change in themselves, or as a tool for helping to achieve the objective of another type of change.

Considering groups and teams during organizational change is important and potentially beneficial for a variety of reasons. As with individual employees, group and team dynamics across an organization are often at risk of being neglected relative to the large-scale structural, strategic and cultural plans initiated from the top. However, groups and teams can exert significant social influence across different parts of the organization, and so it can be important to involve and consider them carefully as part of a change programme. Furthermore, it is unlikely that change agents and managers will always have the time, energy or resources to work in depth with every individual affected by organizational change, so teams represent useful mid-size local units for coordinating change communications and activities more efficiently than one individual at a time.

However, a crucial point for critical reflection here is that teams need to be carefully supported and designed, or they can face serious limitations and be more likely to reduce the effectiveness of change than enable it. Teams can involve biased perspectives, destructive conflicts and experience breakdowns due to poor communication and cooperation processes among their members. While putting people in teams usually makes sense for ensuring people can participate democratically in a change and play a role, teamworking is not automatically an effective choice in and of itself. For example, teams are not always able to manage the individual talents and concerns of their members.

However, when teams are supported and designed with care, they have the potential to drive effective organizational change. Effective teams can collaborate dynamically to deliver strong performances and innovative outcomes that are shared and collective – greater than the total of what individual members could achieve if they were working alone. Many positive conditions need to be in place in an organizational environment to maximize team effectiveness.

High-performing teams need a high-performance environment to achieve and sustain improvements and successful outcomes. For example, a study of an elite Olympic swimming team by Fletcher and Streeter (2016) attributed its success to a high-performance environment with four core components: *leadership* (vision, support, challenge), *performance enablers* (information, instruments, incentives), *people* (attitudes, behaviours, capacity) and *organizational culture* (achievement, wellbeing, innovation, internal processes). Many factors must fit together (in terms of every member of a team feeling supported and understanding each other's roles and goals), if the team is to continue striving for achievements and innovations.

Teams can be understood as needing *inputs* (tasks, members, resources), engaging in *processes* (conflicts, norms, leadership) and generating *outputs* (innovations, reactions, behaviours, performances), often summarized as *input–process–output (IPO)* models. Going from research evidence to practice requires managers to consider a variety of focused interventions for teams that will help build relationships, train team skills, set goals and facilitate debriefings for members' learning (CIPD, 2023). These interventions will ensure that teams are able to harness the diversity of their members, establish healthy working dynamics and communicate and share knowledge effectively.

Various tools for helping teams connect, adjust, diagnose, develop and reflect on their situation are available. Increasingly, teams in many organizational change contexts will have relatively diverse members in terms of personalities, demographic backgrounds, expertise, attitudes and values. Team members may be from different countries, professions, functions (*cross-functional teams* are a common and influential type of team) and even organizations and industries. Depending on the purpose, many team configurations are possible, and most organizations contain entire networks of different teams, with many people being members of more than one team at the same time.

As with individuals, teams may use personality survey tools to profile their different members. A very popular extension of this approach is *team role inventories,* which team members can use to rate themselves and each other on different styles and preferences for playing different roles within a team. Ideally, teams will be aiming for a balanced set of responsibilities for team relationships, tasks and information.

One widely used example is *Belbin's team role model*, first developed by Meredith Belbin in the 1980s and 1990s (Aritzeta, Swailes and Senior, 2007). The model helps team members understand their potential strengths and weaknesses, and how they might best assign roles to support interactions with each other and facilitate the progress of the team. Specifically, the model consists of the following nine roles: *completer finisher, implementer, team worker, specialist, monitor evaluator, coordinator*, *plant*, *shaper*, and *resource investigator* (Aritzeta, Swailes and Senior, 2007). Despite their popularity, it is important to keep in mind the limitations and criticisms of such tools – the roles may overlap, for example, and will not be able to fully predict all behaviours and changes a team might face. However, team role and personality inventories can be used as one tool making up part of a broader toolkit.

Another area where teams can reflect is in terms of how they themselves are developing through various team stages and processes. One of the most influential stage models has been Tuckman's (1965) *stages of group development*, which originally consisted of four steps until a fifth was later added (Tuckman and Jensen, 1977). These steps are explained in Figure 4.5:

1. *Forming* – team members get to know each other, define rules and boundaries.
2. *Storming* – team members attempt to explore conflict and resolve differences.
3. *Norming* – team members' cooperation and commitment to team goals grows.
4. *Performing* – team members make decisions and achieve common goals.
5. *Adjourning (or mourning)* – team members complete task, break up, redeploy.

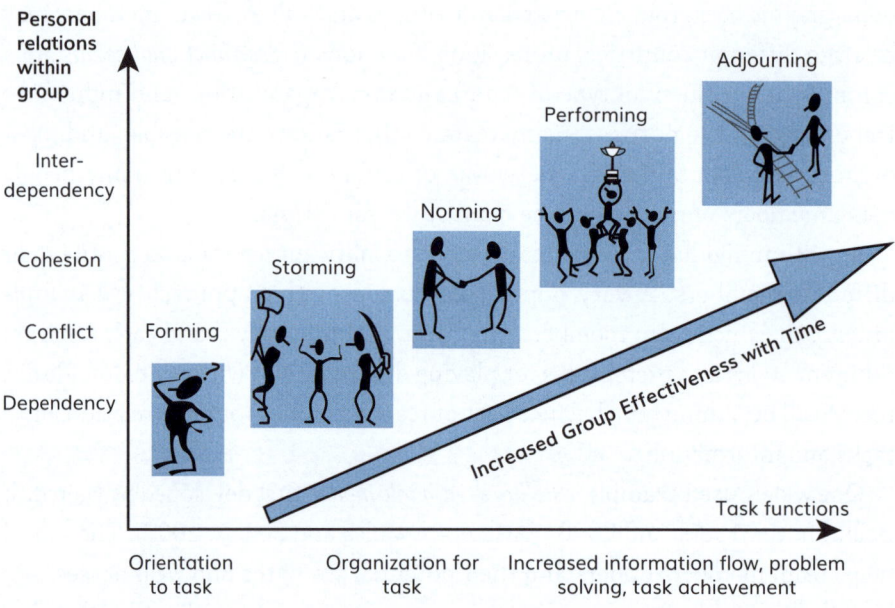

**Figure 4.5** Stages of group and team development. Based on Tuckman's Stages of Team Development (1965).

## ACTIVITY 4.5

1. Think of a team with which you are familiar. This could be at work or socially, perhaps a sports team or a team that you are part of, for example, to deliver group work at a university. Explain the various phases of your team's development by reference to the stages outlined in Figure 4.5.

2. How productive do you think your team was during the various stages? Please explain.

These stages can be a helpful general framework for teams to manage the gradual series of changes involved in moving between one phase of development and another, right from the point at which members start working on something together. However, besides developing in stages, teams can experience time, change and transitions in many other forms. For example, teams can change by stopping and starting more suddenly in response to contextual events such as crises or deadlines. Teams are also going through continuous *processes* of change as members interact with each other and undertake activities, which may involve completing pieces of work in cycles, or changing directions in how they work together and what they work on. Finally, change can *emerge* in teams through members coming to share thoughts, feelings and motivations, and experiencing shared team states such as team trust, confidence and commitment.

## Team Types

In the twenty-first century, as organizations have continued to change their structures and designs and respond to change in their environments, it is important to recognize the changing variety and range of *team types* that can be found in different contexts. Team types can be defined in terms of how diverse their members and tasks are, how long they work together for, and how flat or hierarchical they are in terms of their status, authority and leadership arrangements (Hollenbeck, Beersma and Schouten, 2012). Teams' core work might be manufacturing or developing products, but also producing knowledge and services. Teams may have members working in different parts of the world, using digital technologies to work in a virtual, remote and dispersed fashion. Fundamentally, most organizations have multiple types of teams at different hierarchical levels and in different parts of their structure – be it senior management teams of executives, mid-level managerial and project teams, or teams of supervised frontline workers, engaged in daily customer-facing or operational work.

Special purpose teams can be set up specifically to explore possibilities for innovation and change that the rest of the organization might not be aware of or have time to learn about and investigate. Examples include the scenario team at oil and gas company Shell, that uses experts to assess possible visions of the future, and the 'Nike Goddess' team, who were inspired after a trip to Japan to design a successful new footwear product for the women's sportswear market (Cunha and Chia, 2007).

One general suggestion made is for organizations to give some teams more freedom from traditional working structures to explore potential blind spots and new perspectives for developing and inspiring changes that might not otherwise be considered. These teams have also been called 'x-teams', because part of their purpose is to reach out *externally* to stakeholders both inside and outside their organization – testing technologies, researching products for different countries or markets and building relationships with executives, departments and customer communities (Ancona and Bresman, 2023). Teams can be established for developing or implementing almost any form of organizational change imaginable; whether it concerns organizational learning, culture change, quality improvement, product development, policy reforms or something else. These teams are effective as they tend to be more rapid, entrepreneurial and creative than formal structures with more stable responsibilities, but a lot depends on how well the teams are designed and supported.

## Agile, flexible and dynamic teamwork

For example, one of the most radical approaches to flexible and dynamic teams related to organizational change is that of *agility*. Agile approaches (originally developed in software development contexts after 2001) involve restructuring significant parts of an organization around rapid cycles of high-quality product development, giving teams the freedom to work together across functions, learning and experimenting around how to be most responsive to customers (e.g. Mergel, Ganapati and Whitford, 2021). Often new terminology is adopted to describe dynamic patterns of collaboration. A case in point being that the digital music company Spotify has experimented with organizational agility from 2012 in an approach where small teams become 'squads', while also potentially being part of 'tribes', 'chapters' and 'guilds' depending on links with related business areas, specific domains or communities with shared interests, respectively (Thilak, 2023).

However, there are often critical debates about how well such dynamic approaches might work in different organizations, and what they might look like. For example, one study of agile practices adopted for large-scale software development in a multinational telecom company over a five-year period found at least six unintended problems limiting any desirable learning and innovation outcomes (Annosi, Foss and Martini, 2020):

1. Team identities and norms not fitting with management goals.
2. Teams feeling pressure to prioritize most urgent issues over learning.
3. Team members struggling to build up in-depth knowledge in specific areas.
4. Team members struggling to share and integrate knowledge with daily operations.
5. Team members struggling to identify who to approach for advice and expertise.
6. Team members lacking confidence with frequent failures on different products.

To address complex teamwork challenges during organizational change then, managers need to diagnose and respond to these problems by ensuring that the work environment surrounding the team reduces tensions of workload and balances any competing goals, responsibilities and demands. In fact, most teams face dilemmas around the potential changes in roles, boundaries, diversity and leadership arrangements.

Teams do not exist in a vacuum – they are embedded within other networks and relationships inside and outside of an organization. Some organizations have used *large-group interaction methods,* often technology-supported, to plan and implement major change efforts (Bryson and Anderson, 2000). These include 'hackathon' or 'crowdsourcing' events, which can involve thousands of people periodically breaking out into different groups to compete and collaborate in brainstorming ideas for change. For example, the popular 'Like' button product feature on the Facebook social media website was initially conceived of as part of a hackathon project, among others (Chang, 2012). In this way, organizations can experiment with the very idea of teams forming and reforming themselves into networks and other forms of collaboration of varying size and scale.

In any case, most teams, whatever type or form they take, are likely to benefit to some extent from various *team-building* interventions, as well as other teamworking *tools* and *techniques,* to help boost their effectiveness. Although teamwork is affected by many factors related to an organization's structures and practices – job roles, selection processes, rewards, performance measures – research has generally shown medium additional positive effects of formal and informal interventions that bring team members together to practise their problem-solving and relationship-building skills, particularly if they have more than ten members (Klein et al., 2009). The importance of emotional intelligence (EI) skills for personal development is explored further in Chapter 6, but EI can also be the focus of team-building efforts. Building team EI might involve members taking extra time together outside of regular work (e.g. engaging in physical challenges and exercises outdoors) to become more aware of each other's emotions and how to manage them to support trust, confidence and a sense of shared identity (Druskat and Wolff, 2001).

Even when teams are not engaged in extra team-building activities, there are many tools for supporting and changing their general ways of working. Broadly, tools are likely to vary from the basic to the complex, and be focused on either the tasks the team is working on or the processes of group interaction. For team tasks, such tools could vary from simple flowcharts through to more complex statistical analyses of time and efficiency. For group interactions, tools could vary from simple brainstorming or goal-setting meetings, through to more complex 'groupware' technologies that enable virtual or hybrid cooperation.

Building international teams that can handle organizational change means considering that members may face language barriers, cross different time zones and express different cultural norms. Here, recruiting, building and managing the team may take more time and resources to address these issues. However, they also offer the potential value of global diversity and talent. Similarly, resilient teams that manage to be successful in a digital age tend to do so because they build an appropriate level of confidence in the team, have a detailed plan of roles everyone understands, have a capacity to improvise when needed, and are sustained by a sense of morale and purpose for overcoming difficulties (Kirkman and Stoverink, 2021).

Ultimately, teams require ideal conditions to thrive through change, from leadership actions, interventions and other management support systems in the wider organizational environment (Marks and Richards, 2012). Without support systems, teams are likely to break down from a lack of appropriate influence, cooperation, motivation or skills. So-called team members will not truly feel or act like a team, even though managers have sought to establish them as one. This holds true regardless of whether teams have existed in the organization for a long time, whether they are being newly established as a restructured way of working, or whether they are formed specially to deal with a change project or programme.

## Limitations and Challenges of Addressing Human Aspects of Change

It is important to acknowledge and keep in mind the considerable challenges and limitations in addressing human aspects of organizational change. Many changes end in partial successes or fail to meet their stated objectives, and the reasons for this are often related to human and social issues associated with the experience of the change. Those planning and implementing change may forget or neglect to deal with the human aspects of change, or feel ill-equipped to deal with complex, diverse and time-consuming local issues. The different types of change situations and interventions interacting with many different individual personalities and capabilities may make it very difficult to figure out appropriate responses, especially with limited resources and competing needs, interests and pressures. It may feel impossible to know how to change many different people's attitudes and behaviours, under what circumstances it is appropriate to do so, and by which method. It may also be difficult to stay informed and sensitive to the many different things affecting people across the organization.

However, understanding *why* human aspects of change can be very difficult to deal with is itself part of a human response to the situation, and can still guide us back to potential solutions, because at least we are acknowledging the deeper difficulties. For instance, leaders and managers may eventually become aware that people in the organization are experiencing pain, loss and exhaustion from repetitive and demanding change on a large scale – and decide to stop some planned changes entirely, or break them down into smaller, more gradual parts with more supportive components (Abrahamson, 2004).

Every person involved in a change is going through their own individual process of interpreting and perceiving the situation. They will be guided by their own past experiences, the information available to them and what seems to make the most sense to them according to their perceptions and beliefs about the world. Changing these mental structures or psychological *schemas* is a fragile process, because people are trying to understand what may be new about an experience using pre-existing mental patterns, which can be biased and require difficult updates and modifications. In one model of this process, George and Jones (2001) specified *seven* closely linked steps individuals might ultimately go through to change genuinely, while also suggesting seven corresponding ways that people can resist and refuse to change at every single step:

1. Encountering a change situation and recognizing a discrepancy or inconsistency *but* finding a way to rationalize the change without having to change your mind about it.
2. Having an emotional reaction to the discrepancies in the changing environment as it interrupts your goals *but* feeling helpless to do anything about it yourself.
3. Getting your emotional reactions under control and paying more positive attention to the change issues and concerns *but* denying the change by postponing or distracting yourself.
4. Processing information about the change situation more deeply and in a less intense mood *but* still feeling complacent or getting distracted by more pressing workload and demands.
5. The change persists in more directly challenging your pre-existing schemas about the world, *but* you still treat the situation as an exception and not of broad relevance to you.
6. Processing the change more deeply to see how you might need to change your expectations and views, *but* still passively accepting some events as uncontrollable or unpredictable.
7. An actual schema change where new forms of information and emotion associated with the change are stored for future use in responding to new situations, events and change cycles.

Furthermore, if differences between individual people lead to them resisting, refusing or getting stuck at different stages of processing a change, it may be difficult to decide which approaches or interventions are best for helping facilitate change for them personally. Change agents may feel there are too many different interventions to choose from, may lack time to properly diagnose or experiment with what works best for people and may not have much definitive evidence to make an informed decision.

Nevertheless, facing these decisions is a common predicament and more importantly, a potential opportunity for change agents to deal with human change issues and interventions as professionally and responsibly as possible, by being *evidence-based*. Being evidence-based means trying to gather the best available evidence from multiple sources (e.g. academic research, company data, different people's experiences, experts), weighing up how well it applies to the current situation, deciding what might be the best course of action and evaluating and learning from it for future use (Barends, Janssen, ten Have and ten Have, 2014). Otherwise, careless decisions may get made, people may get harmed more often than they get helped, resources will be wasted on ineffective interventions, and desired change processes and outcomes are unlikely to be achieved.

As we have seen, similar issues are true for addressing the use of teams as part of organizational change. Teams cannot automatically solve human change issues, despite people having optimistic expectations about them, and they need to be carefully designed to align with other processes and circumstances. For example, if teams are imposed by managers as a way of getting people to work harder or longer, the strong peer pressure of being a 'team player' to meet targets and fit in may become part of a negative and stressful work culture. Rather than boosting individual efforts, entire teams may be biased or resistant to change in ways that undermine the potential for more positive individual changes to spread or gain momentum.

## Good Practices in Managing the Human Aspects of Organizational Change?

Thinking critically about how some areas of human change may border on being 'unmanageable', however, does not need to represent an extremely pessimistic or cynical view. It also does not mean we should not try to address human aspects of change, however imperfectly. Instead, such critical awareness can create a space for more open-ended reflections on the limits of what is realistic, ethical, desirable or knowable and lead to an awareness of alternative possibilities. One example of this is recognizing that there are many *covert* irrational human aspects of organizational change – hidden opportunities or issues that may be difficult to notice or put into words compared to the more *overt* rational plans, analyses and arguments that change is obviously needed and a good idea (Marshak, 2006). Covert processes at work may involve more irrational, intangible, uncertain and private aspects. Marshak (2006) proposes five covert dimensions of organizational change that need to be managed. If not, they will block even the best-planned change efforts:

1. *Politics:* individuals and groups considering their own needs and interests (e.g. 'this change might be good for executives' bonuses, but what about the impact on us and our sales teams?').

2. *Inspirations:* people's values-based and visionary aspirations (e.g. 'I don't want to focus on percentages of customer satisfaction or market share, I want to know how this change can help me fulfil a bigger purpose and be part of doing good things!').

3. *Emotions:* people's moods and feelings in reaction to the change (e.g. 'I understand some of the reasons for us to change the organization's name, but I still feel quite sad and afraid about what will happen if we do').

4. *Mindsets:* people's beliefs and assumptions that they rely on for guidance. However, they may be unaware that they could be less helpful under changed conditions (e.g. 'I have always started by thinking about what our organization can offer a customer, not that customers might want something different from us').

5. *Psychodynamics:* people's deep-seated anxieties and defence mechanisms based on past feelings and patterns of behaviour that they may not be aware of (e.g. 'I lead change by changing others, but I find it hard to change myself because I feel I always must be in control').

Tackling these covert issues directly may be time-consuming and uncomfortable in the short-term, but discovering them could remove obstacles that would block the change and lead it to fail in the longer term. Furthermore, for some complex organizational change issues, such as promoting greater *equality, diversity and inclusion* (EDI) across different minority groups, there may be human and social *paradoxes* that are impossible to fully or permanently resolve but need to be managed by continuously balancing the tensions between different views (Ferdman, 2017). For instance, diverse employees may want to be supported to both 'stand out' and 'fit in'; or to feel 'safe' while being pushed 'out of their comfort zones'. Such demands require thinking about how two different things are connected at the same time and seeking 'both/and' solutions that try to get the best from them while avoiding the worst.

Sometimes organizational change is inherently likely to be difficult in human terms, almost by definition, because it is triggered by a crisis or deteriorating conditions and is likely to involve harm of some sort. One of the most striking examples of this is when an organization and its leadership decide it needs to engage in a *downsizing* strategy to reduce its size and costs, and plans to do so through *layoffs*, involving the temporary suspension or permanent termination of employment for a percentage of its workforce. Clearly, this is a 'bad' or harmful change in human terms to the extent that employees are very unlikely to feel entirely positive about being told their job is not secure or that they are to be dismissed. This raises questions about trying to prevent or prepare for such challenging circumstances, and about how to 'make the best of a bad situation' once such organizational changes are underway.

## CASE STUDY: THE NOKIA BRIDGE PROGRAMME'S FAIR AND HUMANE APPROACH TO LAYOFFS

Positive examples of managing change through downsizings and layoffs can be hard to find, as it is nearly always a difficult and emotional process, involving challenging economic and strategic conditions, and uncertain effects on organizational productivity and profitability. Aspects of organizational leadership, politics and ethics can also be criticized in relation to how cost- and job-cutting decisions are made and the damaging effects they can have on the organization, victims and survivors alike. The COVID-19 pandemic brought on fresh rounds of downsizing and layoffs across many industries, particularly big US technology companies, who had over-hired new employees during earlier periods of optimism about continuing growth (Duffy, 2023).

Nevertheless, in 2011, the Finnish multinational telecommunications company Nokia took an approach that shows there are better, more positive ways to deal with layoffs. Nokia was failing in the mobile smartphone market and needed to undergo a massive restructuring to avoid bankruptcy, which would involve laying off 18,000 employees in thirteen countries (Sucher, 2019). A group of senior leaders created a change programme called 'Bridge' to help employees facing layoffs achieve a smoother transition and to know what their next steps would be as soon as they left the organization.

As a large employer, Nokia took responsibility for the effects of layoffs on its employees and their communities, being as transparent as possible about job losses many months in advance. Local managers who were also going to lose their jobs were involved, and a trusting two-way relationship with executives was built around a commitment for the workforce to keep working hard in exchange for a lot of help finding new jobs (Sucher, 2019). At the core of the Bridge programme was an offer for employees to follow one of five paths:

1. *Find another job at Nokia* – some sites remained open and advertised the required jobs and skills, using independent selection committees to identify and nominate candidates fairly. There were also retention programmes designed to keep star performers in future-oriented areas like research and development (R&D).
2. *Find another job outside of Nokia* – extensive job, career and application support was offered, including coaching, clinics and fairs, as well as the establishment of networking groups on popular online platforms.

3. *Start a new business* – grants and funding were offered to employees for starting their own business in any industry, along with coaching and networking supports for assessing and approving the business plan.
4. *Learn something new* – grants and financial support for learning new professions or upgrading existing skills.
5. *Create your own path* – financial support for other plans and personal goals employees might have, such as volunteering.

The Bridge change programme was successful on a variety of measures, with high satisfaction rates among global participants and relatively low costs per person, while at the same time drops in productivity, engagement, quality and revenues were avoided (Sucher, 2019).

Such programmes have powerful implications and lessons for companies trying to avoid causing excessive pain and anger through layoffs (which is also often much more costly and risky), and for government policies trying to encourage employers to pursue best practice in retraining and repositioning employees for alternative jobs and work. More generally, as economic and competitive conditions change, organizations and their leaders need to think strategically about how this will affect their workforce. This includes taking responsibility for disciplined approaches to hiring and performance management and considering creative and collaborative stakeholder solutions to cost-cutting, retention and transformation, building trust with the people most affected (Sucher and Gupta, 2018).

However, unlike Nokia, many organizations still think of staff reduction as a quick and decisive way to cut costs. Yet, there is increasing risk of the rapid spread of bad publicity online, closer scrutiny of poor decision-making and greater criticism about why certain organizations have not considered smarter, fairer, more humane options (Sucher and Westner, 2022). A crucial point is that often conditions recover, and laid-off employees can be both costly to exit and to replace or rehire, raising the question of whether it would have been more effective to retain them in the first place. In the short-term, there are many cost-cutting *alternatives* to layoffs, including pay cuts/freezes, reduced working hours or temporary furloughs, and delaying or reducing other expenses. These measures can help see the organizations and employees through a difficult period and recover to growth, while minimizing job losses and protecting human capability and relationships.

To the extent that a downturn in conditions may be more permanent and significant layoffs more inevitable, an organization should still seek to take a socially responsible approach like that of Nokia, offering retraining, redeployment and transition support. In many contexts there will be government policies, employment laws and HR guidelines that should be followed to ensure that layoff decisions are made in a reasonable, non-discriminatory fashion – in terms of preparation, evaluation, communication, empathy, fairness and other forms of employee 'outplacement' assistance and support (e.g. Campion, Guerrero and Posthuma, 2011; Cascio, 2009; Feldman and Leana, 1994). Ultimately, this should help sustain individuals, organizations, economies and societies through difficult periods of change, protecting people's wellbeing and ensuring greater resilience over the longer term.

## Organization Development and Soft Systems Approaches to Change

As outlined at the start of this chapter, change management has a relatively long history of approaches with a more human-centred emphasis. One of the most prevalent and enduring of these is organization development. The term 'soft systems' might also be used to broadly describe how social relationships and actions in and around organizations are implicated in change management, as relevant decision-makers come together to reflect on problems and decide how to address changing perspectives, goals and purposes. The 'systemic' emphasis is on bringing different people together to get a fuller, more holistic view of the many parts involved in a change, and the 'soft' emphasis is on human preferences, values, activities and relationships, rather than just physical, structural engineering considerations (Checkland, 2000).

As a general field, OD puts people at the heart of organizational change, but has been called a 'magpie profession' because of the wide variety of other fields, practices and tools it can draw from (Rouch, 2023). Typically, the goal is to help organizations align their 'hard' structures and strategies with 'soft' people, behaviour and culture issues, supporting individuals' capability development, collaboration and empowerment to meet personal and business goals.

People practising OD in change management often put themselves in the change and get involved in ongoing activities, meetings, interventions and analyses. Approaches named 'action learning' or 'action research' refer to people working with managers and employees in cycles of meetings, interventions and discussions to try to solve change issues together – taking actions and reflecting on the results, then adjusting actions and repeating the cycle until satisfactory learning and change has taken place. A variation of these approaches with a more explicit positive emphasis is 'appreciative inquiry', where people collaborate to build on their strengths and what is already working well in their organizations while also aspiring to dreams and visions of making them even better.

Often, OD professionals are working as consultants and change agents alongside people affected by the change, and their agenda is to explore how organizational changes will affect different people and how those people can get more involved in shaping the change. More specifically, this agenda might include building community, managing multiple cultures or culture clashes, supporting career development, transmitting feedback and even challenging the decisions of top management if they risk damaging employee relations and trust (Burke, 1997). One distinction in how OD approaches have evolved is in terms of how they try to combine more traditional *diagnostic* efforts, which involve collecting data to solve problems and reach goals, with more emerging *dialogic* efforts, which involve exploring and questioning ideas for change through stories and conversations 'in dialogue' with those affected (Bushe and Marshak, 2009).

In practice, OD can involve many different types of intervention with individuals and groups, including those discussed in this chapter, and a process that brings people along with a planned change as active participants. In the twenty-first century, OD is increasingly overlapping and convergent with the two adjacent fields of Human Resource Development (HRD) and Human Resource Management (HRM). All three fields treat systems of people as central to change, and seek to build, integrate and align their capabilities with organizational strategies and growth (Ruona and Gibson, 2004).

One other insightful approach aligned with OD worth mentioning is 'sociotechnical' systems thinking. As the name suggests, sociotechnical approaches try to build up a detailed and balanced picture of a work environment's 'social' and 'technical' factors – people, tasks, goals, technologies, spaces/layouts, buildings and other circumstances. In terms of organizational change, a key principle of sociotechnical approaches is to heavily involve the 'users' of the change in the design of the change. This ensures that change is not 'pushed' onto people by distant technical experts, but 'pulled' through in a more user-friendly way that better serves the changing needs and demands of different individuals and groups locally (Clegg and Walsh, 2004). Therefore, a sociotechnical systems approach to change in a hospital might involve trialling new work arrangements and gathering feedback with nurses and patients to help design the change, or from delivery drivers, store managers and warehouse workers if it was a change to a logistics and distribution process.

Ultimately, managing human aspects of change as comprehensively as possible means bringing together issues from across multiple levels of the organization, multiple phases of organizational change and multiple interventions. Only then can we get a sense of how different individuals, teams and divisions are reacting and participating across the organization. Thinking across levels can yield important additional 'interlevel' data and insights about strengths and weaknesses affecting the momentum of the change overall. A very simple tool can be to run through some personal pronouns in assessing the change from different perspectives – that of 'I', 'you' (singular), 'he/she', 'we', 'you' (plural) and 'them/they'. It may be that new relationships and initiatives are taking shape as part of the wider change, while others are finishing or disbanding. Multiple changes are likely to be going on at the same time, or at least overlapping, and in some areas, there may be achievements and progress, while in others there may be stressful points, weak links or setbacks. Considering how levels of human experience of change knit together may involve some of the following (Coghlan, 2000):

→ *Individual:* issues around someone's role, job, career path, motivations or performance.

→ *Team:* issues around a team's roles, goals, processes or relationships.

→ *Department(s):* issues around resource allocation, information exchanges, communications and politics.

→ *Organization:* issues around survival, profitability, mission, stakeholder relationships, culture or vision.

Each individual or group, from the top to the bottom of the organization, may be going through very different change processes and some influences may spread and have wider influences, while others remain contained. Some experiences of the change may have common stages, while others may be highly diverse and varied in their pace and content. Overall patterns and questions may arise concerning the drivers, obstacles, momentum, synchronization and sustainability of organizational change based on all patterns of human activity within and across levels of the change system (Whelan-Berry, Gordon and Hinings, 2003).

In theory, there is some sense of what an ideal human-centred organization or change programme might look like. We might suggest it would be one where people are ready for future change and cooperation, interact with enlightened leaders, are well-organized, flexible, creative, comfortable, inclusive of diversity, supportive of personal growth, empowered and rewarded fairly (O'Malley, 2022). Openness, authenticity, resilience and purpose may be emphasized as most important to people, while also being difficult to achieve and sometimes in conflict with each other (Goffee and Jones, 2013). The challenge with implementing human change lies in balancing people's competing priorities and remaining attentive and responsive to their needs and values, so that they do not become demotivated and frustrated.

### CASE STUDY: TULSA REMOTE AND DESIGNING PEOPLE-CENTRED CHANGE

Patterns of remote work or 'work from anywhere' flexible arrangements have continued to change over time, given a significant boost in attention through the remote work experiences engendered and necessitated by the COVID-19 pandemic. Improving the distribution of local and regional economic development and talent requires organizations and governments to work on developing public policy and change programmes to attract remote workers to small towns and other specific localities where communities, economies and industries can be rebuilt and re-energized.

One such innovative change programme is *Tulsa Remote*, started in 2018 and sponsored by a non-profit charitable organization, with the aim of attracting and supporting remote workers to relocate to the US city of Tulsa, in the state of Oklahoma (Kreiter and Lewis, 2022). Workers with jobs that allow them to work from anywhere can apply to the programme and receive $10,000 for relocation to Tulsa, as well as various forms of support with finding housing, access to coworking space and establishing community connections through networks and events.

Begun as an experiment, the programme has become a transformational change success story within a few years, attracting thousands of applications to live and work in a more low-cost city with people at its centre, bringing significant skills, jobs, income and entrepreneurial activity into Tulsa's local economy. The programme has also attracted very diverse applicants, with most of those relocating (around 90 per cent) staying in Tulsa after the year-long programme was completed. Throughout the COVID-19 pandemic the programme adjusted to safety guidelines while still enabling participants to connect with people sharing personal and professional interests (e.g. through outdoor events and experiences). Participants also reported benefits associated with independence, family life, community, living standards and productivity.

At the same time, before the programme was launched, preparations were made to ensure Tulsa would represent an attractive enough location to attract a range of remote workers. This meant aligning Tulsa Remote with appealing public spaces and social infrastructure, such as waterfronts, parks, museums, art galleries and restaurants. Highly paid outsiders also need to build bridges with local communities to ensure that the benefits of job creation, income and spending are shared as fairly and equally as possible, and so applicants are screened for diversity and civic engagement accordingly (Frick, 2023).

Follow-up studies over 2018–22 have further confirmed the benefits of the Tulsa Remote change programme for both the relocating workers and the city's economy (Frick, 2023). The programme also compares favourably to other public policy change interventions, such as cutting taxes to attract big corporations. However, more broadly, there are other similar programmes in the US from other states and cities that can offer comparable subsidies and inexpensive housing, so competition is likely to be a factor affecting Tulsa Remote's success, as well as post-pandemic 'return to office' mandates, and the powerful attractions of larger national cities. Yet the relative success of Tulsa Remote over a period of years reflects adaptations to changing human experiences and ambitious possibilities for the so-called future of work.

### ACTIVITY 4.6

1. In view of the above case study, draw on your learning from this chapter to explain the importance of the human aspects for successful organizational change.

 **CONSULTANCY IN THE CHAIR**

#### Cup of Kindness Activity

The M&A has taken its toll on many individuals within CUP. As a result, there has been increased absences due to illness and a negative impact on productivity as indicated by key accounting measures. The CEO especially would like your advice on why this is happening and, moreover, when there will be improvement in interpersonal relationships and productivity.

 ## Competency-based Interview Questions

1. Can you describe a situation in which you led a successful team?
2. Why do you consider the team to be successful?
3. How do you maintain good working relationships with your colleagues?

## Chapter Summary

In conclusion, this chapter has covered several important areas relating to managing the human aspects of organizational change. To briefly recap, these include:

- The general importance of individuals and teams in managing organizational change given their inevitable role in engaging with and experiencing it.

- Various models and frameworks indicating how individuals cope with and adjust to change in their organizations and their lives, sometimes similarly and sometimes differently, and how to best address and offer support with these experiences.

- How teams and groups relate to organizational change in different ways and come in different forms, representing distinct units with specific roles and processes to be supported through change.

- The inherent challenges and limitations associated with trying to address human aspects of change, given that it can involve very messy, diverse personal struggles and intangible concerns.

- The general importance of organization development and related fields offering different human interventions and frameworks that put people at the centre of organizational change, making up a social environmental system of relationships, goals, values, behaviours, emotions, issues and conversations.

## Useful Resources

- Change Activation: A Simple Guide to Personal Transformation. Changeactivation.com. https://changeactivation.com/downloads/a-simple-guide-to-personal-transformation (accessed 12 April 2025).

- Mind Tools: The ADKAR® Change Management Model. Mindtools.com. https://www.mindtools.com/aou2mjr/the-adkar-change-management-model (accessed 12 April 2025).

- Academy to Innovate HR (AIHR). What is Organizational Development? A Complete Guide. https://www.aihr.com/blog/organizational-development (accessed 12 April 2025).

## Bibliography

Abrahamson, E. (2004), 'Avoiding Repetitive Change Syndrome'. *MIT Sloan Management Review*, 45(2): 93–5.

Allport, G. W. (1927), 'Concepts of Trait and Personality'. *Psychological Bulletin*, 24(5): 284–93.

Ancona, D. and Bresman, H. (2023), 'Turn Your Teams Inside Out'. *MIT Sloan Management Review*, 64(2): 24–9.

Annosi, M. C., Foss, N. and Martini, A. (2020), 'When Agile Harms Learning and Innovation: (and What Can Be Done About It)'. *California Management Review*, 63(1): 61–80.

Aritzeta, A., Swailes, S. and Senior, B. (2007) 'Belbin's Team Role Model: Development, Validity and Applications for Team Building'. *Journal of Management Studies*, 44(1): 96–118.

Bareil, C., Savoie, A. and Meunier, S. (2007), 'Patterns of Discomfort with Organizational Change'. *Journal of Change Management*, 7(1): 13–24.

Barends, E., Janssen, B., ten Have, W. and ten Have, S. (2014), 'Effects of Change Interventions: What Kind of Evidence do we Really Have?' *The Journal of Applied Behavioral Science*, 50(1): 5–27.

Biggs, A., Brough, P. and Drummond, S. (2017), 'Lazarus and Folkman's Psychological Stress and Coping Theory', in C. L. Cooper and J. C. Quick (eds), *The Handbook of Stress and Health: A Guide to Research and Practice* (pp. 349–64), Oxford: Wiley-Blackwell.

Bryson, J. M. and Anderson, S. R. (2000), 'Applying Large-Group Interaction Methods in the Planning and Implementation of Major Change Efforts'. *Public Administration Review*, 60(2): 143–62.

Burke, W. W. (1997), 'The New Agenda for Organization Development'. *Organizational Dynamics*, 26(1): 7–20.

Burnes, B. (1996), 'No Such Thing as ... a "One Best Way" to Manage Organizational Change'. *Management Decision*, 34(10): 11–18.

Burnes, B. and Cooke, B. (2013), 'Kurt Lewin's Field Theory: A Review and Re-Evaluation'. *International Journal of Management Reviews*, 15(4): 408–25.

Bushe, G. R. and Marshak, R. J. (2009), 'Revisioning Organization Development: Diagnostic and Dialogic Premises and Patterns of Practice'. *The Journal of Applied Behavioral Science*, 45(3): 348–68.

Campion, M. A., Guerrero, L. and Posthuma, R. (2011), 'Reasonable Human Resource Practices for Making Employee Downsizing Decisions'. *Organizational Dynamics*, 40(3): 174–80.

Chang, A. (2012), 'Deep Inside a Facebook Hackathon, Where the Future of Social Media Begins'. Wired. July 20. https://www.wired.com/2012/07/

facebook-gears-up-next-big-thing-in-three-day-camp-hackathon (accessed 12 April 2025).

Checkland, P. (2000), 'Soft Systems Methodology: A Thirty Year Retrospective'. *Systems Research and Behavioral Science*, 17(S1): S11–58.

Chin, R. and Benne, K. (1969), 'General Strategies for Effecting Change in Human Systems', in W. Bennis, K. Benne and R. Chin (eds), *Planning of Change* (pp. 22–45), New York: Holt, Rhinehart and Winston.

CIPD (2014), *Neuroscience in Action: Applying Insight to L&D Practice*. November 3. Research Report. Chartered Institute of Personnel and Development.

CIPD (2023), *High-Performing Teams: An Evidence Review*. May 31. Research Report. Chartered Institute of Personnel and Development.

Clegg, C. and Walsh, S. (2004), 'Change Management: Time for a Change!' *European Journal of Work and Organizational Psychology*, 13(2): 217–39.

Coghlan, D. (2000), 'Interlevel Dynamics in Clinical Inquiry'. *Journal of Organizational Change Management*, 13(2): 190–200.

Cunha, M. P. and Chia, R. (2007), 'Using Teams to Avoid Peripheral Blindness'. *Long Range Planning*, 40(6): 559–73.

Druskat, V. U. and Wolff, S. B. (2001), 'Building the Emotional Intelligence of Groups'. *Harvard Business Review*, 79(3): 80–91.

Duffy, C. (2023), 'How Big Tech's Pandemic Bubble Burst'. CNN Business. January 22. https://edition.cnn.com/2023/01/22/tech/big-tech-pandemic-hiring-layoffs/index.html (accessed 12 April 2025).

Elrod, P. D. and Tippett, D. D. (2002), 'The "Death Valley" of Change'. *Journal of Organizational Change Management*, 15(3): 273–91.

Erikson, E. (1959), 'Identity and the Life Cycle'. *Psychological Issues*, 1: 18–164.

Feldman, D. C. and Leana, C. R. (1994), 'Better Practices in Managing Layoffs'. *Human Resource Management*, 33(2): 239–60.

Ferdman, B. M. (2017), 'Paradoxes of Inclusion: Understanding and Managing the Tensions of Diversity and Multiculturalism'. *The Journal of Applied Behavioral Science*, 53(2): 235–63.

Fletcher, D. and Streeter, A. (2016), 'A Case Study Analysis of a High Performance Environment in Elite Swimming'. *Journal of Change Management*, 16(2): 123–41.

Frick, W. (2023), 'Tulsa's Big Bet on Remote Workers'. *Harvard Business Review*. January 13. https://hbr.org/2023/01/tulsas-big-bet-on-remote-workers (accessed 12 April 2025).

Furnham, A. (2020), 'Myers-Briggs Type Indicator (MBTI)', in V. V. Zeigler-Hill and T. T. K. Shackelford (eds), *Encyclopaedia of Personality and Individual Differences* (pp. 3059–62), London: Sage.

Garrety, K. (2007), 'Beyond ISTJ: A Discourse-Analytic Study of the Use of the Myers-Briggs Type Indicator as an Organisational Change Device in an Australian Industrial Firm'. *Asia Pacific Journal of Human Resources*, 45(2): 218–34.

George, J. M. and Jones, G. R. (2001), 'Towards a Process Model of Individual Change in Organizations'. *Human Relations*, 54(4): 419–44.

Goffee, R. and Jones, G. (2013), 'Creating the Best Workplace on Earth'. *Harvard Business Review*, 91(5): 98–106.

Hiatt, J. (2006), *ADKAR: A Model for Change in Business, Government, and our Community*. Fort Collins, CO: Prosci.

Hollenbeck, J. R., Beersma, B. and Schouten, M. E. (2012), 'Beyond Team Types and Taxonomies: A Dimensional Scaling Conceptualization for Team Description'. *Academy of Management Review*, 37(1): 82–106.

Holm, J. E. and Holroyd, K. A. (1992), 'The Daily Hassles Scale (Revised): Does it Measure Stress or Symptoms?' *Behavioral Assessment*, 14(3–4): 465–82.

Holmes, T. H. and Rahe, R. H. (1967), 'The Social Readjustment Rating Scale'. *Journal of Psychosomatic Research*, 11(2): 213–18.

Horvath, J. C. (2022), 'The Limits of Neuroscience in Business'. *MIT Sloan Management Review*, 64(1): 1–4.

Ivancevich, J. M. (1986), 'Life Events and Hassles as Predictors of Health Symptoms, Job Performance, and Absenteeism'. *Journal of Organizational Behavior*, 7(1): 39–51.

Katzenbach, J. R. and Smith, D. K. (2005), 'The Discipline of Teams'. *Harvard Business Review*, 83(7): 162–71.

Kegan, R. (1998), *In Over Our Heads: The Mental Demands of Modern Life*. Cambridge, MA: Harvard University Press.

Kirkman, B. L. and Stoverink, A. C. (2021), 'Building Resilient Virtual Teams'. *Organizational Dynamics*, 50(1): 100825.

Klein, C., DiazGranados, D., Salas, E., Le, H., Burke, C. S., Lyons, R. and Goodwin, G. F. (2009), 'Does Team Building Work?' *Small Group Research*, 40(2): 181–222.

Kreiter, D. and Lewis, G. (2022), 'Tulsa's Innovative Program Supports Remote Workers and Economic Development through COVID-19 and Beyond'. McKinsey. January 11. https://www.mckinsey.com/featured-insights/future-of-work/tulsas-innovative-program-supports-remote-workers-and-economic-development-through-covid-19-and-beyond (accessed 12 April 2025).

Kübler-Ross, E. (1969), *On Death and Dying*. New York: Touchstone.

Lazarus, R. S. and Folkman, S. (1984), *Stress, Appraisal, and Coping*. New York: Springer.

Lewin, K. (1952), *Group Decision and Social Change: Readings in Social Psychology*. New York: Henry Holt and Co.

Mansell, A., Brough, P. and Cole, K. (2006), 'Stable Predictors of Job Satisfaction, Psychological Strain, and Employee Retention: An Evaluation of Organizational Change Within the New Zealand Customs Service'. *International Journal of Stress Management*, 13(1): 84–107.

Marks, A. and Richards, J. (2012), 'Developing Ideas and Concepts in Teamwork Research: Where Do We Go from Here?' *Employee Relations*, 34(3): 228–34.

Marshak, R. J. (2006), *Covert Processes at Work: Managing the Five Hidden Dimensions of Organizational Change*. Oakland, CA: Berrett-Koehler Publishers.

McKinsey (2003), 'The Psychology of Change Management'. June 1. https://www.mckinsey.com/capabilities/people-and-organizational-performance/our-insights/the-psychology-of-change-management (accessed 12 April 2025).

McKinsey (2016), 'The Four Building Blocks of Change'. April 11. https://www.mckinsey.com/capabilities/people-and-organizational-performance/our-insights/the-four-building-blocks--of-change (accessed 12 April 2025).

McKinsey (2020), 'When One Size Doesn't Fit All: How to Make Change Personal'. October 26. https://www.mckinsey.com/capabilities/people-and-organizational-performance/our-insights/the-organization-blog/when-one-size-doesnt-fit-all-how-to-make-change-personal (accessed 12 April 2025).

Mergel, I., Ganapati, S. and Whitford, A. B. (2021), 'Agile: A New Way of Governing'. *Public Administration Review*, 81(1): 161–5.

Michie, S., Van Stralen, M. M. and West, R. (2011), 'The Behaviour Change Wheel: A New Method for Characterising and Designing Behaviour Change Interventions'. *Implementation Science*, 6(1): 1–12.

Neumann, J. E., Holvino, E. and Braxton, E. T. (2004), 'Evolving a "Third Way" to Group Consultancy: Bridging Two Models of Theory and Practice', in S. Cytrynbaum and D. A. Noumair (eds), *Group Dynamics, Organizational Irrationality, and Social Complexity: Group Relations Reader 3* (pp. 383–401). Portland, OR: A. K. Rice Institute.

O'Malley, M. (2022), '10 Principles of Effective Organizations'. *Harvard Business Review*. August 8. https://hbr.org/2022/08/10-principles-of-effective-organizations (accessed 12 April 2025).

Pasmore, W. A. and Fagans, M. R. (1992), 'Participation, Individual Development, and Organizational Change: A Review and Synthesis'. *Journal of Management*, 18(2): 375–97.

Quinn, R. and Sonenshein, S. (2008), 'Four General Strategies for Changing Human Systems', in T. Cummings(ed), *Handbook of Organization Development* (pp. 69–78). New York: Sage.

Rouch, G. (2023), 'How to Start Your Career in Organisation Development'. HRZone. September 5. https://www.hrzone.com/talent/development/how-to-start-your-career-in-organisation-development (accessed 12 April 2025).

Ruona, W. E. and Gibson, S. K. (2004), 'The Making of Twenty-first-century HR: An Analysis of the Convergence of HRM, HRD, and OD'. *Human Resource Management*, 43(1): 49–66.

Schneider, D. M. and Goldwasser, C. (1998), 'Be a Model Leader of Change'. *Management Review*, 87(3): 41–6.

Scully, J. A., Tosi, H. and Banning, K. (2000), 'Life Event Checklists: Revisiting the Social Readjustment Rating Scale after 30 Years'. *Educational and Psychological Measurement*, 60(6): 864–76.

Smith, M. (2020), 'Social Psychiatry Could Stem the Rising Tide of Mental Illness'. The Conversation. June 3. https://theconversation.com/social-psychiatry-could-stem-the-rising-tide-of-mental-illness-138152 (accessed 12 April 2025).

Sucher, S. (2019), 'There's a Better Way to do Layoffs: What Nokia Learned, the Hard Way'. LinkedIn. May 3. https://www.linkedin.com/pulse/theres-better-way-do-layoffs-what-nokia-learned-hard-sandra-sucher (accessed 12 April 2025).

Sucher, S. J. and Gupta, S. (2018), 'Layoffs That Don't Break Your Company: Better Approaches to Workforce Transitions'. *Harvard Business Review*, 96(3): 122–9.

Sucher, S. J. and Westner, M. M. (2022), 'What Companies Still Get Wrong About Layoffs'. *Harvard Business Review*. December 8. https://hbr.org/2022/12/what-companies-still-get-wrong-about-layoffs (accessed 12 April 2025).

Svejenova, S., Planellas, M. and Vives, L. (2010), 'An Individual Business Model in the Making: A Chef's Quest for Creative Freedom'. *Long Range Planning*, 43(2–3): 408–30.

Thilak, A. P. (2023), 'A Glimpse Into the World of Agile: Squads, Chapters, Tribes and Guilds'. LinkedIn article. May 7. https://www.linkedin.com/pulse/glimpse-world-agile-squads-chapters-tribes-guilds-thilak- (accessed 12 April 2025).

Toubiana, M., Ruebottom, T. and Hakak, L. T. (2022), 'When a Major Life Change Upends Your Sense of Self'. Harvard Business Review Digital Articles. https://hbr.org/2022/01/when-a-major-life-change-upends-your-sense-of-self (accessed 12 April 2025).

Tuckman, B. W. (1965), 'Developmental Sequence in Small Groups'. *Psychological Bulletin*, 63(6): 384–99.

Tuckman, B. W. and Jensen, M. A. C. (1977), 'Stages of Small-Group Development Revisited'. *Group & Organization Studies*, 2(4): 419–27.

Vakola, M., Tsaousis, I. and Nikolaou, I. (2004), 'The Role of Emotional Intelligence and Personality Variables on Attitudes Toward Organisational Change'. *Journal of Managerial Psychology*, 19(2): 88–110.

Whelan-Berry, K. S., Gordon, J. R. and Hinings, C. R. (2003), 'Strengthening Organizational Change Processes: Recommendations and Implications from a Multilevel Analysis'. *The Journal of Applied Behavioral Science*, 39(2): 186–207.

# Intercultural Management and Effective Change

**5**

### Learning Outcomes

At the end of this chapter you will be able to:

1. Better understand cultural differences.
2. Use theoretical frameworks for analysing cultural differences.
3. Gain insight into how differences in national cultures impact the way in which organizations are managed.
4. Gain insight into how and why national cultures impact perceptions and responses to substantive organizational change.
5. Appreciate the importance of cultural competence and intelligence for better managing organizational change.

## Introduction

National boundaries are flexible and permeable and what happens in one part of the world impacts another. For example, a natural disaster, pandemic or war in any country can result in bottlenecks, delays and disruptions in the supply chain. This can impact the most fundamental of needs including access to basic foodstuffs and the price of utilities, which has change implications for everyone, no matter where located. Similarly, organizations, be they private, public or voluntary and community, operate in a globally interconnected world. An upside of this is that organizations interface with people from diverse cultural backgrounds in their day-to-day operations and, where managed well, these relationships add richness and depth, including optimal performance through evaluating different ways of working, arriving at creative solutions and making informed and inclusive decisions. Realizing the benefits from a heterogenous workforce has implications for the way in which organizations are structured, and in which leadership and management takes place. This is alongside how people communicate, and how remuneration and reward systems are configured, as well as many routine and non-routine systems and processes.

For substantive change to be successful, organizations need to be mindful of the impact that cultural differences have upon how change is managed. Cultural differences should influence the way in which change is initiated, communicated and implemented. In light of this, we will focus on national cultures and how differences impact and influence the lens through which change is perceived, interpreted and understood. This chapter critically evaluates and examines different models and theories of national cultures, including the long-standing work of Hofstede (1980), the World Value Survey (Haerpfer et al., 2022) and Gelfand's (2011) concept of cultural 'tightness' and 'looseness'. This chapter will also emphasize the importance of cultural intelligence, unpacking what it is and how to develop it, as well as its importance in managing change effectively. As a means of facilitating our understanding of *how* and *why* behaviour appears in specific cultural contexts, we draw upon a portfolio of research fields including anthropology, sociology, cross-cultural psychology and management researchers. Such insights are derived from studies conducted during the 1970s and 1980s in addition to more contemporary work. Amongst all of this, it should be remembered that whilst the insights from early studies are influential, they have naturally been the subject of much debate and criticism.

## Culture: What Is It? Can It Ever Be Defined?

Socialization is the process by which the culture of a society is transmitted. Every child is socialized into their *own* culture and language. Culture is *not* a choice and happens from birth. By the time a child has become a teenager, the socialization process has already happened.

Various definitions of culture are put forward. However, whilst some are more meaningful than others, there is fluidity in as much as there is little by way of common agreement as to a definition that is universally accepted. Culture may therefore be defined amongst other things as:

'*the framework out of which we were (are) socialized and developed, and the lens through which we look out on the world.*' (Anon)

or

'*those customary beliefs and values that ethnic, religious, and social groups, transmit fairly unchanged form generation to generation.*' (Guiso et al., 2006: 23).

However national culture is defined, an important implication is that culture provides a framework by which we can work out our existence with others. In this way, a critical constituent of culture is its explicit and implicit messages and signals. Every culture gives clear messages and sends out implicit signals as to what is expected from its community, from what to eat, what to wear and what is expected from different genders. Furthermore, each culture has cultural tasks that are again both explicit and implicit. This includes what is expected and what is considered desirable for people to do/be in their lives, their work and their relationships with others. These cultural messages, signals and tasks form the foundation upon which people make sense of their lives and their experience, and influence how each person defines and judges themselves and others. Every child begins by assuming that their own culture is 'normal'.

## The Importance of Culture for an Understanding of Self

Culture also organizes the way in which individuals conceptualize themselves and the world, and therefore informs the very essence of the self, including thinking, feeling and reasons for actions (discussed in more detail later in this chapter). There are a number of different ways to identify and classify cultures. The most common is to distinguish between independent and interdependent cultures. Models that can be used in this respect include Hofstede's well-known cultural dimensions (1980, 1991, 2001), alongside other models such as Inglehart's (1997) model of cultural change and Gelfand's (2012) 'tight and loose' cultures. An important lesson for all organizations is that differences in cultural understandings can have profound effects on personal and working relationships. They also affect how change is interpreted and perceived by individuals and groups in a variety of different contexts.

## Differences Between Independent and Interdependent Cultures

North American and Western European cultures predominantly assume an **independent** view of self in which establishing and maintaining independence from others, and discovering and expressing unique inner attributes, is prioritized. This is philosophically rooted in the dualistic tradition characteristic of Western thinking, in which the self is viewed as separate from objects and from the natural world. Emotional maturity is characterized by the capacity to express one's own views and opinions, and behaviour is organized and made meaningful predominantly by reference to one's own **internal** repertoire of thoughts, feelings and actions.

In contrast, other cultural traditions, such as those in Japan, China and Africa, socialize their children into a predominantly **interdependent** experience of self. This view of self prioritizes the relatedness of individuals and encourages attending to others and living in harmonious interdependence with them. Philosophically, the notion of the interdependent self is linked to cultural traditions in which the person is thought to be of the same substance as the rest of nature. Thus, individual persons are only parts of a greater social whole and cannot be understood separately from it. In societies in which an interdependent view of self prevails, adult emotional maturity is considered to be the control and **reduction** of one's own individual views and needs, with priority being given to the fundamental **connectedness** of human beings to each other. The African word '**Ubuntu**' is often used to describe this – 'I am because you are' or 'I am what I am because of whom we all are'.

## Analysing Culture

There are many approaches to analysing cultural differences. Those relevant to managing organizational change and working with different stakeholders are discussed in the next section of this chapter.

## Hofstede's Cultural Dimensions

Hofstede (1980) included independent and interdependent cultures in his Cultural Dimensions Theory. The other five dimensions in this model are:

- → Power distance.
- → Uncertainty avoidance.
- → Individualism vs. collectivism.
- → Masculinity vs. femininity.
- → Short- vs. long-term orientation.
- → Indulgence vs. restraint.

Hofstede's cultural dimensions originate from a large survey he conducted in the 1960s and 1970s, which examined value differences among different divisions of IBM, a multinational computer manufacturing company. This study encompassed over 100,000 employees from fifty countries across three regions.

He initially identified four dimensions but two further dimensions were added by an analysis of World Value Surveys. This research added long-term or short-term orientation (Bond, 1991). 'Indulgence vs. Restraint' was later added as a sixth dimension (Hofstede and Minkov, 2010). These different cultural dimensions are illustrated in Figure 5.1 and further described below.

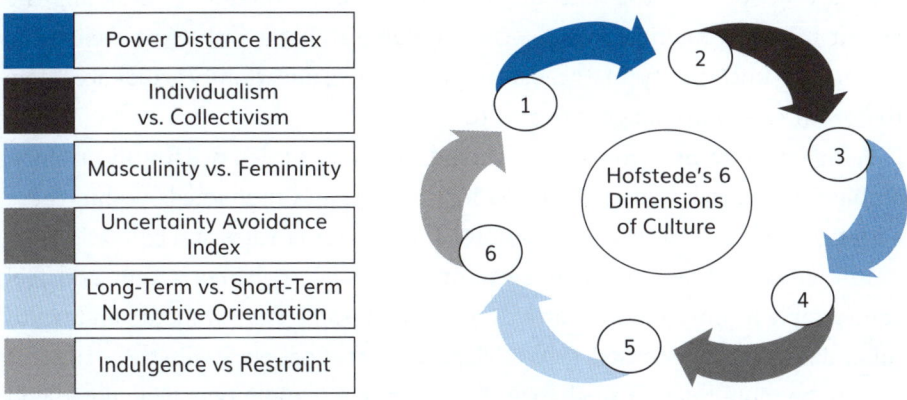

**Figure 5.1** Hofstede's cultural dimensions (Nickerson, 2022).

## Power Distance Index

The power distance index describes the extent to which the less powerful members of an organization or institution – such as a family – accept and *expect* power to be distributed **unequally**. Although there is a certain degree of inequality in all societies, Hofstede (2011) notes that there is relatively more equality in some societies than in others.

Individuals in societies that have a *high degree of power distance* usually accept hierarchies where everyone has a place in a ranking. Parents may expect children to obey without questioning their authority and those of higher status may experience overt displays of subordination and respect from subordinates. Superiors and subordinates are unlikely to see each other as equals in the workplace, and employees assume that those of higher status will make decisions without consultation. Thus, status tends to be more important in high power distance countries than low power distance ones.

However, societies with *low power distance* seek to have a more **equal** distribution of power. The implication of this is that these cultures endorse and expect relations that are consultative, democratic or egalitarian. According to Hofstede, countries with low power distance index values tend to have more equality between parents and children, with parents more likely to accept if children argue or 'talk back' to authority. In addition, in low power distance index workplaces, employers and managers are more likely to ask employees for input and those at the lower ends of the hierarchy usually expect to be consulted.

## Uncertainty Avoidance Index

The uncertainty avoidance dimension of Hofstede's cultural dimensions addresses a society's tolerance for uncertainty and ambiguity, reflecting the extent to which members of a society are able to cope with their anxiety by minimizing uncertainty. In its most simplified form, uncertainty avoidance refers to how threatening change is to a culture.

A high uncertainty avoidance index indicates a low tolerance for uncertainty, ambiguity and risk-taking. Both the institutions and individuals within these societies seek to minimize the unknown through strict rules and regulations.

In contrast, those in low uncertainty avoidance cultures accept and feel comfortable in unstructured situations or changeable environments and try to minimize the number of strict rules. This means that people within these cultures tend to be more tolerant of change. The unknown is more openly accepted and less strict rules and regulations may ensue.

## Femininity vs. Masculinity

Femininity vs. masculinity, also known as gender role differentiation, looks at how much a society values traditional masculine and feminine roles.

Hofstede asserts that a 'masculine' society values assertiveness, courage, strength and competition, whereas a 'feminine' society values cooperation, nurturance and quality of life. Thus, a high femininity score indicates that traditionally feminine gender roles are more important to the culture in question, whereas a low femininity score indicates that those roles are less important. For example, a country with a high femininity score is likely to have better maternity leave policies and more affordable childcare.

## Short-Term vs. Long-Term Orientation

The long-term and short-term orientation dimension refers to the degree to which cultures encourage delaying gratification of the material, social and emotional needs of its members.

Societies with long-term orientations tend to focus on the future in a way that delays short-term success in favour of success in the long-term. These societies emphasize traits such as persistence, perseverance, thrift, saving, long-term growth and the capacity for adaptation.

Short-term orientation in a society, in contrast, indicates a focus on the near future, involves delivering short-term success or gratification, and places a stronger emphasis on the present than the future. There tends to be an emphasis on quick results and respect for tradition.

## Indulgence vs. Restraint

The restraint and indulgence dimension considers the tendency and extent to which a society fulfils its desires. This dimension is a measure of societal impulse and control of desires. High levels of indulgence indicate that a society allows relatively free gratification.

Conversely, restraint indicates that a society tends to suppress the gratification of needs and regulate them through social norms. For example, in a highly indulgent society, people may tend to spend more money on luxuries and enjoy more freedom when it comes to leisure time activities. In a restrained society, people are more likely to save money and focus on practical needs (Hofstede, 2011).

### ACTIVITY 5.1

1. Use Hofstede's cultural dimensions to analyse the national culture that you were born into. For example, is your culture high or low on power distance and why? Do this for all of the dimensions and explain your thinking.

2. Use Hofstede's cultural dimensions to analyse a different national culture. This could be the national culture of a friend or colleague. Compare and contrast your national culture with that of your colleagues'. Again, please explain your thinking behind your analysis.

3. Go to Hofstede's home page, then scroll to where it says 'different countries' and type in both the name of your country and the name of the country you compared with your own culture. Compare your own analysis with Hofstede's country comparison index. What does this reveal to you about your insightfulness to your own culture and to that of others?

## Critique

Although the cultural value dimensions identified by Hofstede are useful ways to think about culture and cultural psychology, given that this theory is prolific in the published literature, it is to be expected that it has been questioned and critiqued. A predominant criticism has been directed at the methodology of Hofstede's original study. Orr and Hauser (2008), for example, note that Hofstede's questionnaire was not originally designed to measure culture, but workplace satisfaction. Furthermore, Hofstede conducted his study using the employees of a multinational corporation, who – especially when the study was conducted in the 1960s and 1970s – were overwhelmingly highly educated, mostly male and performed so-called 'white collar' work (McSweeney, 2002). Hofstede's theory has also been criticized for promoting a static view of culture that does not respond to the influences or changes of other cultures. As Trompenaars and Hamden-Turner (1997) have envisioned, the cultural influence of Western powers such as the United States is likely to have influenced the rise of individualism in Japan, previously conceptualized as primarily a collectivist culture.

Overall, however, it is widely accepted that Hofstede's work has stimulated a great deal of cross-cultural research and provides an important and useful framework for the comparative study of cultures. In addition, as Orr and Hauser (2008) point out, Hofstede's dimensions have been found to correlate with actual behaviour in cross-cultural studies, which supports the validity of his research.

## Inglehart's Theory of Cultural Change

Another interesting contribution to understanding cultural differences is the work of Inglehart (1997), whose key contribution consists of a *dynamic* theory of cultural change. Inglehart was the first to document a massive generational shift in cultural orientations among the public of affluent Western democracies, from a priority on existential security (i.e. 'materialist' values) towards a priority on expressive freedom (i.e. 'post materialist' values). Inspired by Maslow's (1954) 'hierarchy of human needs', the findings of Inglehart and his co-authors (Inglehart and Norris, 2003; Inglehart and Welzel, 2005) demonstrate what they consider to be a universal principle in the functioning of the human mind. This is the 'utility ladder of freedoms', as Welzel (2013) has described it. According to this model, when both security and freedom are in short supply people prioritize security because security is necessary for survival. However, Welzel (2013) argues that as soon as people feel safe they begin to prioritize freedom because freedom is essential for a person to thrive, and also allows for ingenuity, creativity and recreational pleasure. Hence, socioeconomic transformations occur when the nature of life changes from a source of threats into a source of opportunities. This nurtures a generational shift in priorities from 'survival' to 'emancipative' values.

Inglehart and Norris (2003) have summarized these findings in a 'revised theory of modernization'. Welzel (2013) has developed this theory further into an 'evolutionary theory of emancipation', pointing out some key qualifications of emancipatory value change. According to Welzel (2013), for such a change to happen no agent, no campaign, no programme and no particular political system – such as democracy – is needed, because emancipatory value change is self-driven. In other words, it is a process by which the human mind adjusts to changing existential conditions. He considers that this automatism is not culture-specific but a species-wide universalism of humanity. Hence, evolution has infused human existence with a 'utility-value link' through which we adjust our subjective values to life's objective utilities. This link is vital for human liveability and for keeping our goals in touch with reality. The utility-value link is also a precondition for our development because it makes moral progress possible. Moreover, human existence is upwardly directed on the utility ladder of freedoms: we are evolutionary hard-wired to stay on the lower rungs where we prioritize security only as long as necessity dictates such stagnation, but we climb toward the higher rungs where we seek freedom as soon as opportunity allows.

Adaptive value shifts of this kind happen to some extent within generations, but they usually proceed much more profoundly *between* generations, because people tend to stick more strongly to their adopted values as they age. This theoretical framework has been confirmed by recent findings in psychology, which utilize completely different data. Grossman and Varnum (2015), for instance, infer an increase of individualism from changing word frequencies documented in the Google-Ngram Database in the US. Ngram Viewer uses a yearly count of n-grams found in printed sources published between 1500 and 2019. The program can search for a word or a phrase, including misspellings or gibberish and supports searches for parts of speech. It is routinely used in research to track changes in word use in various languages. In addition, Zhou et al.'s (2018) series of interviews of Chinese grandmothers strongly suggest an intergenerational shift from collectivism toward individualism in China (Zhou et al., 2018).

Though highly influential, Hofstede's and Inglehart's works are still criticized and debated. While Hofstede has been questioned for presuming a too stable notion of national culture, his framework has also been questioned for overestimating the number of dimensions, misinterpreting their meaning and using data of questionable quality (Ailon, 2008; Baskerville, 2003; Baskerville-Morley, 2005; Fang, 2003; McSweeney, 2002, 2009; Taras et al., 2012; Venaik and Brewer, 2010). Inglehart, on the other hand, has been criticized for a flawed dimensional understanding of culture that reduces cross-national variation to two 'miss-specified' dimensions and for overestimating the generational replacement dynamic in cultural change (Alémen and Woods, 2016; Flanagan, 1987; Flanagan and Lee, 2003).

A paper attempting to synthesize Hofstede's cultural dimensions with Inglehart's dynamic theory of cultural change (Beugelsdijk and Welzer, 2018), utilizing all data from the World Values Surveys (WVS) and European Values Studies (EVS), confirmed concerns regarding the number and meaning of the original Hofstede dimensions. The authors put forward a set of three cultural dimensions – Collectivism/Individualism, Duty/Joy and Distrust/Trust. For a more nuanced account, see a synthesis of the work conducted by Beugelsdijk and Welzer, 2018).

## Tight and Loose Cultures

Another contribution to a meaningful understanding of cultural differences is made by Gelfand et al. (2011). Utilizing data from thirty-three nations, Gelfand et al. (2011) illustrate the differences between what are called 'tight' cultures (those which have many strong norms and a low tolerance of deviant behaviour) versus 'loose' cultures (those which have weak social norms and a high tolerance of deviant behaviour). Gelfand et al. (2011) argue that the tightness–looseness concept is part of a complex, loosely integrated multilevel system that comprises distal ecological and historical threats (e.g. high population density, resource scarcity, a history of territorial conflict and disease and environmental threats), broad versus narrow socialization in societal institutions (e.g. autocracy, media regulations), the strength of everyday recurring situations, and micro-level psychological affordances (e.g. prevention self-guides, high regulatory strength, need for structure).

Gelfand's theory was based on early anthropological research, such as Pelto (1968). Pelto studied twenty-one traditional societies, and documented wide variations in the expression of, and adherence to, social norms. He found that The Hutterites, Hanno and Lubara were among the tightest societies, with very strong norms and severe sanctions for norm violation, whereas the Kung Bushman, Cubeo and the Skolt Lapps were among the loosest societies, with ambiguous norms and greater permissiveness for norm violation. He speculated that these societies may have different ecologies, with tight societies having a higher population per square mile and a higher dependence on crops compared to looser societies. Later research showed that agricultural societies (e.g. the Temne of Sierra Leone) require strong norms to foster the coordination necessary to grow crops for survival, had strict child-rearing practices and children who were high in terms of conformity. However, hunting and fishing societies (e.g. the Inuit) had more lenient child-rearing practices and children who were low in terms of conformity.

Despite evidence of the importance of this contrast in traditional societies, Gelfand et al. (2011) argue that these studies gave no insights into how tightness–looseness operates in modern nations. The goal of his research was to fill this gap. He proposed that tightness–looseness is part of a complex, loosely integrated system that involves processes across multiple levels of analysis.

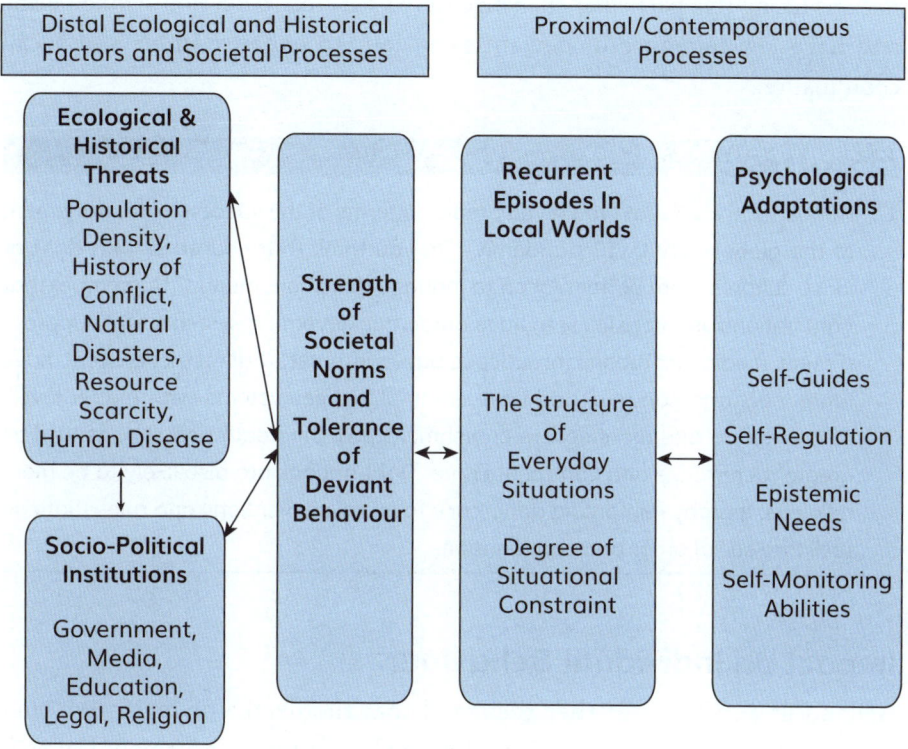

**Figure 5.2** A systems model of tightness–looseness (Gelfand et al. 2011).

He also theorized that the strength of social norms and tolerance of deviant behaviour – the core distinction between tight and loose cultures – is affected by numerous distal ecological and human-made societal threats, societal institutions and practices. The strength of social norms and tolerance of deviant behaviour is further reflected and promoted in the predominance of strong versus weak situations that are recurrent in everyday local worlds, and is reinforced through psychological processes that are attuned to situational requirements. Gelfand predicted that tightness–looseness is afforded by a broad array of ecological and human-made societal threats (or lack thereof). Ecological and human-made threats increase the need for strong norms and punishment of deviant behaviour in the service of social coordination for survival – whether it is to reduce chaos in nations that have high population density, deal with resource scarcity, coordinate in the face of natural disasters, defend against territorial threats or contain the spread of disease.

Research conducted by Gelfand et al. (2021) analyses the relationship between managing the global pandemic COVID-19 and the tightness or looseness of cultures. The strength of social norms – or cultural tightness–looseness – is associated with countries' success in limiting cases and deaths. In his model, nations facing this particular challenge were predicted to develop strong norms and have low tolerance of deviant behaviour to enhance order and social coordination.

### ACTIVITY 5.2

1. Retrospectively, what would you predict in terms of the successful management of the global COVID-19 pandemic? Do you think that countries with tight or loose cultures were better placed to manage this phenomenon? Remember that tight nations are more likely to have autocratic governing systems that suppress dissent, media institutions (broadcast, paper, internet) that restrict content, have more laws and controls, and have criminal justice systems with higher levels of monitoring and more severe punishment (e.g. the death penalty), as well as greater deterrence and control of crime. Tight nations are also likely to be more religious, thereby reinforcing adherence to moral conventions and rules that can facilitate social order and coordination.

## Impact on Individual Behaviour

Gelfand et al. (2011) further theorized that the degree of regulation that exists at the societal level is mirrored in the higher (or lower) amount of self-regulation at the *individual* level. Such psychological processes simultaneously reflect and support the strength of social norms and tolerance of deviance in the larger cultural context. Tight nations are expected to have a much higher degree of situational constraint, which restricts the range of behaviour deemed appropriate in everyday situations (e.g. classrooms, libraries, public parks, etc.). By contrast, loose nations were expected to have a much weaker situational structure, affording a much wider range of permissible behaviour across everyday situations. The socialization of individuals within a particular culture affects individual behaviour as it reflects and supports the degree of order and social coordination in the larger tighter, or smaller looser, cultural context.

## Implications of This Model

Gelfand's model of tight and loose cultures and their effects on both institutions and individual behaviours illustrate the multitude of differences between cultures. From the management of international organizations and personal and professional relationships, it is crucial to accept that, from either system's vantage point, the 'other system' could appear to be dysfunctional, unjust and fundamentally immoral. In addition, such divergent beliefs can contribute to major misunderstandings and even, potentially, to cultural conflicts. It must also be recognized that tight and loose cultures may be, at least in part, functional in their own ecological and historical contexts.

Understanding tight and loose cultures is critical for fostering cross-cultural coordination, and for understanding and working with others in a world of increasing global interdependence.

## Cultural Differences in Expressing Emotions

While it is important to understand how cultural differences can impact how change is perceived and interpreted, it is also essential to understand the crucial role of individual emotional expression and language. Anyone who has travelled to other countries will know that cultures express their emotions differently, ranging from the 'exuberance' of some southern European cultures to the 'restraint' in emotional expression of many cultural traditions in Asia. Lewis's (2006) model (Figure 5.3) identifies the main ways in which different cultures both express emotions and respond to interpersonal demands. In other words, what can be spoken about in different cultures, what can be challenged and how socially appropriate it is to speak openly about difficult issues.

| LINEAR-ACTIVE | MULTI-ACTIVE | REACTIVE |
| --- | --- | --- |
| Talks half the time | Talks most of the time | Listens most of the time |
| Does one thing at a time | Does several things at once | Reacts to partner's action |
| Plans ahead step by step | Plans grand outline only | Looks at general principles |
| Polite but direct | Emotional | Polite, indirect |
| Partly conceals feelings | Displays feelings | Conceals feelings |
| Confronts with logic | Confronts emotionally | Never confronts |
| Dislikes losing face | Has good excuses | Must not lose face |
| Rarely interrupts | Often interrupts | Doesn't interrupt |
| Job-oriented | People-oriented | Very people-oriented |
| Sticks to facts | Feelings before facts | Statements and promises |
| Truth before diplomacy | Flexible truth | Diplomacy over truth |

**Figure 5.3** Lewis's model of cultural categories of emotional expression (Lewis, 2006).

## Language and Worldview

We all share a common humanity and every human has continuous conversations and thoughts in their mind, in their own language, which no one can hear. Which language we speak profoundly determines **how** we understand the world, how we **make sense** of our experience and how we **attribute meaning to our lives**. Thus, there is an intimate connection between language and psychology. The type of language spoken affects an individual's way of seeing the world. Culture and behaviour also influence the way someone thinks and speaks. Thus, each language creates its own worldview. However, every language contains concepts and words that cannot be directly translated into another language. Consequently, any logical train of thought is related to the language of the thinker and their country's culture. For example, the Americans and the Chinese often take the position that **their** logic is the only true logic, forgetting that **their** logic is based on **their own** particular language and culture. There are certain fundamental differences between the English and Chinese languages that may lead to widely divergent world views. Furthermore, vocabulary that is commonplace in one country may be uncommon in another, which can cause communication problems.

*'A literal translation of a metaphor often makes no sense. In other cases, the intrinsic nature of a concept becomes distorted because no word can be found to convey the exact meaning. Italians call this phenomenon "traduttore-traditore" (translator traitor).'* (Yen Mah, 2001: 173).

### ACTIVITY 5.3

1. Imagine you are managing a substantial organizational change initiative with subordinates from various national cultures. Outline what you think are the greatest challenges in the effective management of the change.
2. How you would address these challenges?

## Cultural Competence and Cultural Intelligence

In addition to the models of differences outlined earlier, each culture has specific words and concepts that may have no equivalent in another language, which contributes to an even greater potential for fundamental misunderstandings. Thus, in working with those from different cultural backgrounds and languages, self-awareness of one's own culture and worldview is essential, along with an acceptance that one's own worldview is also a product of one's own culture and language. The development of this *self-awareness* and sensitivity to work with those from different cultures is often described as 'cultural/intercultural competence' or cultural intelligence. The definitions of the terms 'cultural competence' and 'cultural intelligence' overlap to some degree and tend to be used in different contexts – cultural competence is used in many areas of healthcare, whereas cultural intelligence tends to be used in business and organizational contexts. Both will be outlined here. As outlined at the beginning of this chapter, culture does not only refer to nationality, ethnicity or religion. **Cultural competence** has been defined as:

*'The ability to understand and effectively interact with people from cultures different from our own. It also means being able to negotiate cross-cultural differences to accomplish practical goals.' (APA, 2015)*

*'The ability to understand, appreciate and interact with people from cultures or belief systems different from one's own.' (APA, 2015)*

Cultural competence has four major components: *Awareness, Attitude, Knowledge* and *Skills*. According to this approach, multicultural competency requires the following:

→ A basic understanding of your own culture and ethnicity.

→ A willingness to learn about the cultural practices and worldview of others.

→ A positive attitude towards cultural differences.

→ A willingness to accept and respect these differences.

Cultural Intelligence (CQ) is similar, but identifies slightly different components, putting a greater focus on adaptation. Consequently, cultural intelligence is defined as **'the ability to recognize and adapt to cultural differences'** (Earley and Ang, 2003).

## Components of Cultural Intelligence

For a person to be culturally intelligent (Figure 5.4), they cannot simply be aware of different cultures. Crucially, they must also be able to culturally adapt, effectively work and relate to people across a variety of cultural contexts. Cultural intelligence is linked to emotional intelligence – the capacity to sense the emotions, wants and needs of others – but people with high cultural intelligence are also attuned to the values, beliefs and styles of communication of people from different cultures. They use this sensitivity to relate to others with empathy and understanding, which is especially important in to the successful management of substantive organizational change.

Cultural intelligence has been described as including:

→ The skill to relate and work effectively in culturally diverse situations.

→ The capability to cross boundaries and prosper in multiple cultures.

→ Skillsets and capabilities needed to successfully realize your objectives in culturally diverse situations.

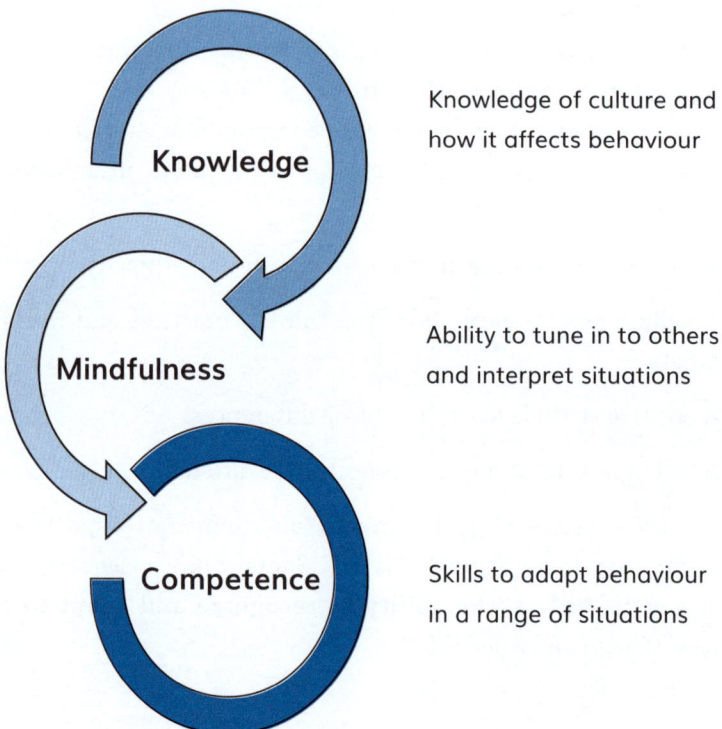

**Figure 5.4** Creating intercultural intelligence.

## Intercultural Competence

Intercultural competence is determined by the presence of cognitive, affective and behavioural abilities that directly shape communication across cultures. These essential abilities can be separated into five specific skills that are obtained through education and experience:

- → Mindfulness: the ability to be cognitively aware of how the communication and interaction with others is developed. It is important to focus more on the process of the interaction than its outcome, while maintaining in perspective the desired communication goals. For example, it would be better to formulate questions such as 'What can I say or do to help this process?' rather than 'What do they mean?'.

- → Cognitive flexibility: the ability to create new categories of information rather than keeping old categories. This skill includes openness to new information, taking more than one perspective and understanding personal ways of interpreting messages and situations.

- → Tolerance for ambiguity: the ability to maintain focus in situations that are not clear, methodically determining the best approach at the situation evolves, rather than becoming anxious. Generally, low-tolerance individuals look for information that supports their beliefs while high-tolerance individuals look for information that helps them to understand the situation and those involved.

- → Behavioural flexibility: the ability to adapt and accommodate behaviours from a different culture. Although knowing a second language could be an important element of this skill, it does not necessarily translate into cultural adaptability. The individual must be willing to assimilate into the new culture.

- → Cross-cultural empathy: the ability to visualize with imagination the situation of another person from an intellectual and emotional point of view. Demonstrating empathy requires the ability to connect emotionally with people, show compassion, think in more than one perspective and listen actively.

## Self-awareness

Self-awareness allows you to more objectively explore what you may subconsciously be bringing to your interpersonal interaction. Components of self-awareness include:

- → Understanding your personal background and culture.
- → Awareness of your assumptions, biases and judgments.
- → Awareness of how others might perceive you and your role.

- → Knowledge of strengths and limitations.
- → Ability to recognize your personal biases, cultural incompetences or exclusive behaviour.
- → Capacity for self-reflection and intervention.

The capacity for awareness of the self and of others is deeply connected to *cultural humility*, in which we are able to recognize that our perspective is just that: our own perspective. Cultural humility is the ability to admit what you don't know and embrace opportunities to learn. Many of us have blind spots or unconscious biases when it comes to our personal beliefs and values. This is why it's vital to examine diversity-related values. We need to bring awareness to stereotyping and prejudices that can create barriers in the workplace and, as a consequence, create issues in the effective management of change.

### ACTIVITY 5.4

1. Given your responses to Activity 5.1, do you think that you are culturally intelligent? Please explain.
2. If you are not quite there yet in terms of cultural intelligence, do you think that this can be developed? If so, how would you go about doing this?

## Managing Stakeholders Across Different Cultures in Organizational Change

Having reviewed different theories of national cultures, it is clear that every culture has its own 'worldview'. This is the lens, including language, through which everything is perceived and made sense of. Although the theories outlined earlier in this chapter have been challenged and critiqued, it is also agreed that they have important validity when considering differences between cultures. However, culture is not static. Western powers have had, and continue to have, a great influence worldwide and the significant changes to culture made by social media are increasingly being studied. Despite increasing knowledge and understanding, working within a multicultural work environment and implementing organizational change remain significant challenges.

Unfortunately, many theoretical paradigms on organizational change do not necessarily address the important role of 'organizational culture', despite there being extensive literature on change processes in organizations. For example, Balogun and Hope Hailey (2008) describe different change processes, including attempting to change the values of employees and others, emphasizing behavioural change or seeking to change the performance objectives or outputs of employees. However, specific issues relating to navigating change across different cultural backgrounds is rarely addressed. From your learning in this chapter, however, you should now understand that addressing different cultures in the change process has a unique set of challenges including communication, management of expectations and implementation of change.

As in all organizations, organizational culture and communication style is very much determined by senior staff who act as role models for other staff. However, key questions need to be asked of a leadership team that is managing substantive change including:

- Are senior staff culturally competent/do senior staff display cultural intelligence?
- Can senior staff adapt their communication style to different individuals, groups and cultures?
- Are senior staff able to use active listening skills?
- Most importantly, are senior staff able to implement processes that promote organizational cultural competence and inclusion?

If the answer to any of these questions is 'no', then perhaps organizations need to consider if they have the 'right' people leading the change.

## How Valuable are the Insights From Cultural Theories?

Hofstede's cultural dimensions are useful in predicting how people from different cultures will interact with each other during the change process. For example, if two people from cultures with different levels of power distance meet, they may have difficulty communicating because they have different expectations about who should be leading the change (Hofstede, 2011). In addition, if an organization is undergoing a process of change, those from cultures who have a high uncertainty avoidance may experience more difficulties with the ambiguity of change and therefore find it more threatening, compared with those from cultures who have a low uncertainty index and are more able to tolerate the change. Another of Hofstede's dimensions which may be useful in the change process is the distinction between individualistic and collectivist cultures. Those from collectivist cultures may find it more difficult to express individual opinions regarding the change processes, as their priority may be the benefit of the whole, i.e. their team, rather than their own individualistic views. Furthermore, Kirsch et al. (2012) point to national differences where high resistance to change is associated with high power distance, low individualism and high uncertainty avoidance. These countries include Portugal, Korea, Japan, France, Spain, Greece, Turkey and Arab and Latin American countries. Juxtaposed with these are the Northern European countries such as the Netherlands where resistance to change is lower. These countries tend to feature low on power distance, high on individualism and low on uncertainty avoidance.

Nonetheless, Hofstede's theory still has a few enduring strengths. As McSweeney (2002) notes, Hofstede's work has 'stimulated a great deal of cross-cultural research and provided a useful framework for the comparative study of cultures' (p. 83). Additionally, as Orr and Hauser (2008) point out, Hofstede's dimensions have been found to correlate with actual behaviour in cross-cultural studies, suggesting that it does hold some validity. All in all, as McSweeney (2002) points out, Hofstede's theory is a useful starting point for cultural analysis, but there have been many additional, and more methodologically rigorous, advances made in the last several decades. Furthermore, as we have seen in this chapter, cultural theories can be utilized to illuminate the process and pitfalls of organizational change, or at least to start a meaningful discussion on managing cultural differences during substantive change.

## CASE STUDY

### MUTUAL MISUNDERSTANDINGS: THE IMPACT OF LIMITED CULTURAL AWARENESS ON THE FUNCTIONING OF THE OFFICE OF AN INTERNATIONAL AID ORGANIZATION IN PAPUA NEW GUINEA

### Introduction

This case study uses a small number of examples to indicate the potential barriers that cultural misunderstandings may have on managing change within an international organization. These examples are based on the first author's experience of different cultures and the issues that arose during a consultancy project in Papua New Guinea (PNG).

As this chapter indicates, cultural activities comprise everything we do and experience from birth. Therefore, constant cultural ambiguity and negotiating meaning is simply part of being human. How different people interpret their world (including their working environment) and give it meaning can differ. When staff in an organization come from very different cultural backgrounds, mutual misunderstandings may ensue. This can negatively affect many aspects of the work of the organization including its ability communicate and lead and manage people effectively. This case study focuses on some of the potential effects of a lack of understanding of different cultural perspectives in the work environment.

## Background

PNG has a population of 8.7 million, which includes many different tribal groups. Although English is the language of business and government, over 700 local languages are spoken. Tribal identities and cultural traditions are still essential components of everyday life, including for those with higher levels of education living in urban settings. The working environment in PNG is considered to be high risk, due to the high levels of robbery and violence. Armed robbery and domestic violence at home are common.

The office has thirty-nine staff – fourteen international staff (mainly from Western countries) and twenty-five local staff (those who live permanently in PNG). A recent Global Staff Survey identified this office as the worst performing. The Head of Office had been removed for bullying staff, two temporary replacements had been appointed and there had been six Operations Managers in eighteen months. Many staff expressed disillusionment with the work of the organization, and anger about what had happened in the office. There had been far too much change and many staff felt helpless. These difficulties were exacerbated by cultural misunderstandings.

## Daily Life

How someone performs at work cannot be separated from their personal situation. In addition to differences in salary, differences in everyday life between national and international staff are profound, as we can see from the summary below.

## National Staff Experience

- Long-distance commuting often requiring more than one bus. Public transport does not operate after 6pm.
- Cultural and family obligations, including the Wontok clan/family traditions, which often involve having to provide money at significant events.
- High cost of living, particularly rent, healthcare and school fees.
- Potential risk from security issues, for example, attacks and robbery.

- Male-dominated society with high rates of domestic violence.

## International Staff Experience

- Much higher quality of accommodation and shorter commuting times.
- Lack of freedom of movement due to security concerns.
- Difficulty in forming friendship or support networks.
- Separation from family and sometimes children.
- Lack of intimacy and personal support.

## Overview of Local Cultural Traditions/Assumptions

## The Wantok System

The Wantok (one talk) system, which is the basis for all social systems in PNG, is extremely complex. Clan loyalty is very strong, and an intricate web of cultural and financial obligations binds people together. If a person needs assistance they can ask, but they are also obliged to assist others. Power is created by *giving* to others, which creates obligations for those who have been given to. The Wantok system pervades all activities – from the highest government office to each individual in a village. Government ministers fill posts with wantoks – personal loyalty to the same clan is prioritized above qualifications. This system is very useful in a subsistence economy but does not work well in commerce or Western organizations. It also places great strains on working people – having to share money with wantoks and having to give priority to unqualified wontaks of the same clan. Revenge and payback are also integral parts of traditional culture, and everyone in a clan shares a collective responsibility for payback. This explains why staff from different tribes are likely to become nervous and suspicious of each other.

## Impact of Cultural Misunderstandings on the Work Environment

Local staff thought managers did not understand local culture, particularly the implications of the 'Wantok' system.

> *'The Wantok culture means your own tribal group is always favoured'*
> *'Programme assistants are from different tribes so they do not help each other'*
> *'Management do not understand the culture and its effects on team building'*

International staff also complained about national staff.

> '*PNG staff react emotionally and take things personally*'
> '*Staff do not speak up*'

## 1 Communication and 'Speaking Up'

International staff were experienced and confident in expressing their views in meetings but complained specifically that local staff did not speak up. Cultural reasons for this inhibition included fear of losing their job, but more specifically cultural assumptions as to who is perceived to hold knowledge and power.

> '*Elders are the only ones who have the "right" to speak as they have the knowledge*'
> '*Cultural obligations are unspoken, everyone knows what is expected so no one needs to speak*'
> '*National staff sometimes think that international staff are the ones with the expertise, and this contributes to national staff "taking a back seat"*'

These underlying assumptions contributed to national staff believing that international staff have greater expertise and, as a consequence, they undervalued their own contributions. This resulted in national staff being reluctant to speak up in the face of an incompetent leader. If also led to intense disappointment and 'puzzlement' as to how someone who does not have the necessary knowledge is in a more powerful position than themselves. This issue of who holds knowledge was compounded by some international staff not **actively valuing** the knowledge of local staff, which created even greater anxiety about speaking up.

Another aspect of local culture of relevance to 'speaking up' is the notion of 'payback'. This is a collective responsibility for each clan. If staff are from different tribes/clans, they may fear speaking up in case they offend someone from another clan, which may encourage some form of 'payback'. It was also clear that those experiencing harsh child-rearing practices and possible domestic violence were encouraged not to 'speak up' for fear of punishment.

Some staff expressed great anxiety about 'speaking up' in meetings as they felt that their own knowledge and experience was not valued or acknowledged. These issues severely affected the capacity of national staff to give 360 feedback to their supervisor when requested. To encourage staff to 'speak up', and help them overcome some of these factors/barriers, international staff must **listen** sensitively and constructively.

This fear of speaking up permeated all aspects of the work. It was not only a source of frustration for international staff, but also contributed to the despair of national staff who felt that their own knowledge and experience was not valued.

## 2 Impact on Work Tasks

How decisions were made differed greatly between national and international staff. In local PNG culture, decision-making is always collaborative and takes time, whereas Western organizations tend to have hierarchical structures with linear decision-making practices. Local staff perceived these procedures as 'rigid'.

> 'Procedures are hierarchical in roles and responsibilities, too much vertical'
> 'PNG staff cannot express their views because decisions are not consultative'

Local PNG staff come from a predominantly egalitarian environment. Everyone interacts with others, and everyone knows each other. Entering a formal environment with rigid rules of behaviour and seemingly rigid procedures and can severely inhibit the behaviour and attitudes of local staff, as well as the achievement of work tasks. International staff also described their own frustrations with national staff, describing them as having a *'lack of capacity'*, *'lack of motivation'* and *'lack of professionalism'*.

## 3 Relationships

The effects of cultural misunderstandings on relationships were profound.

> 'Everything in PNG is built on relationships built over years with partners. Supervisors need to listen to national staff about how to do relationships. Some partners are not interested in working with us anymore as the relationship has been lost'

## Impact on Staff Morale, Work Tasks and Relationships Between Expat and Local Staff

As well as lack of understanding of fundamental cultural issues, many other aspects of the past and present office environment contributed to low staff morale. There was still much anger and distrust as to how staff had behaved in the past.

## Relationship Between National Staff and Supervisors

The relationship between national staff and expatriate supervisors was particularly poor.

> 'Everything in PNG is built on relationships built over years with partners. Supervisors need to listen to national staff about how to do relationships. If we are always going back to them asking questions, partners experience it as questioning their integrity. Some partners are not interested in working with this INGO any more as the relationship is lost'
> 'Too many questions/interrogations'
> 'Lack of trusting relationships in the office – superficial, no human side, creates extra stress. Supervisors interrogate staff on work and personal issues making staff feel less competent. There is also a lack of support'

National staff assume that relationships are built over time, including relationships with external organizations. This is very different in Western organizations where work relationships usually depend on the *positions occupied* and are hierarchical in nature. Due to the stability of family networks and cultural traditions, national staff are far more averse to change and find constant changes of international staff very difficult, whereas international staff often have twelve or twenty-four month contracts and expect to be moving on.

### ACTIVITY 5.5

1. Using the cultural patterns described in this chapter, how would you describe the cultures of both national and international staff?
2. What do you think are the key issues here?
3. If you were appointed Head of Office, how would you address the issues highlighted?

### CONSULTANCY IN THE CHAIR

#### Cup of Kindness Activity

You are again called on by the CEO for advice. It appears that the overwhelming demographic for middle management in the North European and US branch of the organization are mostly White Anglo-Saxon Males (WAMs), and some of the changes that they have tried to implement in line with the requirements of the CEO have not been well received by the cross-cultural workforce. The CEO would like you to unpack what is causing the bottleneck and what your solution(s) might be?

**Competency-based Interview Questions**

1. Please give an example of a time you successfully handled conflict in the workplace. What was your approach?
2. Why do you think your approach was successful?
3. Is there anything that you would improve upon next time around and, if so, what?

## Chapter Summary

This chapter has critically evaluated the complexities surrounding the understanding of cultural differences. We have reflected and critically evaluated cultural differences which we have framed through important theoretical paradigms such as those of Hofstede (1980), Gelfand (2011) and Inglehart (1997). This learning has provided insight into how differences in national cultures impact the way in which organizations are managed, and specifically how change is managed and perceived by different national cultures. To put us in touch with our own awareness of cultural differences, we have used a diagnostic tool to compare different national cultures. The importance of managers and leaders having cultural intelligence in general, and specifically in the context of substantial organizational change, has been reflected by way of better managing the change process.

## Useful Resources

https://www.hofstede-insights.com

## Bibliography

Ailon, G. (2008), 'Mirror, Mirror on the Wall: Culture's Consequences in a Value Test of Its Own Design'. *Academy of Management Review*, 33: 885–904.

Alémán, J. and Woods, D. (2016), 'Value Orientations from the World Values Survey: How Comparable Are They Cross-nationally?' *Comparative Political Studies*, 49: 1039–67.

American Psychological Association (2015), *Monitor on Psychology*, 46(3).

Balogun, J. and Hope Hailey, V., Johnson, G. (ed), and Scholes, K. (ed) (2008), *Exploring Strategic Change*, third edition. London: Prentice-Hall.

Baskerville, R. F. (2003), 'Hofstede Never Studied Culture'. *Accounting, Organizations and Society*, 28: 1–14.

Baskerville-Morley, R. F. (2005), 'A Research Note: The Unfinished Business of Culture'. *Accounting Organizations and Society*, 30: 389–91.

Beugelsdijk, S. and Welzer, C. (2018), 'Dimensions and Dynamics of National Culture: Synthesizing Hofstede With Inglehart'. *Journal of Cross-Cultural Psychology* 49(10): 1469–505.

Bond, M. H. (1991), *Beyond the Chinese Face: Insights From Psychology*. New York: Oxford University Press.

Earley, P. C. and Ang, S. (2003). *Cultural Intelligence: Individual Interactions Across Cultures*. Redwood City, CA: Stanford University Press.

Fang, T. (2003), 'A Critique of Hofstede's Fifth National Culture Dimension'. *International Journal of Cross Cultural Management*, 3: 347–68.

Flanagan, S. (1987), 'Value Change in Industrial Society'. *American Political Science Review*, 81: 1303–19.

Flanagan, S. and Lee, A. R. (2003), 'The New Politics, Culture Wars, and the Authoritarian-Libertarian Value Change in Advanced Industrial Democracies'. *Comparative Political Studies*, 26: 235–70.

Gelfand, M. J. (2012), 'Culture's Constraints: International Differences in the Strength of Social Norms,' *Current Directions in Psychological Science: A Journal of the American Psychological Society*, 21(6): 420–4.

Gelfand, M. J., Raver, J. L., Nishii, L., et al. (2011), 'Differences Between Tight and Loose Cultures: A 33-Nation Study'. *Science (American Association for the Advancement of Science)*, 332(6033): 1100–4. DOI: https://doi.org/10.1126/science.1197754.

Gelfand, M. J., Jackson, J. C., Pan, X., et al. (2021), 'The Relationship Between Cultural Tightness–Looseness and COVID-19 Cases and Deaths: a Global Analysis'. *The Lancet Planetary Health*, 5(3): e135–e144.

Grossmann, I. and Varnum, M. E. W. (2015), 'Social Structure, Infectious Diseases, Disasters, Secularism, and Cultural Change in America'. *Psychological Science*, 26: 311–24.

Guiso, L., Sapienza, P. and Zingales, L. (2006), 'Does Culture Affect Economic Outcomes?', *The Journal of Economic Perspectives*, 20(2): 23–48.

Haerpfer, C., Inglehart, R., Moreno, A., Welzel, C., Kizilova, K., Diez-Medrano, J., Lagos, M., Norris, P., Ponarin, E. and Puranen, B. (2022), 'World Values Survey Wave 7 (2017–2022) Cross-National Data-Set. Version: 4.0.0. World Values Survey Association'. DOI: doi.org/10.14281/18241.18.

Hofstede, G. (1980), *Culture's Consequences: International Differences in Work-Related Values*. Beverly Hills, CA: Sage.

Hofstede, G. (1991), *Cultures and Organizations: Software of the Mind*. London: McGraw-Hill.

Hofstede, G. (2001), *Culture's Consequences: Comparing Values, Behaviors, Institutions and Organizations Across Nations*. Thousand Oaks, CA: Sage (co-published in the PRC as Vol. 10 in the Shanghai Foreign Language Education Press SFLEP Intercultural Communication Reference Series, 2008).

Hofstede, G. (2011), 'Dimensionalizing Cultures: The Hofstede Model in Context'. *Online Readings in Psychology and Culture*, 2(1). DOI: https://doi.org/10.9707/2307-0919.1014.

Hofstede, G. and Minkov, M. (2010), 'Long- Versus Short-term Orientation: New Perspectives'. *Asia Pacific Business Review*, 16(4): 493–504.

Inglehart, R. (1997), *Modernization and Postmodernization: Cultural, Economic, and Political Change in 43 Societies*. Princeton, NJ: Princeton University Press.

Inglehart, R. and Norris, P. (2003), *Sacred and Secular*. New York: Cambridge University Press.

Inglehart, R. and Welzel, C. (2005), *Modernization, Cultural Change and Democracy: The Human Development Sequence*. New York: Cambridge University Press.

Kirsch, C., Chelliah, J. and Parry, W. (2012), 'The Impact of Cross-Cultural Dynamics on Change Management', *Cross Cultural Management: An International Journal*, 19(2): 166–95.

Lewis, R. D. (2006), *When Cultures Collide: Leading Across Cultures*. Boston, MA: Nicholas Brealey International.

Maslow, A. H. (1954), *Motivation and Personality*. New York: Harper and Row.

McSweeney, B. (2002), 'Hofstede's Model of National Cultural Differences and Their Consequences: A Triumph of Faith – a Failure of Analysis'. *Human Relations*, 55: 89.

McSweeney, B. (2009), 'Dynamic Diversity: Variety and Variation Within Countries'. *Organization Studies*, 30: 933–57.

Nickerson, C. (2022), *Hofstede's Cultural Dimensions Theory*. Simply Psychology. www.simplypsychology.org/hofstedes-cultural-dimensions-theory.html (accessed 18 April 2025).

Orr, L. M. and Hauser, W. (2008), 'A Re-Inquiry of Hofstede's Cultural Dimensions: A Call for 21st Century Cross-Cultural Research'. *Marketing Management Journal*, 18: 1–19.

Pelto, P. J. (1968), 'The Differences Between "Tight" and "Loose" Societies'. *Trans-action* 5, 37–40. DOI: https://doi.org/10.1007/BF03180447.

Taras, V., Steel, P. and Kirkman, B. (2012), 'Improving National Cultural Indices Using a Longitudinal Meta Analysis of Hofstede's Dimensions'. *Journal of World Business*, 47: 329–41.

Trompenaars, F. and Hampden-Turner, C. (1997), *Riding the Waves of Culture*, second edition. Boston, MA: Nicholas Brealey.

Venaik, S. and Brewer, P. (2010), 'Avoiding Uncertainty in Hofstede and GLOBE'. *Journal of International Business Studies*, 41: 1294–315.

Welzel, C. (2013), *Freedom Rising: Human Empowerment and the Quest for Emancipation*. New York: Cambridge University Press.

Yen Mah, A. (2001), *Watching the Tree*. New York: Broadway Books.

Zhou, C., Yiu, W. Y. V., Wu, M. S. and Greenfield, P. M. (2018), 'Perception of Cross-generational Differences in Child Behavior and Parent Socialization: A Mixed-method Interview Study with Chinese Grandmothers'. *Journal of Cross-Cultural Psychology*, 49: 62–81.

# Understanding Power and Politics in Organizational Change and Effectively Managing Resistance

**6**

## Learning Outcomes

At the end of this chapter you will be able to:

1. Appreciate the relationship and differences between power and politics.
2. Understand the role of power and politics as an important resource in the change process.
3. Be aware of the dark side of organizational politics and how this can be detrimental to a change initiative.
4. Appreciate that organizational politics can be used in a positive way to influence and optimize the successful outcome of a change initiative.
5. Understand the nature and role of emotional intelligence in organizational change.
6. Recognize and evaluate the role of resistance in the change process and how this can be perceived and managed more effectively by managers and leaders.

## Introduction

To further facilitate your insight and manage the process and interpersonal relationships around change effectively it is essential to understand the challenges, role and dynamics that power and politics play. As we have seen from earlier chapters, change is not straightforward. Where change is significant, power and politics take a pivotal role. This chapter critically evaluates power as an interpersonal resource that should be utilized by organizational stakeholders to successfully conduct transformational change. Central to a meaningful discussion on power and change is the role of organizational politics. Not all organizational stakeholders acquire power from legitimate sources, so organizational politics is instead used to gain power. Whilst workplace politics can be used to benefit an organization, a toxic element can also develop, involving political manoeuvring and short-term tactics. Individuals and groups may use organizational politics to maintain the status quo or to hijack a change initiative, with the intention of taking the initiative in an entirely different direction. This may be because they think the change would not benefit them. Another important aspect of this chapter involves exploring resistance to change and the different lenses through which resistance is perceived. Understanding resistance as part of the change process is integral for change to be managed effectively.

## Different Approaches to Power: What Is It and Who Has It?

Power is a critical resource in making transformational change happen. At the macro level of the organization, it is typically senior and middle management that have power. This level of management has control over valued, and sometimes limited, resources that can be used to drive change in a meaningful way. Of all the resources that this level of management has access to, one of the most important is people. Change can never be truly successful without acceptance from key organizational stakeholders, such as employees. Whilst change can be 'pushed' through by altering systems, procedures and processes, without employees' buy-in there is always some residual resentment in those who are not properly involved in the process of change. This can lead to suboptimal outcomes for an organization, and ultimately result in good workers feeling demotivated. As a result, they often decide to leave, which can prove costly for any company. Furthermore, where power is used in an unethical way, the media inevitably reports it, which may damage an organization's reputation (see in particular the P&O case study in Chapter 9 on organizational change and ethics).

An important resource that managers can use to motivate workers to engage in transformational change is power. Power can be described as having the authority to get things done, through and with others. Whilst there is no universally recognized definition of power, much is made of Weber's (1978) definition, who described it as 'the probability that one actor within a social relationship will be in a position to carry out "their" own will despite resistance, regardless of the basis on which this probability rests' (Weber, 1978: 53). In other words, the power dynamic is relational, interpersonal and concerns the interconnectedness of us all. In a workplace context, someone may consistently have more power than another because they occupy a recognized position of authority within the organization's hierarchical structure and reporting lines. However, that individual or group of people are not likely to be in a position to exercise that power on a 'forever' basis. Whilst this holds true in formal relationships between employer and employee, in more informal relationships (such as those we have with friends), who holds the power tends to depend on the circumstances. Consequently, power is more likely to oscillate from one person to another. For example, if you are unable to attend a lecture you may need to get a set of notes and recording from a peer student colleague. At that point they have the power to either share or withhold what you need. Regardless, they only hold power for that moment because they might call on you for the same in a few weeks' time when they are unable to attend. In this way, the power oscillates from one person to another and does not generally reside more consistently in one individual.

In more formal relationships, such as those between employees in organizations, it is line managers and those more senior who consistently have more power over individuals and groups. For example, line managers have the power to give or withhold rewards such as promotions. Managers use their power in a subtle and not so subtle way to influence subordinates' behaviour towards engaging and participating in new work practices. By doing so, change is brought about and new organizational objectives are met. In this respect, power might be interpreted as 'an ability to get another person to do something that he or she would not otherwise have done' (Dahl, 1957: 158), and thus contains an element of control whereby a person or group of people are coerced into performing the requisite behaviour. Whilst some may view power as coercing employees into new behaviours to bring about change, there is also a practical element here. A degree of control, when exercised in an ethical way, has the ability to reduce uncertainty and bring about clarity in ensuring that employees understand what can be reasonably expected from them before, during and after the change process. Employees can thus do their best to make meaningful contributions towards organizational goals and objectives. Furthermore, when exercised in an ethical way, power can assure organizational survival by improving efficiency and effectiveness. In this way, employees' behaviour can be positively influenced towards attaining an organization's vision. Where managers do not have sufficient power they are unable to bring about transformative change, which might lead to an organization's demise in which managers are unable to intervene on behalf of employees to bring about favourable outcomes for them. Where managers have sufficient power, they can:

- Facilitate a favourable outcome for an employee who might need help.
- Get agreement for expenditure for their department that is above a pre-agreed budget.
- Enhance the reputation of their department by positively influencing the rest of the organization favourably towards them.
- Protect their department by acting as a buffer between their people and the rest of the organization.
- Make certain that their department is given a voice at crucial meetings by getting their needs and concerns on the agenda.
- Have access to more senior managers so that they are well-informed of strategic shifts in advance.

Juxtaposing this are leaders and senior managers who abuse their power in their interpersonal relationships to get change done (more of this in Chapter 9). These unethical methods are most likely be used against individuals and groups that object to the proposed change. Leaders and managers might use a number of toxic methods to 'manage' these individuals and groups including public humiliation, ostracizing them from important meetings so dissenting voices are unheard, giving these individuals and groups poor performance feedback, refusing promotion and generally making their workplace life unbearable. If you have ever been on the receiving end of such unethical behaviour you may be glad to know that there is empirical evidence to suggest that such abuses of power in interpersonal relationships are flagged as a key factor in derailing leaders' and managers' careers.

## An Observation on Power and Influence

Influence is often subsumed under a broad conception of power. However, it is suggested that the two concepts are different though power can produce influence and vice versa. Willer et al. (1997: 573) define influence as 'the socially induced modification of a belief, attitude or expectation effected without recourse to sanctions'. In other words, whilst power involves external positive or negative sanctions, influence takes place by persuasion and advice. Therefore, change can occur as a result of influence if it benefits the person or the group to which they belong, whereas power occurs where the interest of two parties are complementary, i.e. neither can benefit without reaching some agreement.

Various influence tactics can be used to achieve change in organizational settings ranging from the use of rational discussion for example, offering to make sacrifice or help to get the job done to the use of clandestine tactics such as manipulating information or making the target feel important. The choice of influence tactic varies depending on the power of the target or counterpart where the tactics of self-presentation and supporting data may be used to influence superiors whereas, training, demanding and explaining can be used to influence subordinates.

We now set out conceptualizations of power by way of better understanding this complex phenomenon.

## Compliance Theory of Power

Etzioni's (1975) conceptual paradigm of power is framed by compliance theory. This theory emphasizes the relational aspect of power and, in particular, the power granted to leaders by virtue of their position in the organizational hierarchical structure. Importantly, compliance theory provides a framework for considering power dynamics in relationships between those that hold power and those that are subject to it. Fundamental to this theory is the assumption that power is held by those who have a position of authority in the organizational structure. There are three types of power that can be used to ensure compliance from subordinates in regards to proposed changes. These are:

- Coercive;
- Utilitarian;
- Normative.

Coercive power involves the express/implied threats and punishment of subordinates when, for example, a rule is disobeyed or when an order from a senior manager is not carried out. An obvious example of this type of power is illustrated by the military, in which a person with authority can demand additional physical exercises from a subordinate who disobeys or does not carry out an order correctly. Utilitarian power is where managers and leaders control subordinates' behaviour through extrinsic rewards. Depending on the individual or group, it is more likely they will cooperate with change if rewarded through increased financial remuneration, bonuses and promotion. Finally, normative power is more subtle than coercive and utilitarian power. Normative power is focused on intrinsic rewards. However, just as with coercive and utilitarian power, it is used to control subordinates' behaviour. Intrinsic rewards in a workplace context involve the feeling of fulfilment subordinates get from completing a task satisfactorily. In other words, the pleasure, pride and emotional wellbeing that flows to an individual from performing the task. In this way normative power is symbolic and figurative. It involves managers and leaders ensuring compliance with change by reminding subordinates of a shared identify through the articulation the organization's vision, mission, goals and objectives. A manager might also use normative power by calling upon the work group that the non-compliant subordinate is a member of to encourage compliance through group norms.

## Subordinate Involvement in Coercive, Utilitarian and Normative Power

The underlying objective of these three types of power is compliance from subordinates. However, the extent to which they are effective depends on subordinates' positive or negative involvement. Accordingly, subordinate involvement in change can be:

- Alienative;
- Calculative; or
- Moral.

Alienative involvement occurs in employees who feel estranged from the organization in which they work and, as far as any proposed change is concerned, they are unaccepting and hostile, experiencing a highly negative reaction. At the same time, because of the type of power that managers and leaders exert, subordinates will have no choice other than to follow instructions for change.

Calculative involvement involves a more ambivalent response from subordinates. They may respond positively or negatively to the proposed change, but, whatever their response, their involvement in it will *not* involve any commitment or loyalty.

The opposite of alienative and calculative involvement is moral involvement, which triggers an intense positive response from subordinates. These subordinates are loyal without question to the organization. They have internalized and assimilated the organizations norms, professed values and beliefs and are therefore wholly engaged in any change.

## Common Compliance Power Relationships

Organizations are compelled to be efficient and managers are tasked with achieving organizational goals with fewer and fewer resources. Three types of compliance relationships between managers, leaders and subordinates that purport to enable the efficient use of resources are Coercive-Compliance, Utilitarian-Compliance and Normative-Compliance. Coercive-compliance relationships cause alienation, yet subordinates have no choice but to carry out orders and follow rules. In this way, the power relationship is effective. Utilitarian-compliance is also deemed to be effective because subordinates are given financially remunerative benefits to carry out instructions. Likewise, normative compliance demonstrates an effective power relationship because subordinates are wholly committed to achieving organizational goals and objectives and will, without question, follow instructions from senior managers. Accordingly, these types of compliance relationships are efficient in achieving organizational change. Subordinates have no choice but to follow instructions for change, are given extrinsic benefits to achieve change, or have internalized the organization's beliefs and norms to an extent that no threat of punishment or offer of extrinsic rewards is required to carry out the change.

### ACTIVITY 6.1

1. Given the emphasis upon efficiency and effectiveness within organizations, do you think that compliance theory is a true representation of how power operates between senior managers and subordinates? Please explain and provide examples.

2. Identify three types of organization (perhaps by reference to different industrial sectors) that illustrate the three power compliance relationships outlined above.

3. Do you think that the three compliance relationships outlined above illustrate the dynamics of power relationships within organizations during change initiatives? Please justify your response.

## Power as Getting Things Done Through Co-operation

As we have learnt so far, power is traditionally associated with the upper echelons of management, especially in larger organizations where power typically resides at the top of the hierarchical structure. In this way, the senior management team has power over subordinates, which is expressed in a mono-directional way from the top of the hierarchical structure to those below. However, it was Mary Parker-Follett, a pioneering management thinker in the early part of the twentieth century, who made a significant contribution to the development of contemporary organizational behaviour theory. Juxtaposed with the prevailing theories of the day, which assumed workers to be no more than objects like any other piece of machinery, Follett developed a different concept of management and power. Management, she said is the 'art of getting things done through people'. Follett's underlying assumption emphasizes the symbiotic nature of power. Power is held *with* others and not *over* others. Accordingly, power is bidirectional; it functions in two directions as it flows between management and workers. Workers and managers have skills, views, thoughts and capabilities that need to be respected, so there is an acknowledged interdependence between managers and workers in achieving organizational goals.

Follett's approach fits well with the design of contemporary organizations, which have less bureaucratic structures, fewer people and decentralized communication brought about by changes in IT and artificial intelligence. In this scaled-down, flatter-structured organization, tiers of middle management are stripped to improve efficiency and reduce costs. This is especially the case in macro and industrial sector organizations, which tend to be highly competitive and economically challenged. With a flatter structure and tiers of management removed, organizations save on costs by employing fewer permanent managers and workers. In this way, it is less apparent who power resides with. This is especially true of workers and managers who telecommute (work from home). This presents organizations with a complex set of challenges whereby supervision and authority are opaque. With reduced hierarchical layers those with power need to exercise their power in especially intelligent, empathetic and bidirectional ways to influence employees, meaning interpersonal relationships are crucial to organizational success.

## Determinants of Power

So far in this chapter we have considered the nature of power, what it is and who typically has it. In this next section, we consider power bases. Managers and leaders need power bases to make change happen. This is the case whether power is exercised mono-directionally or bi-directionally. If power is the ability to get others to do what someone else wants them to do, then *how* do managers and leaders do this? From where do managers and leaders acquire their power?

## Sources of Influence: Power Bases

French and Raven (1959) identified five bases which are key to possessing power (see Figure 6.1). These are:

→ Legitimate power bases;
→ Reward power bases;
→ Coercive power bases;
→ Expert power bases;
→ Reference power bases.

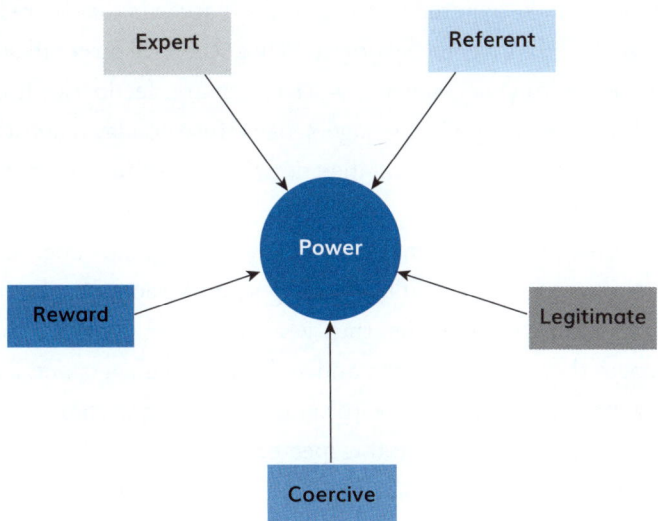

**Figure 6.1** Sources of power. Based on French and Raven's (1959) Five Bases to Power.

To persuade people that transformational change is required, managers and leaders need power from all five bases. Legitimate power is the power someone derives from the very nature of the role and position that they occupy within the organization's structure. For example, consider the position of Student Voice Leaders who represent the rest of the cohort on undergraduate or postgraduate programmes. These individuals, by virtue of the position they hold at the university, have the power to represent the rest of the cohort's views, for example, on how effective the programme of study is at formal university meetings. Likewise, academic colleagues, by virtue of the position they hold at the university, have the power to set and evaluate assessments. It is more likely that change is accepted and accomplished where it is perceived as a legitimate exercise of a manager's or leader's authority.

Reward power is where an individual has the authority to give or withhold rewards within an organization. This may include the authority to increase remuneration, including pay, salary and bonuses such as private medical care. It also includes the power to give non-financial rewards such as verbal praise, which many value above and beyond financial remuneration. In this way, managers and leaders have power to praise individuals that have been proactively engaged in the transformational change process.

We touched on coercive power earlier in this chapter. Coercive power is the power that a manager or leader has to 'punish' others. This may take the form of verbal reprimands, for example, if a subordinate is uncooperative and refusing to engage in behaviours required by the change. It appears that there is a sinister undertone associated with coercive power. Whilst coercive power may be utilized in a positive sense (to give constructive criticism and feedback), it can also be used in a toxic way. For example, managers may refuse holiday requests or change work patterns in an effort to 'get change done', even if this does not align with workers' best interests.

Another source of power comes with being a recognized specialist. This is called expert power and is a result of managers and leaders having recognized specialist skills and competencies that very few in an organization possess. Workers respect these competencies and skills, and managers and leaders have the ability to influence workers towards engaging with the change in a positive way because they are listened to and respected.

Reference power is much undervalued by organizations who operate in dynamic and short-term macro environments. In comparison to the four other types of power, reference power is more informal in nature. It is power that flows to managers and leaders as a result of their personality. This type of power can be described as the 'likeability' factor. Some managers and leaders are good people to be around; they are trustworthy and show respect for others by doing what they have committed themselves to. They are pleasant and remember informal conversations with workers. They have attractive personal qualities which result in them being held in favourable regard by others. Where this is the case, it is more likely that workers will follow managers and leaders and show their commitment to change by engaging proactively in new behaviours.

### ACTIVITY 6.2

1. Recall a time (either in your personal or professional life) when you possessed power. Describe the situation as you recall it.
2. Using the five power bases that French and Raven (1959) put forward, analyse where your sources of power emanated from.
3. How did having this power make you feel?
4. Now recall a time (either in your personal or professional life) when you did not possess power. Describe the situation as you recall it.
5. Explain why you did not have power, and how this made you feel.

## The Power of Lower Subordinates

By way of an icebreaker to this section of the chapter, please reflect on the following questions:

### ACTIVITY 6.3

1. Is there any organization that you can think of where power actually resides with subordinates?
2. Is there any workplace situation that you can think of where power is likely to reside with subordinates?

These are interesting and challenging questions and, as you respond, you may alter the lens through which you would otherwise perceive organizational power and dynamics. As we have seen so far in this chapter, those that have power in the workplace tend to be managers and leaders. However, there are certain circumstances and situations where this power dynamic is flipped, giving power to subordinates who would not ordinarily have it. A case study that illustrates this is British Airways (BA). BA's response to increasing competition from cheaper providers was to reduce HR costs and, in particular, the cost of lower subordinates in organizational hierarchical terms. This included reducing the number of air cabin staff and removing their core conditions including, for example, travel perks. The air cabin staff went on strike for a period of 22 days. During this time BA lost £150 million in travel disruptions, which would have undoubtedly damaged their reputation as a high-quality service provider. These lower-level subordinates would typically have limited power given their place in the organization's hierarchical structure. However, on this occasion, due to their strike the power balance flipped from residing in the senior management team to the air cabin crew, resulting in many of their core conditions being reinstated. In response to this victory, Len McCluskey Unite's General Secretary said;

**'I hope it sends a message to employers everywhere that working with your workforce is the only way to secure productive change.'**

### CASE STUDY: BRITISH AIRWAYS

To recap the BA case study, please read through the summary published by *The Guardian* and respond to the following questions:

1. What do you think of Len McCluskey's statement? To what extent do you believe organizations are interested in working alongside their employees to secure productive change? Please explain, using examples from your own experience of either being a subordinate or a manager.
2. Why do you think it's a good idea for organizations to work alongside their employees in a substantive change initiative?
3. Why do you think it's not a good idea for organizations to work alongside their subordinates during a substantive change initiative?
4. How does the success of the lower-level subordinates in the BA case study make you feel?
5. If you were a lower-level subordinate and unhappy about a substantial change initiative, what would you do? How would you increase your chance of being successful in preventing the proposed change from happening if you thought it was not in the organization's best interests?

The concept of lower-level subordinates having power is not new. In 1964 Crozier conducted research into power and lower-level organizational participants. The perception was that maintenance workers in a French tobacco factory were at the bottom of the organizational hierarchy and workplace processes, and as such had no or very little power. However, this was only a perception, and did not represent the reality. In fact, the organization was wholly dependent on the continued efficient and effective manufacturing process to complete orders. Therefore, if a machine broke down and the production workers decided to go on strike, their power would quickly become evident because the organization is wholly dependent on these 'subordinates' to fulfil orders and therefore survive.

## Organizational Politics and Change

Organizational Politics (OP) is used in both negative and positive ways during significant organizational change. There are two juxtaposed perspectives held about OP. One is that OP is a toxic tactic that individuals without power use to further their *own* interests. The other is that OP is a useful social skill that can be used positively by employees, leaders and managers to further the legitimate interests of the organization and key stakeholders.

## The Darker Side of Internal Organizational Politics

There is a common understanding between employees and organizations that there are mutual benefits to acting cooperatively, as it helps them to meet agreed collective goals. However, from time to time, individual and team agendas may differ from those of the organization. It is at this point that those with (or indeed without) power may use OP to protect their interests. These individuals, without any thought for colleagues or the organization, may engage in this behaviour as a means of either protecting or enhancing their position. In this way we would define OP as 'the actions which persons undertake, in pursuit of certain personally significant outcomes, to influence others whom they see as having the power of various kinds to facilitate or hinder those outcomes and also different and potentially conflicting concerns to their own' (Jones, 1987: 118). Consequently, OP is often seen as self-serving, highly manipulative and encouraging of exploitative behaviour. Is it any wonder that the following common value judgements are associated with OP?

- → 'Back-stabbing'
- → 'Vindictive'
- → 'Self-serving'
- → 'Exploitative'
- → 'Manipulative'
- → 'Underhand'
- → 'Lacking integrity'
- → 'Veiled in secrecy'
- → 'Self-interest'

→ 'Deliberate obfuscation'

→ 'Deception'

Individuals that use OP in a negative way have little by way of an internal moral compass to stop themselves from damaging others' reputation, so that they are perceived in a more favourable way by those typically higher up the hierarchical structure, and who therefore have the power to make decisions in these individuals' favour. A result of using OP in this way is that good colleagues are passed over for promotion as they are kept in inferior positions. Another consequence is that organizations, over a long period of time, are nudged in directions that add no value. Ultimately, individuals that are less qualified but good at the dark side of OP reap the benefits in terms of promotions, and therefore increased remuneration.

## What Causes Dark Side Organizational Politics?

There are two key reasons as to why dark side OP happens in the workplace. Firstly, the inherent nature of some individuals means that they are geared up for self-preservation and survival. In this way, OP might be seen as a natural response in assuring continuation and protection of an individual's workplace position. However, OP used in a negative way (for the benefit of certain individuals) is only possible in an already toxic workplace environment. For example, when a company is characterized by limited resources, poor organizational practices, lack of transparency as to how decisions are made and poor leadership, it is more likely that dark side internal politics will follow (Vredenburgh and Shea-VanFossen, 2010). In this environment, dark side internal politics is more likely to be accepted and, unfortunately, even expected.

## The Associated Cost of Dark Side Organizational Politics

Dark side OP can be seen as legitimizing illegitimate and unethical behaviour, so that the unacceptable becomes acceptable. This can be costly for organizations in terms of transparency, decency and ultimately the commitment of good employees, and often results in underlying feelings of unfairness and inequitableness in the way in which decisions are made, resources are used and, ultimately, who benefits. An understandable reaction to an organization that is highly politicized is that good employees withhold or restrict important information, views and opinions so that suboptimal decisions are made. Employees become fearful of being transparent in their views and the information they hold as they feel threatened by individuals that use their illegitimate influence for opportunistic gain. This is ultimately linked to poor job satisfaction, organizational commitment and job performance. In this sort of environment, significant organizational change is likely to fail as employees withdraw their efforts from a process in which they have little confidence.

## Organizational Politics as a Social Skill That Can Aid Transformational Change

So far we have seen how OP, when used for selfish gains, can skew and block the success of transformational change. However, OP is a two-sided coin. On the other side is the idea that for transformational change to be successful, positive workplace OP is a necessary skill and social function. Whilst OP has a poor reputation (due to what we outlined earlier on in this section), when used positively to influence others it can help managers effectively manage the process of transformational change. Snell et al. (2014: 756) consider managers' political skills to be a 'critical driver' of successful change. Their view is that not being aware of an organization's political nature leads to missed opportunities and unsuccessful change, as others that are more talented in this respect take the change initiative in an unwanted direction for the benefit of a few stakeholders.

Positive workplace OP can be defined as '… a combination of social astuteness, interpersonal influence, networking ability and apparent sincerity' (Snell et al.: 757). Social astuteness is the ability to understand and deal with the competing views and agendas of various stakeholder groups within an organization and, importantly, to create agreement between these various factions. This is about being able to make sense of their environment and understand what can be said to whom in order to get change done. We have already seen that a hallmark characteristic of power is its interpersonal nature and, likewise, its OP. Positive workplace OP can be used to positively influence the views and opinions of colleagues. Being able to influence and facilitate others to take on board new ways of working that are creative, time saving and involve the good use of resources is imperative to transformational change. Positive workplace OP can therefore be used to help bring about the organization's vision and strategy in the process of transformational change. Another aspect of positive workplace OP is the connectedness formed through the leveraging of network alliances. To be successful in transformation change a diverse lateral network of internal contacts is imperative. This means having a network of supporters at all levels of the organization. An objective is to leverage the network for additional support to encourage a positive outcome in transformational change. For example, those higher up in the network might be willing to support additional resources, whilst others might be willing to verbalize their support for change to positively influence others.

### ACTIVITY 6.4

1. Would you say that you are a 'political person'? Why/why not? Please explain.
2. Think about a recent situation in which you have used politics to positively influence a situation. Please explain.
3. Think about a historic situation where you have used politics in a not so good way to influence the outcome to your own advantage. Please explain.
4. How do you think positive workplace OP can influence a change initiative?
5. How do you think negative workplace OP can influence a change initiative?

## Understanding Resistance to Change

It is hardly surprising that not all transformational change projects succeed. One of the most commonly cited and complex issues associated with this type of change is employee resistance. Crail's (2007) survey of HR managers found that 91 per cent identify employee resistance as a significant problem in the effective management of change. Resistance occurs when individuals and groups passively or actively refuse to accept or comply with the organizational change initiative. Their objective is to maintain the status quo. Employee resistance to change, whether at an individual or group level, is commonly understood as something that must be overcome, and at any cost. This is illustrated by Clegg and Hardy (2004: 343) who state that: 'If employees don't want to change, then managers must use power – the ability to make them change despite their disinclination – against their resistance'. This view typically exists in the senior management team at the macro level of the organization. However, as we have seen, whilst power typically resides with the senior management team, subordinates can be effective in exercising their power, especially when this is done through the collective group. When employees and management clash in this way the workplace can become toxic, resulting in unpleasantness, hostilities and eventually poor workplace morale, all of which eventually combine to effect organizational performance. It is therefore important to understand resistance, to reduce the likelihood of conflict and manage it more effectively.

Resistance to change can sometimes be subtle. For example, employees may resist change by not paying attention to their workplace tasks, by intermittently taking sick leave and, in general, not being committed to the organization in any meaningful or productive way. Resistance to change can also result in more active and hostile behaviour. For example, employees that are part of a trade union may decide to strike to actively prevent change from happening. A well-known example of this is rail strikes, whereby disgruntled employees not only voice their views on the change, but also disrupt the change by going on strike, which draws the public's attention to how they are being treated by their employer.

Resistance to change is perceived differently by individuals and groups within the same organization. Some individuals and groups perceive resistance as deviant and incredibly disloyal to organizational values and senior management imperatives. They may perceive the resisting individuals or group as untrustworthy and may refuse to work, even ostracizing them from important meetings. On the other hand, some may see the resistors as incredibly brave, heroic and morally justified in their resistance. In this next section we unpack and explore the complex nature of resistance to change to develop a better understanding of why resistors resist, how change triggers emotional responses, and whether managers and leaders can alter their lens to accept resistance as being a valuable part of the change process.

## Reasons for Resisting Change

There is a plethora of reasons as to why transformational change is resisted. It might be because people feel uncomfortable when familiar daily work patterns are disrupted and altered, or from having experienced organizational change initiatives that have historically been poorly managed and resulted in ineffective outcomes. Change may also be resisted for any or all of the reasons listed below:

- Uncertainty and fear of the unknown
- Risk aversion
- Need for change not evident, feasible or practicable
- Personal losses including giving up current advantages
- Change and its implications not understood
- Change is juxtaposed against organizational values
- Change is unethical

- Fear of failure
- Lack of trust in leadership
- Resentment toward the initiator
- Inflexibility/low tolerance to change
- Power maintenance
- Structural stability
- Internal rivalries and vested interests
- Organizational culture
- Group and organizational norms

### ACTIVITY 6.5

1. It has been said that 'if employees don't want to change, then managers must use power – the ability to make them change despite their disinclination – against their resistance' (Hardy and Clegg, 2004: 343). What do you think is meant by this?
2. If you were or are currently a manager, how would you use your power to make employees change – despite their disinclination and against their will?
3. Do you think that this is an effective way of managing employee resistance? Please explain.

## Negative Emotions Triggered from Poorly Managed Change

Whatever the reason for resisting change, it appears likely that significant organizational change elicits a range of emotional responses from individuals and groups. Where change is managed well it is more likely that a combination of positive and negative emotions are triggered in people. However, when change is managed ineffectively, negative emotions are triggered in both the individuals and groups experiencing the change. There is a relative imbalance between positive and negative events in terms of triggering emotional reactions. People attach greater significance to negative events due to the potential harmful implications. In addition, negative workplace events (such as experiencing poorly managed change) are overly/obsessively analysed in comparison with positive events (Frijda, 1993). This may result in employees being unable to focus on their job, meaning they have fewer cognitive resources for job performance.

Affective Events Theory (AET) can be used to explain employees' emotions triggered by poorly managed change (Figure 6.2). Employees' affective reactions result directly from things that happen to them in the workplace and indirectly by perceptions of their workplace environment. In this way, an employee's endogenous affective disposition is chiefly influenced exogenously by their workplace environmental context. An affective workplace event triggers negative and positive emotions in employees including anger, fear, joy, love and sadness. There is an interrelationship between a workplace event, immediate emotions and subsequent slower workplace attitude and behaviour (Weiss and Cropanzano, 1996). An affective event is an emotional elicitation process. First, a workplace event occurs. This is subject to an initial appraisal, typically constructed along the lines of: *'what does this mean for me in view of the goals I want to attain?'* Discrete emotions then emanate from a more contextual consideration, typically evaluated in terms of 'the degree of personal control, coping potential, consequences of the event and future expectations about this situation' (Gaddis et al., 2004: 665), which subsequently impact workplace attitudes and behaviours.

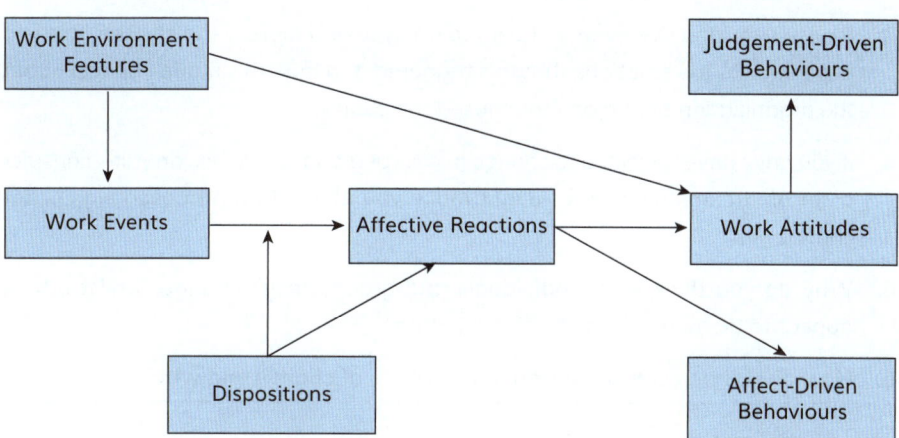

**Figure 6.2** Affective Events Theory (Weiss and Cropanzano, 1996).

Negative discrete emotions such as anger and frustration are linked to health issues such as stress and post-traumatic stress (Shaw, Erickson and Harvey 2011) and, in general, negative emotional responses to negative workplace experiences are associated with depression (Zineldin and Hytter, 2012). In this way, exposure to poorly managed change has been linked to negative personal and professional outcomes for individuals and groups, which eventually results in poor organizational performance. Rafferty and Jimmieson (2017) also found that employee wellbeing can be adversely affected by what they describe as 'exposure to organizational change'. This includes:

→ Poor mental health.

→ Increases in stress-related medication.

→ Poor health in general.

→ Workplace absences.

→ Intention to quit.

→ Hospital admissions.

→ Poor sleep patterns.

### ACTIVITY 6.6

1. Have you ever resisted a change in your professional or personal life? Please explain what the change was, how it made you feel emotionally and your reasons for objecting?

2. Please use Affective Events Theory to analyse and explain the change that you experienced, the emotions that this triggered and how this made you feel about the organization or person that caused the change.

3. If you have never objected to change in your personal or professional life, consider a set of circumstances that might make you object to a proposed significant change.

4. Why do you think some individuals and groups resist change, whilst others appear to be more accepting of a situation?

5. How do you perceive organizational resistors of change and why?

## Managing Resistance Effectively

There are financial and emotional costs of mismanaging transformational change. It is crucial, therefore, that organizations understand resistance and manage it well if they wish to succeed. A good point from which to start is adjusting managers and leaders' lens through which resistance is perceived. Unfortunately, one prevailing view is that resistance is not beneficial to an organization and needs to be overcome. This can result in time-consuming and unproductive clashes between employees, managers and leaders. It may also lead to suboptimal outcomes from poorly thought through change, which has not been challenged in any meaningful way. A more productive approach, despite being counterintuitive and uncomfortable for some managers and leaders, is to adjust their lens to accept resistance as a valid and valued part of the change process that, if listened to, is likely to result in better outcomes.

It is therefore important that managers and leaders recognize employees' emotional resistance cues. As we have discussed, resistance triggers an array of emotional responses in employees. These emotions are laden with informational and behavioural cues. An important characteristic of emotions is that many are interpersonal. This means that during interpersonal exchanges between managers, leaders and employees, emotions serve as an important conduit for transmitting and receiving valuable information. For example, anger as a response to transformational change may send a timely reg flag signal to managers and leaders to at least reflect on the *what* and *how* of change. This may result in taking corrective action such as improving transparency and communication to better manage employees' expectations in the change process, and thereby increasing the likelihood of a successful change initiative.

## Good Practices for Managing Resistance Effectively

### Understanding Individual Cognitive Processes

Resistance is a natural step for some individuals and groups in making sense of change. The cognitive processes that groups and individuals go through in coming to terms with change are illustrated by transition models such as those of Kübler-Ross (1969) and Bridges (2004). These models can be used by managers and leaders to provide insight into how employees may feel throughout the change process, and provide the opportunity to think through potential solutions to make the transition easier and less painful.

One of the classic and most commonly cited and influential transition models is that of Kübler-Ross (1969). See Figure 6.3.

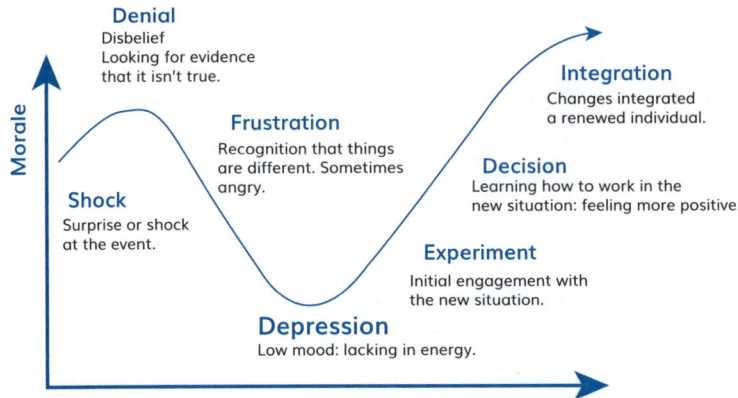

**Figure 6.3** The Kübler-Ross Change Curve (Kübler-Ross, E., 1969).

The Kübler-Ross model shows the various stages that people go through in coming to terms with a bereavement. These are shock, denial, frustration, depression, experimenting and testing. Latterly the model has been used to understand how people react to significant organizational change. The various stages are explained below:

1. Shock

    There has been little by way of communication that there is to be a significant change, so when the announcement is made, it is a considerable source of distress. Groups and individuals feel overwhelmed, they are in shock and thus immobilized. They cannot focus on their day-to-day work routines because their attention is consumed by feeling anxious and uncertain whilst they try to work out what the implication of the change is for them.

2. Denial

    In this stage there is a retreat from the current reality as individuals and groups refuse to believe that the change is happening. They instead immerse themselves in the 'old' ways of doing things from which they find comfort.

3. Frustration and Anger

    At this point, the reality of the change begins to permeate causing anger. People become frustrated as they feel that change is being forced upon them and that they have no choice in the matter.

**4.** Depression

This is the point in which reality sets in and it is understood that things will never be the same again. This causes misery, sadness and dejection. During this stage people are too tired to focus on the day-to-day activities that make up their job. An attitude of 'why bother?' and 'is this really worth the bother?' prevails. Hard-working and conscientious employees may, at this point, make the decision to leave the organization as they do not wish to be part of the change initiative nor part of the organization's future going forwards.

**5.** Experimenting and Testing

Over a period of time those that decide to stay start to experiment with new ways of doing things.

**6.** Decision (Acceptance)

Eventually, where people decide to stay in the organization, the new ways of doing things are accepted and internalized. People take on board new ways of completing tasks, affirming the change through their behaviour. They also demonstrate their acceptance by being proactive.

**7.** Integration

Eventually the change is fully integrated to the extent that it becomes the expected way of doing things.

Another useful framework to help managers and leaders understand the cognitive processes that individuals and groups go through in coming to terms with significant change was put forward by Bridges (2004). This constitutes three separate transition processes:

**1.** Endings.

**2.** Neutral zone.

**3.** New beginnings.

The first transition process is endings. This is about disengaging from the old ways of doing things. This is incredibly painful for people, as not only are they comfortable with their familiar work practices, it is also likely they have been successful in their accomplishments. Moreover, these work practices are part of their perceived identity, which they value and which they feel is being threatened by change. The neutral zone is also an uncomfortable experience whereby people are confronted by the reality of having to let go of old practices and confront the future. In this way, they are stuck between the old and new reality. Whilst painful, this is when the real transition takes place, as people start adjusting and eventually come to terms with the new reality, resulting in transformation. Unfortunately however, some people are unable to move on from the first and second stage. They either get stuck in the old ways or do not give themselves enough time to adjust during the neutral zone. It is likely that these people leave the organization because they cannot or will not adapt. The third stage is about new beginnings. However, similar to the first and second transition process, this is not without difficulties, because new behaviours feel unfamiliar. People do not yet have the required experience to be confident and competent. Nonetheless, this is a more positive stage in the process because people have generally accepted the new reality and are starting to experiment and move forwards.

Throughout the three stages in Bridge's transition model organizational productivity ebbs and flows. During the neutral zone, productivity is poor. However, with the acceptance of new beginnings, productivity increases. See Figure 6.4 for an overview of Bridges' Model.

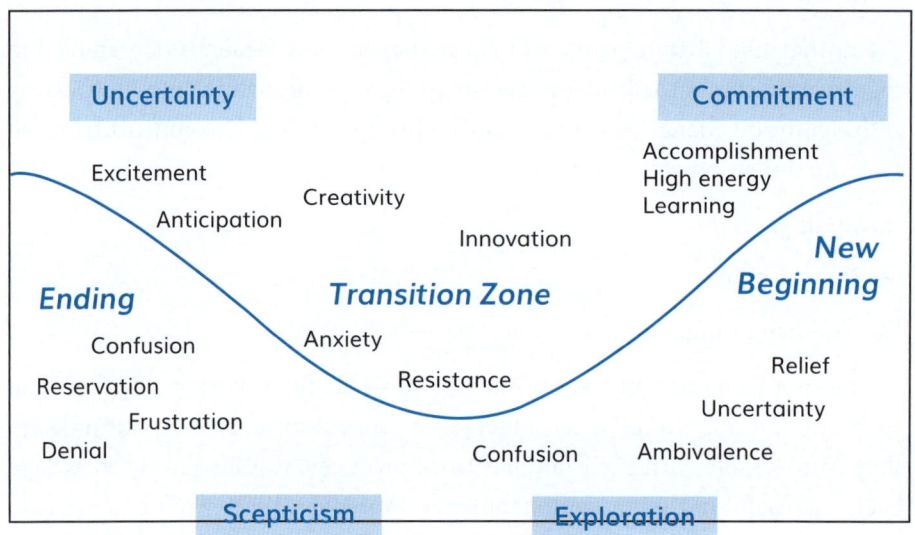

**Figure 6.4** Bridges' Transition Model (Bridges, 2004).

## Emotional Intelligence

For managers and leaders to be successful in understanding the emotive temperature of resistance it is essential they have emotional intelligence. The concept of emotional intelligence was originally put forward by Salovey and Mayer in 1990. However, it was made part of popular psychology in Goleman's 1995 account of Mayer and Salovey (1993) where emotional intelligence is defined as 'the ability to perceive emotions, to access and generate emotions so as to assist thoughts, to understand emotions and emotional knowledge, and to reflectively regulate emotions so as to promote emotional and intellectual growth' (Mayer and Salovey, 1993: 5).

Emotional intelligence is flexible and developed through experience. It is the ability to recognize and understand one's own emotions to make better decisions. For example, after receiving an email that triggers anger, an instinctive reaction is to send a return email that expresses this anger. However, if the recipient has good emotional intelligence, they will recognize that the email has triggered anger and wait until they are calm before sending a response.

Emotional intelligence is made up of four components:

- **Self-awareness** is foundational to the concept of emotional intelligence. This is about being in touch with one's self, including having self-insight, which is the ability to know when you are sad, angry, happy and so forth. Another important aspect of self-awareness is understanding what has triggered the emotional response.

- **Self-management** is the ability to control and manage harmful negative emotions, such as anger and fear. Anger and fear can be destructive in as much as they are an obstacle to being confident and therefore impede good decisions from being made. If, however, you are good at self-management, then you are more able to recognize, managing and control your emotions. Consequently, anger or fear are less likely to act as a roadblock to the successful completion of tasks, goals and objectives.

- **Social awareness** which constitutes empathy, is core to emotional intelligence. Empathy is the ability to 'put yourself in someone else's shoes'. Empathy has two facets: cognitive empathy and affective empathy. Cognitive empathy means being able to understand someone else, so you *know* how others are feeling. Affective empathy is *feeling* how someone else is feeling. For example, if we witness someone falling over and hurting themselves, we can instantaneously identify with the shock the fall has caused alongside the possible humiliation and physical pain. The important point here is that, if we are able to identify with how others are feeling, we can manage them in a more effective way, motivating them towards achieving organizational goals. We are also more able to respond to their concerns and needs.

- **Relationship awareness** is the ability to have effective and positive interpersonal relationships by virtue of being a good role model and having the ability to articulate and persuade others to work towards achieving organizational goals and objectives. A person with relationship awareness manages to get change done through influencing and managing others in way that is responsive and supportive.

- **Self-motivation**, the emphasis here being on 'self', is when individuals are motivated intrinsically to attain personal and professional goals. They are driven by their internally held values to attain high standards, juxtaposed to being driven extrinsically, for example, by high remuneration.

If we are able to recognize and manage our own emotions, we can better recognize, understand and manage the emotions of others as they experience change. Emotional intelligence as a competence is especially desirable in managers and leaders because it enables them to communicate more effectively, including articulating a better future following change, alongside managing conflicts that arise during the change process.

## Working Alongside the Resistors

There is some early and interesting work by Karp (1984) which is relevant to organizations going through substantial change. Karp's view is that resistance needs to be dealt with respectfully. Instead of being labelled as dysfunctional and deviant, resistance should be treated as an asset. Karp's (1984) strategy for working with resistors consists of the following four features:

- Surfacing the resistance;
- Honouring the resistance;

→ Exploring the resistance; and

→ Rechecking the resistance.

'Surfacing' is about bringing 'out in the open' exactly what it is that resistors object to. This can put resistors in a vulnerable position because it likely shines an unwanted spotlight on them. However, if managers and leaders are serious about respecting resistance, then a safe environment can be created as trust develops and grows. An objective of 'surfacing' is gaining clarity and transparency as to what is being objected to, so that it can reasonably be addressed. Listening to the resistors is critical to honouring the resistance. In listening to the resistors, not only is valuable information gained, interpersonal relationships are improved between the resistors and those that are driving the change. Where surfacing and honouring are effective it becomes easier to explore the resistance in more granular detail. In this process, drivers of change need to be conscious and discern between 'faux' (fake) and genuine resistance. Faux resistance is typically associated with the resistor themselves and likely a result of previous bad experiences and poor interpersonal relationships. Genuine resistance, however, is a competent and articulated statement of what is being objected to in the current circumstances. This can then be explored by asking probing questions to gain a better understanding. Finally, rechecking occurs to ensure that everyone has the same understanding. At this point it might be that perceptions, views and objectives have altered on both sides, so it is worth rechecking to ascertain that everyone's understanding is at least similar. Overall, this process allows resistance to be dealt with in a more positive way, making it less likely to act as a blocker to change.

## A Situational Approach to Resistance

Given that resistance can constitute a number of different passive and reactive behaviours, a more considered response to resistance takes on board the context in which change and resistance are taking place. Consideration can then be given to the most appropriate method(s) in the prevailing circumstances. This is supported by Kotter and Schlesinger (2008), who put forward six approaches for managing resistance with the caveat that managers should use more than one method if that is what the situation requires. See Figure 6.5 before completing the activity below.

| Method | How to Use | When to Use | Advantages | Drawbacks |
|---|---|---|---|---|
| Education | Communicate the desired changes and reasons for them | Employees lack information about the change's implications | Once persuaded, people often help implement the change | Time-consuming if lots of people are involved |
| Participation | Involve potential resisters in designing and implementing the change | Change initiators lack sufficient information to design the change | People feel more committed to making the change happen | Time-consuming, and employees may design inappropriatete change |
| Facilitation | Provide skills training and emotional support | People are resisting because they fear they can't make the needed adjustments | No other approach works as well with adjustment problems | Can be time-consuming and expensive; can still fail |
| Negotiation | Offer incentives for making the change | People will lose out in the change and have considerable power to resist | It's a relatively easy way to defuse major resistance | Can be expensive and open managers to the possibility of blackmail |
| Coercion | Threaten loss of jobs or promotion opportunities; fire or transfer those who can't or won't change | Speed is essential and change initiators possess considerable power | It works quickly and can overcome any kind of resistance | Can spark intense resentment toward change initiators |

**Figure 6.5** Methods for Managing Resistance. (Kotter and Schlesinger, 2008).

## ACTIVITY 6.7

1. Look carefully at the various methods for managing resistance outlined in Figure 6.5, alongside their pros and cons. Which of these approaches would you use to best manage the various transition stages in the Kübler-Ross change curve? Please use the table below to complete this activity.

| Kübler-Ross | Method | Rationale |
|---|---|---|
| Stage One: Shock | | |
| Stage Two: Denial | | |
| Stage Three: Frustration and Anger | | |
| Stage Four: Depression | | |
| Stage Five: Experimenting and Testing | | |

##  CONSULTANCY IN THE CHAIR

### Cup of Kindness Activity

Unfortunately, since the merger, CUP has become a highly politicized environment. In your role as an objective consultant, you have conducted many interviews with employees who are disenfranchised with the current situation. Some of the phrases and words employees are using to describe the environment are as follows:

- 'Back-stabbing'
- 'Vindictive'
- 'Self-serving'
- 'Exploitative'
- 'Manipulative'
- 'Underhand'
- 'Lacking integrity'
- 'Veiled in secrecy'
- 'Self-interest'
- 'Deliberate obfuscation'
- 'Deception'

### Question

What advice will you give to the CEO to turn this situation around? What is your recommended approach?

**Competency-based Interview Question**

1. Can you give an example of when you have not managed resistance to change well and what you learnt from this experience, especially in terms of what you would do to improve your approach going forwards?

## Chapter Summary

This chapter has covered the need to be mindful of the pivotal role that power, politics and resistance take in significant organizational change initiatives, no matter the position you occupy within an organization. Power, politics and resistance have been conceptualized through a different, positive lens, which lends insight into how to use these phenomena to influence change in a way that benefits an organization and its key stakeholders. Nonetheless, we must remember that where power and politics are misused, significant change is likely to fail, not least because of the implications of the dark side of power. We have also visualized the individual transition processes that employees go through in coming to terms with significant change, and how managers and leaders need to be aware of emotionally laden signals to help them adjust their approach to managing resistance to change more effectively. Finally, we have proposed some good practices in managing resistance to change in a meaningful way to enhance the likelihood of change being successful and sustainable.

## Bibliography

Bridges, W. (2004), *Transitions: Making Sense of Life's Changes*, second edition. London: Perseus Publishing.

Clegg, S. R. and Hardy, C. (2004), 'Power and Change: A Critical Reflection', in J. J. Boonstra (ed), *Dynamics of Organizational Change and Learning*. Chichester: John Wiley & Sons Ltd.

Crail, M. (2007), 'HR's Role in Managing Organizational Change'. *IRS Employment Review*, 885, November 19.

Dahl, R. A. (1957), 'The Concept of Power'. *Behavioral Science*, 2(3): 201–15. DOI: https://doi.org/10.1002/bs.3830020303.

Goleman, D. (2010), *Emotional Intelligence: Why it can Matter More than IQ*. London: Bloomsbury.

Etzioni, A. (1975), *A Comparative Analysis of Complex Organizations: On Power, Involvement, and Their Correlates*. New York: Free Press.

French, J. R. P., Jr. and Raven, B. (1959), 'The Bases of Social Power', in D. Cartwright (ed), *Studies in Social Power* (pp. 150–67). Ann Arbor: University of Michigan.

Frijda, N. H. (1993), 'The Place of Appraisal in Emotion', *Cognition and Emotion*, 7(3–4): 357–87. DOI: https://doi.org/10.1080/02699939308409193.

Gaddis, B., Connelly, S. and Mumford, M. D. (2004), 'Failure Feedback as an Affective Event: Influences of Leader Affect on Subordinate Attitudes and Performance'. *The Leadership Quarterly*, 15(5): 663–86.

Holbeche, L. (2016), *Influencing Organizational Effectiveness: A Critical Take on the HR Contribution*. London: Routledge. DOI: https://doi.org/10.4324/9781315815862.

Jones, S. (1987), 'Organisational Politics - Only the Darker Side?', *Management Education and Development*, 18(2): 116–28. DOI: https://doi.org/10.1177/135050768701800206.

Karp, H. B. (1984), 'Working with Resistance', *Training & Development Journal (0041-0861)*, 38(3): 69.

Kipnis, D., Schmidt, S. M. and Wilkinson, I. (1980), 'Intraorganizational Influence Tactics: Explorations in Getting One's Way'. *Journal of Applied Psychology*, 65(4): 440.

Kotter, J. P. and Schlesinger, L. A. (2008), *Choosing Strategies for Change*, Harvard Business Review. Boston: Harvard Business School Press.

Kübler-Ross, E. (1969), *On Death and Dying*. New York: Touchstone.

Mansaray, H. E. (2019), 'The Role of Leadership Style in Organisational Change Management: A Literature Review, *Journal of Human Resource Management*, 7(1): 18–31.

Mayer, J. D. and Salovey, P. (1993), 'The Intelligence of Emotional Intelligence'. *Intelligence*, 17(4): 433–42.

Rafferty, A. E. and Jimmieson, N. L. (2017), 'Subjective Perceptions of Organizational Change and Employee Resistance to Change: Direct and Mediated Relationships with Employee Well-being'. *British Journal of Management*, 28(2): 248–64. DOI: https://doi.org/10.1111/1467-8551.12200.

Shaw, J. B., Erickson, A. and Harvey, M. (2011), 'A Method for Measuring Destructive Leadership and Identifying Types of Destructive Leaders in Organizations'. *The Leadership Quarterly*, 22(4): 575–90. DOI: https://doi.org/10.1016/j.leaqua.2011.05.001.

Simpson, J. A., Farrell, A. K., Oriña, M. M. and Rothman, A. J. (2015), 'Power and Social Influence in Relationships', in M. Mikulincer, P. R. Shaver, J. A. Simpson and J. F. Dovidio (eds), *APA Handbook of Personality and Social Psychology, Vol. 3. Interpersonal Relations* (pp. 393–420). American Psychological Association. DOI: https://doi.org/10.1037/14344-015.

Snell, S. J., Tonidandel, S., Braddy, P. W. and Fleenor J. W. (2014), 'The Relative Importance of Political Skill Dimensions for Predicting Managerial Effectiveness'. *European Journal of Work and Organizational Psychology*, 23(6): 915–29. DOI:https://doi.org/10.1080/1359432X.2013.817557.

Vredenburgh, D. and Shea-VanFossen, R. (2010), 'Human Nature, Organizational Politics, and Human Resource Development'. *Human Resource Development Review*, 9(1): 26–47. DOI: https://doi.org/10.1177/1534484309343094.

Weber, M. (1978), *Economy and Society: An Outline of Interpretive Sociology, Vol. I*, ed. Guenther Roth and Claus Wittich. Los Angeles: University of California Press.

Weiss, H. M. and Cropanzano, R. (1996), 'Affective Events Theory: A Theoretical Discussion of the Structure, Causes and Consequences of Affective Experiences at Work', in B. M. Staw and L. L. Cummings (eds), *Research in Organizational Behavior: An Annual Series of Analytical Essays and Critical Reviews*, Vol. 18, 1–74. Oxford: Elsevier Science/JAI Press.

Willer, David, Lovaglia, M. J. and Markovsky, B. (1997), 'Power and Influence: Theoretical Bridge'. *Social Forces*, 76(2): 571–604.

Zineldin, M. and Hytter, A. (2012), 'Leaders' Negative Emotions and Leadership Styles Influencing Subordinates' Well-being'. *The International Journal of Human Resource Management*, 23(4): 748–58.

# The Role of Change Leadership

**7**

## Learning Outcomes

At the end of this chapter you will be able to:

1. Explain the general importance of leadership in organizational change.
2. Distinguish between different types of leadership theory and style that affect organizational change, including leading change versus managing change.
3. Identify ways in which leaders can seek to strategically transform organizations.
4. Understand and explain critiques of change leadership and its limitations.
5. Understand and explain the importance of developing and encouraging diverse change leadership more widely and responsibly in organizations.

## Introduction

This chapter reviews and critically reflects on relationships between leadership and change. The general importance of linking topics of leadership and organizational change is discussed in terms of what is expected from change leaders, and the different styles and activities they may engage in. Leading change is distinguished from managing change to some degree, although both are important to ensuring its effective implementation. The ways in which top leadership teams, particularly chief executives, attempt to lead strategic change are explored, and it is argued that very different types of leadership can be effective at different times and in different change conditions. Leadership development and bottom-up forms of organizational change are explored to challenge the idea that change leadership is always down to strong, charismatic individuals taking decisive action, and can instead be just as effective if shared, democratic and diverse. Critiques of change leadership are summarized in terms of the political and ethical dilemmas surrounding it, and incompetent and destructive forms of change leadership are covered. Finally, perspectives on reimagining change leadership are discussed, illustrating the importance of continuing to debate the kinds of leadership that are needed and hoped for as organizational life continues to change.

## Leadership and Organizational Change

The results of a survey of 259 senior executives in Fortune 500 companies in the US, published by the American Management Association, found that 92 per cent of those surveyed mentioned leadership as an important 'key to successful change', topping corporate values (84 per cent) and communication (75 per cent), the two next most popular responses (Gill, 2002). This indicates that leadership is often perceived as one of the most, if not *the* most, important factor in managing change successfully.

The purpose of this chapter is to ask questions and reflect on the general nature and importance of leadership in relation to organizational change. The two concepts of change and leadership would appear to be intimately related; it is hard to imagine a leader avoiding or not being involved in organizational change, and it is hard to imagine organizational change happening effectively without some form of leadership. Combining the two creates the distinct term *change leadership*, a competency which has been defined as the 'ability to influence and enthuse others, through personal advocacy, vision and drive, and to access resources to build a solid platform for change' (Higgs and Rowland, 2000: 124).

It seems important to acknowledge that change leadership may be difficult to distinguish from leadership in general, and at times be difficult to distinguish from different forms of change *agency* or *competency* that facilitate organizational change. This is because leadership can take many forms and be shown by many different people at different times and under different circumstances. Nevertheless, many stakeholders and people in and around organizations – employees, teams, customers, trade unions, shareholders, communities – look to leaders and leadership for direction and guidance in terms of pursuing goals, solutions and improvements. Leaders are therefore likely to be simultaneously involved in responding to change and setting change agendas.

A relatively simple and helpful way to begin analysing leadership and organizational change context is to break it down into a series of reflections on four main questions:

1. **Person:** Who are they? What types of personality characteristics does the leader have? Do they have values and behaviours reflecting a style of leadership? What is their social and demographic background? What life and career experiences are relevant to their leadership?

2. **Result:** What change outcomes are they seeking to deliver? What are their metrics for success and failure? Do they have a clear vision and set of goals?

3. **Position:** Where are they located in the organization and what roles do they play? How much responsibility and control over key resources do they have? Are they a frontline, mid-level or senior leader? Is their leadership shared or distributed with leaders in other positions? Are they an outsider or an insider relative to the organization and its stakeholders? Who follows them, and who does not?

4. **Process:** How does this leader manage organizational change over time? Do they use tools or interventions? How do they respond when something does not go to plan? How do they keep change momentum going? How do they share work and cooperate with those following them? How do they deal with possible beginnings and ends of change, as well as the stages in between?

In the twenty-first century the field of leadership, whether related explicitly to change or not, has become very extensive, with over 100 years of research and many different theories and perspectives continuing to emerge. In addition, the field has seen the introduction of specialist journals, investments and agendas. Nevertheless, as with the four questions above, it is important not to get overwhelmed, but rather to remain open to different theories. It is also important to recognize that no single leadership theory gives a full picture, but that different types of theory emphasize different pieces of a more complex overall picture of relationships, resources and circumstances.

For instance, some of the most traditional leadership theories do emphasize the individual *person* (e.g. a 'hero' or 'great' figure), while others try to differentiate between various leadership *styles* (e.g. controlling or democratic). Further theories focus on how the effectiveness of different types of leadership is *contingent* ('depends upon'), and how features of the *situation*, such as the type of task or power dynamic/influence between leaders and their subordinates, can impact the success of change. We might also add leadership contingencies based on the *change situation,* because it is easy to imagine different leaders and different forms of leadership being more effective in different types of organizational change context (e.g. a crisis versus a planned restructuring), or during different phases of change (e.g. a launch event versus an end-of-year evaluation). Finally, there are a variety of perspectives that are more *critical* or sceptical about the positive role or general importance of leadership. For example, there is a risk that we overemphasize leadership influences on change, when in fact it is difficult to isolate leaders' influence relative to other factors, such as culture, politics, economics and technology.

## Leadership Styles and Managing Change

Fundamentally, the idea of various leadership *styles* has remained very influential, because it speaks to the idea that we see and experience many kinds of leadership methods, characteristics and behaviours in different organizational change contexts. At the same time, there have always been debates about how to define and measure the many different potential styles, their associated behaviours and dimensions, as well as positive and negative views of their relative advantages and disadvantages in different situations.

One influential – if not *the most* influential – distinction that has been made in recent decades is between *transactional* leadership, based on a series of exchanges or bargains between leaders and followers, and *transformational* leadership, where a leader inspires or transforms followers to go beyond basic exchanges and emotionally and motivationally participate in a shared vision. A third style is *laissez-faire* leadership, which, in contrast to the other two, is typified by an extremely passive avoidance or absence of leadership decision-making and responsibility. All three styles can be, and have been, measured through various versions of a Multifactor Leadership Questionnaire (MLQ), with which leaders can assess themselves, but also be assessed by multiple raters – such as superiors, peers, subordinates and others – in a 360-degree fashion (e.g. see Den Hartog, Van Muijen and Koopman, 1997).

While there has been much emphasis on transformational leadership as a positive style due to its charismatic approach, imbued with qualities of integrity and a commitment to developing followers and inspiring extra effort from them, we should try to avoid simplistic assumptions that it is always the 'best' style in isolation. This is because it is possible to think of different organizational change situations where elements of transactional and laissez-faire styles may represent more effective approaches. For example, a transactional leadership style may be effective in situations where followers need clarity to solve a short-term problem or task quickly, and a laissez-faire style may be appropriate where employees are already highly capable, motivated and independent.

In any case, other related, overlapping leadership styles continue to be proposed and are likely to be considered in combination with transformational leadership. Examples of these other styles include *authentic* leadership, which emphasizes ethics, open communication and self-awareness, and *servant* leadership, where a leader makes considerable effort to empathize with their team and put the team's interests before their own. One other example, particularly emphasized in relation to change crisis situations affecting large numbers of people, such as the COVID-19 pandemic, is *compassionate* leadership, which emphasizes the importance of leaders developing a style that embodies care and support for the wellbeing and inclusion of diverse other people (Ramachandran, Balasubramanian, James and Al Masaeid, 2023).

One classic, traditional leadership debate, often set for students to answer, has been whether (great) leadership is 'born or made'. That is, to what extent certain individuals are 'born' especially suited to leadership in general because of relatively fixed competence, power and personality attributes. However, strong arguments for the 'born to be a leader' view are increasingly being challenged by the argument that many people can, and need to, develop and show many different types of leadership, with learning and adaptations 'made' according to different hierarchical distances, cultural expectations and follower relationships (Blackmore-Wright, 2023).

Nevertheless, a version of this debate persists in thinking about how 'great' leadership involves a challenging path of *development*, where an individual must question their leadership capabilities. To do this effectively they must take their identities, career achievements and relationships into consideration, noting how they affect others in their drive towards organizational success. Becoming a 'great' leader may be a very difficult task, but it is also a very valuable one, if it results in someone becoming a top leader that can move an organization and its people toward greatness.

This approach of striving to become a great leader is championed by Jim Collins in his 2001 book *Good to Great*. Here, a 'level 5 leader' reflects someone in an organization who has an extra executive leadership dimension in their skills and characteristics, beyond the four levels of being a 'good' contributing individual, team member, manager or leader, helping to improve others' performance. Collins draws attention to the distinguished, paradoxical mixture in level 5 leaders of being both humble and highly ambitious and focused at the same time. Collins also advises top leaders to combine their level 5 behaviour with other success factors, such as surrounding themselves with the right people who can perform brilliantly for what is coming next, and creating a culture of discipline in people, allowing them to focus on a shared passion for reaching standards and delivering results (Collins, 2005).

## Distinctions Between Leading and Managing Change

Another classic leadership debate relevant to organizational change concerns the distinction between *leading* change and *managing* change (Table 7.1). Often the two have been contrasted as involving different activities, such that leading is seen as the more proactive and positive work of creating and initiating change through vision, innovation and risk-taking. Conversely, managing roles and activities are more associated with conforming to and controlling the implementation of change. In a famous 2001 article, John Kotter argued that most US organizations were 'over-managed' and 'under-led'. This referred to the idea that managers help keep large complex organizations orderly and controlled in terms of plans and budgets, but when it comes to coping with change, organizations need to develop more leadership, which is what sets a direction and motivates people to engage in it.

| Leading Organizational Change | Managing Organizational Change |
|---|---|
| • Inspiring vision<br>• Entrepreneurship<br>• Integrity and honesty<br>• Risk-taking<br>• Creativity<br>• Experimentation<br>• Using power | • Empowering others<br>• Team building<br>• Managing resistance<br>• Conflict resolution<br>• Networking<br>• Knowledge of the business<br>• Problem solving |
| More common to both leading and managing?<br>• Learning from others<br>• Adaptability and flexibility<br>• Openness to new ideas | |

**Table 7.1** Leading Versus Managing Change (adapted from Caldwell, 2003)

## ACTIVITY 7.1

1. Imagine you are a consultant advising an organization as they go through substantial change. During a meeting with a manager and leader the senior management team ask you to explain their different roles during the process of change. Please use Table 7.1 to help you explain to them how their roles will differ. Please include examples.

The focus of the leading versus managing change debate is about how much the two roles overlap, how much they differ and how to balance or combine the two. It is therefore important not to overemphasize the value of one at the expense of neglecting the other, because both are likely to be *complementary*, with each helping the other. For example, if a leader initiates or envisions a change from the top of an organization, then a manager can help facilitate progress and build support for the change among more specific units and functions in the middle of the organization (Caldwell, 2003). Similarly, if a leader sets out broad principles for future developments, a manager can focus on the more specific and urgent day-to-day plans, tools, needs and impacts for people doing more specific work (McHale, 2020).

Ultimately, there may be a tendency to see leadership as more high status, attractive and effective than management, but this should not lead us to overlook the fact that most leaders or leadership teams will need to be able to switch between and combine the qualities of both in practice. Relatedly, different people may also prefer or be more suited to either managing or leading, in relation to their career paths or strengths.

## ACTIVITY 7.2

1. During substantial change, would you prefer to be a manager or leader? Please explain why.

# Change Leadership Requirements

In general, there are likely to be various change leadership roles, competencies and capabilities required to help manage change across the organization. One way to break these change leadership requirements down and specify them more clearly is by asking questions about the work of *effective change implementation* (Higgs and Rowland, 2000):

1. The **'why'** – making the case for change by establishing purpose, objectives and readiness.

2. The **'where'** – outlining a new future for change by establishing what to focus on, what to ignore and what to create.

3. The **'how'** of implementation – elaborating on how the change will be supported by a strategy, set of interventions, change agents and metrics.

4. The **'how'** of keeping the change going – sustaining the momentum of change by reinforcing, aligning, adjusting and learning new behaviours.

Finally, while leadership styles for managing change are typically defined by what leaders do, they can also be considered in relation to what potential *followers* or *recipients* of change in the wider workforce experience, and the kinds of support or resources they are expecting in their relationship with potential change leaders. For example, in a study of financial services employees working in London, top managers were found to try to lead change by responding to external pressures in ways that would keep the organization cost-efficient, profitable and competitive. However, as well as responding to macro conditions outside the organization, effective change leaders must also pay attention to the energy of employees, particularly in terms of how capable and able to cope they feel regarding changes to *their* jobs and working arrangements. Typically, change leaders need to ensure others are coping effectively with change by equipping them with the necessary resources, relationships, skills, information and recognition they are hoping to receive (Woodward and Hendry, 2004).

A healthy relationship between leaders and followers is conveyed in Steve Cooper's account of how he led the English Premier League football club, Nottingham Forest, through change during his time as manager between 2021 and 2023. Specifically, Cooper has described his leadership style as seeking to drive standards while retaining a sense of humility, gratitude and care towards the team. This involved him sharing leadership with a group of senior players to create a suitable environment for integrating diverse new international players so they can cope with adversity, learn to adjust their performances and understand how to work, play and train together as effectively as possible (Bate, 2023). Latterly, the role of head coach at Nottingham Forest has been taken up by the Portuguese former goalkeeper Nuno Espírito Santo who also appears to be a role model for humble leadership. Nuno has taken Nottingham Forest from fighting against relegation to being third in the Premier League. Forest appear to have undergone some further transformation. This is described in an article published in *The Guardian* as being transformed from 'circus to contenders' (Unwin, 2024). The transformational change is illustrated by some of the stats, including that this is the first time that the club won three consecutive matches in the Premier League since 1999, in other words their best performance for at least a quarter of a century. Nuno's humble leadership is illustrated in an article 'It's about the players – humble Nuno plays down his role as Nottingham Forest reach third place in Premier League' (Gillen, 2024) and by several interviews.

### ACTIVITY 7.3

1. Read through the two online summary articles about Nuno and the transformation at Nottingham Forest. Reflect on any views you have with regard to the type of leadership implied by the articles.

2. Listen to the interview with Nuno and again reflect on any thoughts you have with regard to Nuno's type of leadership.

3. Overall, how do you think Nuno's type of leadership may have transformed Nottingham Forest and why and how?

## Transforming Organizations Through Leadership

To transform an organization through planned, intentional, strategic change requires leaders to make difficult choices about the demands of the situation and the leadership style(s) best suited to meet the circumstances. For instance, if there is sufficient time available and favourable interest in change from groups within the organization, a more collaborative, gradual approach may be suitable. On the other hand, if there is support for change from organizational groups but less time available for participation, a more charismatic and visionary leadership approach may be better. However, in cases where leaders face opposition, they may decide to employ a more coercive, directive style to force evolution, or, more urgently, ensure an organization survives by dictating the fulfilment of some overriding priority (Dunphy and Stace, 1988).

These sorts of varying situational contingencies help us understand why there are contrasting types of leaders in the world around us, as different types of people seek to bring about transformation in different ways, under different conditions, with varying degrees of success or adaptability. For example some leaders do act more like 'tyrants' or 'lone geniuses' that are difficult and demanding for followers to work with, and yet have admirably high ambitions and a record for getting results – we might think of master chefs, movie directors or visionary founders and entrepreneurs as likely to be in this category. At the same time, other successful leaders take a 'mothering' approach to their followers, giving them much freedom and positive encouragement to support them in shared team endeavours (Coget, Shani and Solari, 2014).

This difference in leadership styles raises further questions regarding how transformational organizational change might be accomplished effectively through more than one leader; with change leaders working in combination or through a complementary balance of abilities. Based on forty years' experience studying organizational change, Beer and Nohria (2000) suggested that leading organizational change involves striving to resolve the tensions between two leadership approaches, labelled Theory E and Theory O. *Theory E* refers to the 'E'conomic need to respond to changes in the organization's wider economic and strategic environment, while *Theory O* refers to the 'O'rganizational need to help the organization's internal workforce respond to changes.

In a specific example, Beer and Nohria (2000) suggest that the UK supermarket chain ASDA managed to successfully recover from near-bankruptcy in 1991 and positively transform its structure and culture by having two complementary change leaders working to resolve conflicts between the Theories E and O of change. Theory E was largely addressed by the CEO Archie Norman, while Theory O was largely addressed by Allan Leighton, another executive hired to work closely alongside him. Both leaders shared E and O values but had very different personalities and styles that they could capitalize on – Archie could be 'respected' for making difficult structural and financial decisions from the top of the organization, while Allan could be 'loved' for creating emotional commitment to the change and connection with the organization at large. In practice, combining Theory E and Theory O is likely to be challenging, but having two carefully partnered senior leaders working together to embrace both theories between them offers a powerful suggestion of how to attempt it.

The blending of leadership styles, forms and activities as a necessary part of accomplishing successful transformational change has been supported by other researchers. For example, in a study of several multinational organizations based in Australia, Graetz (2000) found that strategic change leadership typically demanded blending an *instrumental* style or role (focused on technical, design, planning, control, resources and improvement issues) with a *charismatic* style or role (focused on inspiration, trust, emotions and drive issues). It is likely that multiple leadership figures are needed to collectively balance these 'hard' and 'soft' sides of strategic change; to act as role models and ensure buy-in from other potential change leaders, agents and recipients across the organization.

Another key question concerning transformational change leaders and leadership asks where their power, status and influence come from. We dealt with the six main 'bases' of power (e.g. Raven, 1993) in Chapter 6. Do reflect on your learning from this chapter to remind yourself of these bases.

A leader's awareness of these power bases, in relation to themselves and others, can help them think about which forces of influence might help or hinder the leadership of transformational organizational change. The effectiveness of power bases is likely to vary under different organizational conditions, such as the relationships with different targets of influence, and the importance of needing to monitor the compliance of others. Power can also take on more forceful or manipulative forms in more extreme contexts where people are influenced without their full awareness or agreement.

As well as seeking to draw on different power bases to lead change, leaders can also attempt to ensure transformational change by leading their organizations through the phases or steps of well-known stage models of change. Chief among these is the eight-step plan developed by John Kotter in his 1996 book *Leading Change*, based on his work consulting with large US companies (e.g. see Finnie and Norris, 1997):

1. Establish a sense of urgency (identify and discuss crises and opportunities).
2. Create a guiding coalition (form a group with power and skills to work together).
3. Develop a vision and strategy (encourage effort, goals and direction).
4. Communicate the change vision (use channels and key people to get the message out).
5. Empower broad action (remove obstacles and encourage new ideas and activities).
6. Generate short-term wins (show, recognize and reward visible improvements).
7. Join up gains for more change (keep refining new projects, themes and people).
8. Anchor new approaches in culture (make sure employees see and promote results).

These types of stage models are helpful as they suggest areas and sequences for leaders to pay attention to when creating their plans and taking actions to ensure best change leadership practice. At the same time, however, they can be criticized as being prescriptive and idealistic, because they suggest that simply following a series of specific steps will always lead to positive results. Following the steps may offer no guarantees of successful change in particular contexts and circumstances. In addition, such models tend to be based on anecdotes – stories from CEOs at companies that were successful at a given point in time – rather than providing more precise evidence for how leaders' actions cause certain effects in organizational change.

Nevertheless, leading organizations through transformational changes clearly requires planning and sequencing a series of potential activities and interventions with an appropriate focus and in an appropriate order. Good timing from change leaders may help to capture opportunities better, build change momentum and spread or pace effort and energy so there is not a need to do many things at once. Leaders will need to carefully consider how they shift their attention between interventions focused on changing structures, processes, beliefs and relationships in their organizations (Huy, 2001). There may be a need for leaders to think about the *rhythms* of how they lead change and when it makes sense to separate or combine interventions. Some conditions may call for a sudden and dramatic revolution, but often leaders need to plan and make time for change to happen among their followers more gradually and experimentally (Huy and Mintzberg, 2003).

Leading organizations through and out of periods of crisis or underperformance is a common scenario where transformational change leadership is strongly emphasized and expected. This often requires a leader gathering people together (e.g. top teams and boards) to openly acknowledge that the organization is facing a significant problem, discussing critical warning signs that changes may be needed (e.g. to company cashflows, incentives, old ways of working), and coming up with a great change story about the future (Yakola, 2014).

Again, stage models are popular and influential when it comes to repairing and relaunching an organization in trouble. There seems to be a consensus among many successful senior executives that leading change involves building powerful support, having difficult conversations about how to communicate and behave in new ways, tackling major problems with culture/talent/resources, and mobilizing learning, data and results (Boyd, 2011). One consulting model for leading large-scale change has described this in terms of five stages, collectively called the '5As' (Keller and Schaninger, 2019):

1. *Aspire:* where do we want to go?
2. *Assess:* how ready are we to go there?
3. *Architect:* what must we do to get there?
4. *Act:* how do we manage the journey?
5. *Advance:* how do we continue to improve?

Leaders who manage to transform organizations through crises and toward recovery represent influential stories of change management, referred to as *'turnarounds'*, where newly appointed CEOs from inside or outside the organization offer a fresh perspective on what needs to change to spark new plans and conversations. Some leaders even repeat this process multiple times over a period of years or decades, gaining a reputation in their careers as turnaround experts or specialists. There are many real-world examples of change turnaround leaders, such as:

- Alan Mulally's turnaround of Ford Motor Company (2006–14).
- Anne Mulcahy's restoration of Xerox Corp to profitability (2001–9).
- James Daunt's turnaround of struggling bookstore chains Waterstones and Barnes & Noble (2011–19, and 2019–ongoing).
- Jim Continenza's revitalization of Kodak as an industrial manufacturer of advanced materials and chemicals after its fall in the photographic film market (2019–ongoing).

In general, two things are clear when it comes to senior leaders who are at least nominally responsible for leading change management efforts and strategic changes that will affect and transform their entire organizations. One, that it is very hard work; and two, that it involves many more people than just a single leader – typically leadership teams, influencers and followers across the rest of the organization. Another helpful way to summarize the scope and complexity of the hard work and social complexity of leading change is to try to summarize it in the form of a set of underlying principles or rules for guiding behaviour (Table 7.2). Some principles might concern how leaders communicate and make change decisions, others may concern how leaders shape people in the rest of the organization, and finally, there can be principles around how the leaders think about themselves.

| |
|---|
| **Principles for leaders' change decision-making, transparency and innovation** |
| • Distribute responsibility by empowering levels below |
| • Be honest and open about providing and sharing information |
| • Create multiple paths and channels for innovative change ideas |
| **Principles for leading through assessment, hiring and training** |
| • Make it safe for followers to fail, admit errors, learn lessons from experience |
| • Make connections between strategists, experts, teams/peers and unique talents |
| • Hire people for diversity, responsibility and experimentation with change |
| **Principles for leaders changing themselves through personal evolution** |
| • Bring 'whole self' to work, in terms of life lessons, values and authenticity |
| • Make time to reflect on your own biases and assumptions |
| • Be willing to develop yourself and others by being helpful, vulnerable and humble |

**Table 7.2** Principles of Leading Transformational Change (adapted from Leitch, Lancefield and Dawson, 2016)

### ACTIVITY 7.4

1. Why do you think that effective leadership is imperative to successful organizational change? Please list your reasons, and explain why they're important.
2. Do you think 'great' leaders are born or made? Please explain.

## Leadership Development

Although sometimes neglected due to a focus on a singular central leadership figure, an important link between leadership and change concerns how leaders and organizations *change* the leadership abilities of *others* by attempting to enhance them through processes and practices of leadership development. Many organizations tend to invest a lot of resources into leadership development in general, but questions remain about the adequacy and effectiveness of leadership development approaches. Leadership development is crucial for ensuring that organizations do not become overly dependent on individual leaders for their success, so that leadership responsibilities can be shared or transferred as needed, and a culture is developed whereby people can grow and develop as change leaders in different ways.

Establishing leadership development strategies and plans from a change management perspective requires an organization to reflect on desired leadership styles and competencies for both its current and potential future leaders. Often there is a blended emphasis on people leading themselves, leading others and leading areas of the organization. It also requires investing in a variety of formal and informal learning and development practices, such as self-paced online courses, mentoring relationships with other leaders, job rotations, job shadowing for understanding roles and other potential professional courses and established qualifications.

Common problems with designing leadership development programmes, however, can include too much conformity to a single style of leadership, limited opportunities to practice and transfer leadership skills back into work settings, and a lack of support for 'stretch' challenges that really expand leadership skills beyond existing ones (Zaccaro and Banks, 2004). Recommendations of more effective practices for developing leadership and change management skills include frequent supervisory encouragement and feedback, building links between different levels of performance requirements and allowing time and resources for people to discover, learn, adjust and overcome challenges along the way (Zaccaro and Banks, 2004).

At large global and multinational organizations, leadership development frameworks are likely to involve change management assignments in different countries and cultures, departments and groups, with different mentors, roles and assignments comprising steps toward and requirements for career progression. Ultimately, spending on effective leadership development should also be linked to a positive return on investment, in the form of better-quality decisions and recommendations from leaders, leading to improved cost savings, revenues and other forms of impact and value created for the organization.

In change management, a powerful argument for leadership development states that if leaders cannot commit to leadership and change themselves, then they cannot expect others to follow them through a successful change process. Self-assessment is therefore an important component of change leadership and leadership development, and leaders may need to assess themselves honestly in a variety of ways to gain self-awareness and insight (Schneider and Goldwasser, 1998). They should consider:

- Whether they are verbally and nonverbally showing commitment to change.
- Whether they can clearly explain business reasons for change.
- Whether they have dedicated enough time and resources to support change efforts.
- Whether they have built change management activities into their plans.

- Whether they are participating in reaching out to all important change stakeholders.
- Whether they are looking for and dealing with signs of resistance to change.
- Whether they are empowering their team to come up with change ideas.
- Whether they are motivating others to become committed 'change agents'.
- Whether other managers/supervisors understand their roles in the change process.
- Whether they understand how this change relates to other company initiatives.

More critically, some leaders may find themselves thinking about how meaningful leadership relates to their own identities and personal sense of purpose. Not everyone, particularly those in minority groups, see themselves as a leader or someone who might become a leader, because they do not fit the stereotype of a 'white, heroic man at the top' (Zaar, Van den Bossche and Gijselaers, 2020). Leadership development should therefore be more personalized and involve open exploration – not just narrow formal requirements for skills and knowledge that people may or may not have. Put another way, *leadership itself can change*, if people are empowered to develop different perspectives and possibilities on what leadership might look like for them.

### ACTIVITY 7.5

1. Imagine yourself as a leader in the workplace, of a sports team or a group project. What does or would leadership 'look like'? Please explain.

## Bottom-Up Forms of Leading Organizational Change

Change leaders that simply add new vision and direction from the top of the organization and expect everyone to be ready to follow it are very one-sided and *top-down* in their approach. In contrast, adopting more *bottom-up* forms of leading organizational change requires that leaders let go of more of their control as individuals, and listen and pay more attention to ongoing shared issues and relationships in the change environments in the wider context of the organization (Karp, 2006). Rather than looking for a quick fix or a big personal success, bottom-up change leaders are more willing to display 'minimum intervention', leading change through a few basic principles while finding the right people, resources and signals for spreading and experimenting with changes in ways that make it seem more natural and more likely to last (Karp, 2006).

In many organizational change contexts top-down leadership is flawed from the outset, because top leaders by themselves do not have all the resources to come up with innovations or analyse complex and uncertain situations quickly to determine a decisive course of action or judgement call. More thoughtful, patient approaches may be needed where long-term investments in research and development (R&D) are involved, for example. In crisis or innovation contexts, leaders may need to improvise or change course quickly in response to environmental feedback, or risk serious failure.

One framework that captures some of these ideas is the *cynefin* leadership framework, named after a Welsh word relating to connections with our environment (Snowden and Boone, 2007). The cynefin framework describes five main contexts facing leaders, each suggesting different ways for leaders to make decisions and intervene:

1. *Simple (or obvious) contexts:* these are relatively stable environments with clear connections that everyone understands. Here, leaders can delegate, give simple orders, and follow a course of action people know to be 'best'.

2. *Complicated contexts:* these may involve multiple helpful solutions but require more expert analysis, because not everyone can see all the connections. However, given time, people may come up with various new and creative options and ideas.

3. *Complex contexts:* in this context right answers cannot be established by a leader in advance, because conditions are unpredictable and continuously changing (which is the case for most situations and decisions in organizations!). Leaders should therefore probe and experiment with their followers, patiently waiting to see what useful patterns might emerge.

4. *Chaotic contexts:* these contexts are highly disruptive and unstable and temporarily require decisive top-down action from leaders, but only until a crisis is over and has been steered back to a complex context.

5. *Disordered contexts:* these contexts are difficult to classify and may involve too many different perspectives and arguments. Here, to avoid confusion, leaders may need to gather more information and/or separate out parts of the situation that can be reclassified into one of the four other domains above.

In general, then, leaders are likely to face changing circumstances, and may often need to adjust and rebalance the extent to which they take a 'command and control' approach to managing change, versus bottom-up approaches that are based more on discussing, listening and experimenting through their followers before they act or respond.

Another way of expressing how more bottom-up approaches to change leadership may be common or necessary is to consider the ways in which leadership may be *shared* and *distributed*. This is common to many organizational contexts, although it is particularly evident in public sector settings, where change may require leadership at different levels, across different committees and national, regional and local community structures and services. For example, healthcare partnerships in the UK referred to as 'integrated care systems' involve collaborative leadership between many participating organizations seeking to develop shared plans and joined-up services across sectors and geographical areas. The aim is to serve a common good; to ensure patients and populations are provided with the best possible physical, mental and social support. Here there is both *vertical* and *horizontal* leadership in relation to global and national policy, partner organizations located in similar places or offering related services, and individual leaders and managers distributed throughout a wider system of organizational and professional groups (Moore, Elliott and Hesselgreaves, 2023).

In the hierarchy of any organization, many managers, especially *middle managers*, are likely to see themselves as *connecting leaders*, or leaders and followers at the same time, involved in upward and downward change influence activities, and therefore important and valuable in their potential for bringing multiple levels of the organization closer together (Jaser, 2021). This change leadership is likely to be most effective to the extent that upward and sideways leadership is not being neglected relative to traditional downward command and control. If nothing else, senior leaders cannot give 100 per cent of their time and energy to a change or hope to understand 100 per cent of the issues themselves. They might think instead of their leadership in terms of the *Pareto Principle* (or 80/20 rule). This might take various forms, but in essence means that leaders need to be selective in how they prioritize and focus their leadership. For example, it might be that they make a crucial 20 per cent of decisions or communicate directly with a crucial 20 per cent of their followers, and it is this focus that will lead to more effective results, because the remaining 80 per cent is expected to be delivered by the rest of the organization, in response.

Furthermore, it is not always those in formal leadership positions that act or are seen as change leaders. More *informal* and *emergent* theories of leadership suggest that anyone can become a leader without official status, provided they are perceived as having useful experience and knowledge so that people approach them for answers and follow their guidance as they interact over time. This might also be particularly apparent in contexts where people are organizing more public and political movements for leading social change, and many people may volunteer to tell stories or put values into action in different times and places – a highly participatory leadership culture where 'you can make a difference' (Ganz, 2010).

One of the biggest challenges to the conventional idea of a charismatic, strong-willed individual leader guiding change from the top down comes from *substitutes for leadership theory* (Kerr and Jermier, 1978). This theory proposes that certain aspects of organizations, followers and tasks are more or less likely to substitute for leadership, making leadership itself less important/necessary. Such factors include:

→ *Subordinates* that are highly knowledgeable or professionally independent.

→ *Tasks* that are unambiguous, routine, offer direct feedback or are intrinsically satisfying.

→ *Organizational structures* with clear plans and rules, cohesive work groups and subordinates working far from superiors' control or ability to reward them for their efforts.

While these theories may not describe typical leader-centric situations with powerful, charismatic figures, they nevertheless go some way toward explaining why we see some change leaders in organizations that are apparently more successful by adopting quieter, more patient and more understated approaches.

### CASE STUDY: QUIET CHANGE LEADERSHIP

Shantanu Narayen is an Indian-American business executive and has been the chairman, president and chief executive officer of the multinational computer software company, Adobe Inc., since 2007. He rarely gives media interviews and has described himself as being 'very comfortable not being out there pounding my chest'. However, he has quietly reinvented Adobe to adapt to changes brought by cloud computing, improving its market capitalization significantly over a ten-year period, and outperforming rival software companies like Microsoft and Salesforce (*The Economist*, 2021). John Donahoe, eBay CEO, who has discussed strategic change with Shantanu Narayen, has described him as 'a quiet person, he leads with his actions rather than his words. He's not a guy with a huge ego, but he has a lot of pride' (Waters, 2015).

In the late 2000s smartphones and cloud computing brought changes to how software products were being used and offered. Narayen embraced the chance for the company to change and innovate, in part by offering a healthy mix of top-down and bottom-up leadership and management. While he sets out the destination for the organization, it is the three managers of Adobe's three subscription-based 'clouds' ('Document', 'Creative', and 'Experience') that decide exactly how to reach the change performance objectives, with the help of their teams of engineers.

Narayen has described Adobe's core values as innovation and people, and is proud of how the company has avoided mass restructurings during recent crises. In 2009 Narayen helped expand Adobe's strategy from content creation to content management, measurement and monetization, partly by trusting his team's instincts that betting on these innovations would be right for the company long term. Around 2011, when Adobe was changing to adopting a Software as a Service (SaaS) business model, he emphasized the success of this transformational change in relation to a companywide effort, involving his leadership team and tens of thousands of employees embracing new priorities, performance indicators and incentives in the wider system (Narayen, 2023). He also describes the importance of finding champions of change, while recognizing quick wins and short-term successes.

More recently Adobe has focused on developing and deploying generative AI technology via its R&D investments and innovating across its portfolio. Narayen has been able to celebrate a 25-year anniversary of working at Adobe and describes his change leadership approach as being a 'flag planter' and 'road builder', which helps 'clear a path for teams to take ownership and execute'. The world continues to give Adobe credit under Narayen's leadership for being the first major software company to change from a desktop-based, perpetual licensing business to a multi-billion-dollar SaaS one (Narayen, 2023).

Like Shantanu Narayen, Ho Kwon Ping is another quiet, understated change leader. A former director of Singapore International Airlines, the company has been successful in its industry for over forty years by letting 'ordinary people' make it into an 'extraordinary company' (Chia, 2014). Then there is also Lars Jørgensen, chief executive of the Danish pharmaceutical company Novo Nordisk and the *Financial Times*' Person of the Year 2023, involved in leading innovative new treatments for obesity, who is frequently described as an understated, thoughtful, patient and responsible leader (Kuchler, 2023).

## Critiques and Limits of Change Leadership

From the late twentieth into the twenty-first century, a growing variety of critical perspectives on leadership and change leadership have continued to emerge. It is important to recognize how organizational change can be risky, unpredictable and unmanageable and leaders can be an influential part of the general uncertainty, failure and destructiveness that might accompany change. Often there is a tendency to generalize about what makes a good leader, and yet, in reality, we see many different types of leaders in organizations facing different types of change circumstances and taking different approaches, with varying degrees of success.

Change leaders are often forced to make sacrifices and face difficult, competing demands on their time, energy, identity, image, resources and interests. It may be tempting for leaders to try to 'be all things to all people' during change, or to say yes to all the change ideas of their followers and allies ('letting a thousand flowers bloom'), but the reality is that most leaders, sooner or later, must figure out how to endure threats, losses and the consequences of difficult decisions that take them to their limits. Many such issues facing change leaders can be described as 'paradoxes', due to the strongly contradictory or opposing nature of the courses of action suggested to them.

One example is the 'information-action paradox'. Here leaders may have some information suggesting the need for change, but not enough evidence to easily convince everyone to follow them into action. However, if they wait for more information to become available before acting, they may lose a crucial window of opportunity, and it becomes too late to take full advantage of the situation or make the necessary changes sufficiently quickly (Siren, Anthony and Bhatt, 2022).

This predicament was experienced by the leadership team of the Australian branch of global law firm King & Wood Mallesons, who were picking up signals that the law market was changing and, as a consequence, they knew that their practice would need to change too. These changes included technology being used to deliver routine services, clients who were dissatisfied with high bills starting to develop some of their own in-house legal capabilities, competition from leading accounting firms and young lawyers getting frustrated with their working hours and tasks. However, many lawyers, partners and other stakeholders could not initially see enough persuasive evidence of the pressures to change. They were therefore inclined to avoid risk until more information became available. Resolving this dilemma took about a year. Leaders had to work hard to build more collective conviction for change, mainly by generating more private data and making efforts to 'lower the threshold of proof' – digging deeper into data to share and discuss, and using predictive models and shared language so trends were not dismissed as noise (Siren, Anthony and Bhatt, 2022).

### ACTIVITY 7.6

1. In relation to the above case study of King & Wood Mallesons, if you were leading change, how might you have used all the sources of your power base to make change happen?

Consulting research has also suggested at least six other major paradoxes of leadership related to complex and fast-changing global contexts (PwC, 2020). These are:

1. *Global-local*. Leaders need to find ways to be both deeply engaged with local cultures and markets while also being connected across the globe.
2. *Integrity-political*. Leaders need to find ways to make change happen when parties have different political interests, while retaining followers' trust in their character and values.
3. *Humble-heroic*. Leaders need to have the confidence to act when there is uncertainty and anxiety while also having the humility to recognize that they can be wrong and need help.
4. *Strategist-executor*. Leaders need to make time to think about strategic choices affecting the future while also being able to execute actions effectively and more immediately when urgent problems need solving along the way.
5. *Techno-humanist*. Leaders need the technical skills to understand technological advances, while also appreciating people's needs at work and the human implications and impacts of technological changes.
6. *Traditional-innovative*. Leaders need to find ways to respect and use the past to guide change, while also having the courage to try new things and push new boundaries in moving toward the future.

In general, to avoid creating crisis and damage from these demanding paradoxes, leaders and their organizations must work together to recognize that these tensions exist, try to understand them, accept that they are ongoing, and map them to multiple leaders' strengths and development plans.

Regardless of the paradoxes and limits that test change leadership, there are also ways in which leadership may be said to have a 'dark side'. While it may not always be completely intentional, leaders can create various liabilities for their followers and organizations in terms of how their needs, visions and management styles become a centre of attention and influence. It is not uncommon for leaders to pursue a personal vision in such a way that they lead their organization into a crisis or a costly 'Pyrrhic victory', where a leader achieves the development and launch of a new product or policy, but at great cost to the organization as a whole, because the timing is wrong, or the responses not very positive (Conger, 1990).

Many limits and critiques of change leadership draw attention to *power*. Leaders can linger on at companies holding powerful boardroom positions, with share ownership and voting rights on the direction of the organization, awarding themselves large bonuses, even though they may have mismanaged or damaged organizational performance. Alternatively, top leaders may drive and preside over successful organizational change for years, only to 'fall from grace' should it emerge that they were neglectful, complicit or involved in a scandal or abuse of power in some way.

One line of critique argues that the leadership industry often confuses how a leader *ought* to be, morally speaking, with how they really *are*, in terms of their careers and political decisions. The reality is that successful leaders are highly imperfect and even unpopular people, but able to drive change effectively by doing what is necessary to achieve their objectives, even if it means sometimes behaving inconsistently, ambiguously and manipulatively in their dealings with others (Pfeffer, 2016). Another line of critique suggests that where elite, powerful figures are perceived and represented as 'leaders', there is a risk that they are celebrated in overly positive ways, which disguises and distracts from deeper conflicts of interest and inequalities (Learmonth and Morrell, 2019).

Consequently, the political and ethical aspects of change leadership still risk being neglected sometimes, in terms of being underexamined or not subjected to more critical scrutiny. Evil and destructive leaders throughout history, such as Adolf Hitler, provide obvious examples of how leaders can be authoritarian, elitist and devastatingly harmful, all while leading transformational change. Often change leaders that might be more peaceful, successful and progressive may not step forward because of fear, uncertainty and doubt about how to deal with the pain and resistance that change might provoke. One way for organizations to try to deal with this is to get better at defining and recognizing forms of 'bad leadership' or 'misleadership' which, because they do not aim at the greater good of helping others and supporting wider communities, should perhaps not be associated with leadership at all.

| Ineffective leadership (fails to use appropriate methods to lead change) |
|---|
| 1. Incompetent – leader lacks the will or skill (or both) to create and sustain change |
| 2. Rigid – leader is inflexible, and unable or unwilling to adapt to new information, ideas or other changes |
| 3. Intemperate – leader lacks self-control and is unable or unwilling to correct their actions when things go wrong |
| **Unethical leadership (may achieve change but fails to distinguish right from wrong)** |
| 4. Callous – leader is uncaring or unkind, ignoring needs and wishes of others |
| 5. Corrupt – leader is willing to lie, cheat or steal and to put their self-interest far ahead of public interest |
| 6. Insular – leader ignores the health and wellbeing of 'others' outside of their own group or organization |
| 7. Evil – leader does psychological or physical harm to others, using extreme violence or wickedness as a way of exercising power |

Table 7.3 Forms of Bad Leadership (adapted from Gini and Green, 2012; Kellerman, 2004)

Leadership can therefore be problematic in many ways and forms, which has implications for the types of environments surrounding the leader, and the types of followers and relationships that are cultivated. Even a leadership style traditionally and widely viewed as positive for change, such as transformational leadership, could be interpreted as having negative effects to the extent that it inhibits follower dissent, encourages too much dependence on the leader, and forms part of a controlling, cult-like set of power relations (Tourish and Pinnington, 2002). The ethics of leadership is about much more than just the leaders themselves. If the organizational change in question involves dealing with risks, disasters or emergencies – related to climate change, for instance – then leaders and followers alike may need to find ways to show mutual vulnerability, care and compassion, instead of denying there is a problem or expecting each other to be resilient as individuals (Crossweller and Tschakert, 2019).

If views of change become too 'leader-centric', they may over-attribute the success or failure of the change to the actions of a single person, overemphasizing the role and influence of leadership relative to other organizational factors – a perception that has been termed the 'romance of leadership' (Meindl, Ehrlich and Dukerich, 1985). This can lead to biased perceptions, distortions and political representations of leadership that simplify the complex relationships of change, crediting leaders with being responsible for change successes, or blaming them for change failures, when they may not deserve either. There is some evidence to suggest that female leaders in particular can be affected negatively by this. They are more likely to be appointed as leaders in 'glass cliff' situations, where the risk of change failure is higher due to challenging circumstances, and even if they do succeed, a man may be reinstated to take credit when company performance improves again (Haslam and Ryan, 2008).

Ultimately, we need to be prepared to question the myths of change leadership. It is not about one individual leader, it is not the only condition needed for successful change, and it does not involve styles that are effective for all types of change. Furthermore, formal leaders may not actually provide leadership, while conversely, other employees not formally referred to as leaders may be acting as change agents and providing considerable forms of change action and influence that many would consider key aspects of leadership (By, Hughes and Ford, 2016). Rarely is organizational change as simple a situation as one where all managers/leaders/agents are on one side and all non-managers/followers/recipients are on the other. And although they are often considered separately, there remains complicated relationships *between* change and leadership. For example, if our very understandings of leadership do not change, are we ourselves failing to engage with change?

The importance of this type of critical thinking about leadership has been neatly summarized as important for challenging 'zombie leadership', so named because older ideas about leadership have been disproven and yet continue to live on, mainly because they are popular and profitable (Haslam, Alvesson and Reicher, 2024). Zombie leadership involves eight main axioms or propositions:

1. *'Leadership is all about leaders'* (no – followership and follower understanding are important too).
2. *'There are specific qualities all great leaders "have"'* (no – followers need to perceive people as intelligent and charismatic in context).
3. *'There are specific things all great leaders do'* (no – leadership requires behaviour which is sensitive to the circumstances and the people or groups being led).
4. *'We all know a great leader when we see one'* (no – there are different perspectives and definitions of 'greatness', not a consensus).
5. *'All leadership is the same'* (no – leadership looks different, and needs to change, across different contexts).

6. *'Leadership is a special skill limited to special people'* (no – treating leaders as highly elite or superior to others can harm followers and relationships).

7. *'Leadership is always good and always beneficial for everyone'* (no – leadership can just as readily support inequality and tyranny as it can universal good).

8. *'People can't cope without leaders'* (no – not everyone needs leadership. In fact, some leadership can make followers and groups disengage and work less effectively).

In turn, there are four strategies for defeating zombie leadership beliefs and issues (Haslam, Alvesson and Reicher, 2024):

1. *Recognizing its key claims and components* that focus heavily on leaders as great, special and the deserving centre of attention.

2. *Returning to the definition of leadership* as a process involving followers and relationships that motivate and shape people's orientations towards collective goals in various contexts.

3. *Recognizing the costs of zombie leadership* in terms of how it can damage leaders' skills, alienate followers and groups and reduce the productivity and health of groups and society.

4. *Championing theoretical and practical alternatives to zombie leadership* that go beyond leadership to include everyone's contributions, in addition to investment in group connections and leadership development.

### ACTIVITY 7.7

1. Consider the terminology that is used to describe ineffectual and unethical change leadership outlined in Table 7.3.

2. Think of a workplace situation in which you have experienced these types of leadership, or a recent example of it in the public domain. How would you advise individuals and groups to respond?

## Reimagining the Future of Change Leadership

Following on from the previous sections, questions and arguments remain about how we might learn from change leadership of the past and present in order to achieve better change management in the future. For instance, some feel that leadership is in crisis because the world continues to have many leaders serving their own narrow interests in elite groups, operating in a highly individualistic, 'masculine' manner that expects to overcome the resistance of managers and workforces (Burnes, Hughes and By, 2018). These leaders deal in corporate clichés such as 'mission' and 'value' while engaging in unethical and even illegal practices that reinforce their own power and privilege.

In contrast to this troubling current reality, it is worth going back to the historical roots of change management, imagining how more ethical change leadership is possible. It would, however, mean changing leadership radically towards more collaborative approaches that are morally engaged with the consequences of change for harming or helping a broader range of stakeholders, and welcoming creative responses to change from subordinates, managers and institutions in wider society (Burnes, Hughes and By, 2018).

The appetite for this more collective form of leadership, where many people come together and take responsibility for finding a more meaningful sense of *purpose* beyond narrow individual and organizational objectives, seems heightened in response to global challenges such as humanitarian and climate crises (By, 2021). Here, change leadership is more likely to involve trying to align and commit people across divides to achieve longer-term goals and outcomes, such as the *UN's Sustainable Development Goals*, which emphasize the need for global partnerships pursuing changes that are good for a larger majority of people (e.g. health, education, equality, equity, peace etc.).

These calls to action and more ethical, purposeful change leadership are certainly not without their challenges. One crucial point is to recognize the global relationships between change leadership and critical equity, diversity and inclusion perspectives. Celebrating leaders with certain privileged demographic backgrounds and characteristics can serve to exclude, silent and exploit minority individuals and groups that do not conform to the same ideals. However, at the same time, leaders from dominant groups and communities can help act as *allies* to minority groups and leaders by acknowledging their privileged positions, listening to and learning from diversity, and working to support minority causes and voices (Liu, 2021).

The profound sense of organizational crisis and change brought about and worked through during the global COVID-19 pandemic and beyond has also invited reflections on the changing nature of leadership. Leaders and their organizations were suddenly thrust into the unknown, confronted with the realities of how health and social inequalities affect people across interconnected societies, dealing with employee health, grief, trust, resilience and rapid digital transformation as part of their leadership. Four areas for ensuring responsible leadership through difficult change are as follows (CIPD, 2022):

1. *Ability* – leaders with the right competencies and abilities to do their jobs.
2. *Benevolence* – leaders that are bothered about others, and who are not entirely self-interested.
3. *Integrity* – leaders are guided in their decisions and actions by an admirable moral code.
4. *Predictability* – leaders have a positive consistency to their approach.

Some lapses in ability and predictability can be considered a normal part of human nature. Consequently, we may be more willing to forgive leaders during difficult times of change. However, problems perceived with leaders' benevolence and integrity are more likely to be seen as serious betrayals and destroy trust rapidly (CIPD, 2022). Some leaders attracted more public support during the pandemic because they were seen as managing change with greater urgency and transparency, taking responsibility for mistakes and keeping the public updated, and acknowledging suffering (Kerrissey and Edmondson, 2020).

One interesting study of pandemic leadership found evidence for activities very unlike 'great hero models' of leadership. These actions were more like what the researchers called 'unleading' – everyday actions undertaken with humility and compassion during uncertain circumstances (Kars-Unluoglu, Jarvis and Gaggiotti, 2022). Many local communities, organizations and individuals were purposefully connecting and collaborating to deal with exceptional change in leader-like ways, but did not tend to explicitly refer to their work as leadership. Initiatives were also often quite spontaneous, including supporting key workers, distributing masks, manufacturing ventilator parts, fundraising, creating health and safety information campaigns, organizing social events, and volunteering (Kars-Unluoglu, Jarvis and Gaggiotti, 2022).

It could be argued that some ways of reimagining leadership stretch quite far away from traditional definitions – but perhaps this is a positive thing. Ultimately, there are many components of *implementing* change. As a consequence, it does typically become the work of many people, if only because change conditions tend to be varied and complex. An integrative framework, such as that put forward by Ford et al., can help makes sense of this (Ford, Ford and Polin, 2021):

- Leadership *functions* – vision, structure, social integration, monitoring.
- Leadership *behaviours* – task-focused, relationship-focused, change-focused.
- Leadership *sources* – individuals, partnerships, collectives.
- Leadership *responses* – the timing, order, patterning and commitment of activities.
- Leadership *situations* – the variety of events arising during a change.
- Leadership *effectiveness* – task accomplishment, group integration, sustained progress.

The most significant change in how many people understand leadership is in terms of its *dynamic* and *relational* qualities – that it can look very different depending on the change context, purpose, unfolding processes and the more active participation of followers and stakeholders. Despite all the past theories and observations about leadership, there is still a lot to understand and discover about the different ways it can be studied and practised with organizations (Higgs, 2022).

### CASE STUDY: JACINDA ARDERN AND LEADING CHANGE DIFFERENTLY

Jacinda Ardern served as the fortieth Prime Minister of New Zealand and leader of the Labour Party from 2017 to 2023. When she announced her resignation in early 2023, many people were surprised; she had steered her country through a series of difficult change situations, including a mass shooting, a volcanic eruption and the COVID-19 pandemic (*The Economist*, 2023).

Ardern has generally been perceived positively. She was seen as having offered a different type of leadership: one that is kinder, more progressive and more humane. Even when explaining her resignation, she drew attention to depleted energy levels and knowing that it was the right time to hand over leadership to a successor – itself a form of change to be managed appropriately. This is a move that other successful leaders have undertaken in recent years, after managing years of demanding change, such as the football manager Jürgen Klopp, and the former CEO of Pfizer, Jeff Kindler. Leaders need time to reflect and be with their families just like any other human being, and it can be a sign of responsible leadership to know the right time to resign, as someone else may be better placed to serve stakeholders and continue a change journey.

During Ardern's leadership, after fifty-one people were shot and killed at a mosque in Christchurch in 2019, she wore a headscarf, embraced grieving families and coined the national phrase: 'They are us.' She was also quick to close New Zealand's borders in early 2020, keeping the death toll from the pandemic there relatively low. Her ratings in polls reached the highest of any party in the country's history since 1951, and she garnered high levels of global popularity for New Zealand overseas.

Following this however, Ardern faced struggles and decreases in popularity due to dissatisfaction with rises in the cost of living, inflation and issues with crime, despite well-intentioned policies and New Zealand faring better than many other countries dealing with these changes. As the world's youngest serving female leader at the time, and the second woman to give birth while holding elected office, she also had to endure criticism directed at her coloured by discriminatory sexist and misogynistic attitudes towards women (Wilson, 2023). Her change leadership legacy of reforms has included reducing child poverty and improving conditions for workers, although is more mixed in areas such as housing, water infrastructure governance and reducing emissions to address climate change.

In her emotional resignation speech, Ardern addressed her family directly, saying she was looking forward to having time to be with her daughter when she starts school, and to finally get married to her partner. She also summarized her leadership principles by stating 'I hope I leave New Zealanders with a belief that you can be kind but strong, empathetic but decisive, optimistic but focused ... And that you can be your own kind of leader – one who knows when it's time to go' (McClure, 2023).

From a change management perspective, Ardern's leadership offers many topics for further learning and discussion. These include the challenges faced by women leaders, how unity and confidence can be inspired through communication during a crisis, how to show cultural sensitivity and emphasize inclusion for social change, and how compassionate leadership can help others to cope with change and recover from stress.

 **CONSULTANCY IN THE CHAIR**

**Cup of Kindness Activity**

The CEO calls you into their office for your advice on which leadership styles they should assimilate throughout the programme of change at CUP. How would you respond?

**Competency-based Interview Question**

1. Can you give an example from a recent workplace or personal experience that demonstrates your ability to lead others?

## Chapter Summary

In conclusion, this chapter has covered several important areas relating to the role of leadership in organizational change. To briefly recap, these include:

- → The general importance of leadership for ensuring more effective organizational change, as well as how to define and observe change leadership in context.
- → Various concepts and frameworks for analysing different change leadership styles, components and activities, including similarities and differences between leading change and managing change.
- → How change leaders and change leadership can involve seeking to transform organizations by using various forms of power, influence and planning to establish stages and combinations of change activities that will improve organizational performance.
- → The importance of establishing leadership development programmes and support for more 'bottom-up' forms of change leadership in wider organizational environments beyond just the top senior leaders, so that leadership can be shared and complex change environments and conditions can be dealt with.
- → How to critique change leadership in terms of difficult change dilemmas, biased perceptions, forms of incompetence and harmful abuses of power that increase the likelihood of destruction or failure.
- → How to reimagine possibilities for doing leadership differently in future, which might involve more ethical approaches to managing organizational change, more diverse and representative leadership figures, and more active collaboration with followers and stakeholders.

## Useful Resources

→ Mind Tools. *Leadership Styles: Choosing the Right Approach for the Situation.* Available at: https://www.mindtools.com/a7m23wp/leadership-styles (accessed 19 April 2025).

→ Leitch, J., Lancefield, D. and Dawson, M. (2016), '10 Principles of Strategic Leadership'. *Strategy + business.* May 18. https://www.strategy-business.com/article/10-Principles-of-Strategic-Leadership (accessed 19 April 2025).

→ PwC (2020). Six Paradoxes of Leadership. April. https://www.pwc.com/gx/en/issues/assets/pdf/six-paradoxes_brochure.pdf (accessed 19 April 2025).

## Bibliography

Bate, A. (2023), 'Steve Cooper Interview: Nottingham Forest Boss on Leadership, Managing Change and the Team's Style of Play'. Sky Sports. September 30. https://www.skysports.com/football/news/11727/12973060/steve-cooper-interview-nottingham-forest-boss-on-leadership-managing-change-and-the-teams-style-of-play (accessed 19 April 2025).

Beer, M. and Nohria, N. (2000), 'Cracking the Code of Change'. *Harvard Business Review*, 78(3): 133–41.

Blackmore-Wright, J. (2023), 'Are Great Leaders Born or Made?' *Management Today*. September 25. https://www.managementtoday.co.uk/great-leaders-born-made/classroom/article/1834711 (accessed 19 April 2025).

Boyd, D. P. (2011), 'Lessons From Turnaround Leaders'. *Strategy & Leadership*, 39(3): 36–43.

Burnes, B., Hughes, M. and By, R. T. (2018), 'Reimagining Organisational Change Leadership'. *Leadership*, 14(2): 141–58.

By, R. T. (2021), 'Leadership: In Pursuit of Purpose'. *Journal of Change Management*, 21(1): 30–44.

By, R. T., Hughes, M. and Ford, J. (2016), 'Change Leadership: Oxymoron and Myths'. *Journal of Change Management*, 16(1): 8–17.

Caldwell, R. (2003), 'Change Leaders and Change Managers: Different or Complementary?' *Leadership & Organization Development Journal*, 24(5): 285–93.

Chia, R. (2014), 'In Praise of Silent Transformation – Allowing Change Through "Letting Happen".' *Journal of Change Management*, 14(1): 8–27.

CIPD (2022), 'Responsible Business Through Crisis: Has COVID-19 Changed Leadership Forever?' Chartered Institute of Development report. November. https://www.cipd.org/globalassets/media/knowledge/knowledge-hub/reports/responsible-business-crisis-1_tcm18-112209.pdf (accessed 21 April 2025).

Coget, J. F. A. H., Shani, A. B. R. and Solari, L. (2014), 'The Lone Genius, or Leaders who Tyrannize Their Creative Teams: An Alternative to the "Mothering" Model of Leadership and Creativity'. *Organizational Dynamics*, 43(2): 105–13.

Collins, J. (2005), 'Level 5 Leadership: The Triumph of Humility and Fierce Resolve'. *Harvard Business Review*, 83(7): 136–46.

Conger, J. A. (1990), 'The Dark Side of Leadership'. *Organizational Dynamics*, 19(2): 44–55.

Crosweller, M. and Tschakert, P. (2019), 'Climate Change and Disasters: The Ethics of Leadership'. *Wiley Interdisciplinary Reviews: Climate Change*, 11(2): e624.

Den Hartog, D. N., Van Muijen, J. J. and Koopman, P. L. (1997), 'Transactional Versus Transformational Leadership: An Analysis of the MLQ'. *Journal of Occupational and Organizational Psychology*, 70(1): 19–34.

Dunphy, D. C. and Stace, D. A. (1988), 'Transformational and Coercive Strategies for Planned Organizational Change: Beyond the OD Model'. *Organization Studies*, 9(3): 317–34.

Finnie, B. and Norris, M. (1997), 'On Leading Change: A Conversation with John P. Kotter'. *Strategy & Leadership*, 25(1): 18–24.

Ford, J., Ford, L. and Polin, B. (2021), 'Leadership in the Implementation of Change: Functions, Sources, and Requisite Variety'. *Journal of Change Management*, 21(1): 87–119.

Ganz, M. (2010), 'Leading Change: Leadership, Organization, and Social Movements', in N. Nohria and R. Khurana (eds), *Handbook of Leadership Theory and Practice* (pp. 527–68). Brighton, MA: Harvard Business Press.

Gill, R. (2002), 'Change Management – or Change Leadership?' *Journal of Change Management*, 3(4): 307–18.

Gillen, S. (2024), 'It's About the Players – Nuno Plays Down his Role as Nottingham Forest Reach 3rd Place in the Premier League'. https://www.youtube.com/watch?v=vN67gcQ5UbA (accessed 19 April 2025).

Gini, A. and Green, R. M. (2012), 'Bad Leaders/Misleaders'. *Business and Society Review*, 117(2): 143–54.

Graetz, F. (2000), 'Strategic Change Leadership'. *Management Decision*, 38(8): 550–64.

Haslam, S. A., Alvesson, M. and Reicher, S. D. (2024), 'Zombie Leadership: Dead Ideas That Still Walk Among Us'. *The Leadership Quarterly*. DOI: https://doi.org/10.1016/j.leaqua.2023.101770.

Haslam, S. A. and Ryan, M. K. (2008), 'The Road to the Glass Cliff: Differences in the Perceived Suitability of Men and Women for Leadership Positions in Succeeding and Failing Organizations'. *The Leadership Quarterly*, 19(5): 530–46.

Higgs, M. (2022), 'Insomnia? Try Counting Leadership Theories'. *Journal of Change Management*, 22(4): 355–72.

Higgs, M. and Rowland, D. (2000), 'Building Change Leadership Capability: "The Quest for Change Competence".' *Journal of Change Management*, 1(2): 116–30.

Huy, Q. N. (2001), 'Time, Temporal Capability, and Planned Change'. *Academy of Management Review*, 26(4): 601–23.

Huy, Q. N. and Mintzberg, H. (2003), 'The Rhythm of Change'. *MIT Sloan Management Review*, 44(4): 79–84.

Jaser, Z. (2021), 'The Real Value of Middle Managers'. *Harvard Business Review*, 99(3): 124–33.

Karp, T. (2006), 'Transforming Organisations for Organic Growth: The DNA of Change Leadership'. *Journal of Change Management*, 6(1): 3–20.

Kars-Unluoglu, S., Jarvis, C. and Gaggiotti, H. (2022), 'Unleading During a Pandemic: Scrutinising Leadership and its Impact in a State of Exception'. *Leadership*, 18(2): 277–97.

Keller, S. and Schaninger, B. (2019). 'A Better Way to Lead Large-scale Change'. *McKinsey*. July 10. https://www.mckinsey.com/capabilities/people-and-organizational-performance/our-insights/a-better-way-to-lead-large-scale-change (accessed 19 April 2025).

Kellerman, B. (2004), *Bad Leadership: What it is, How it Happens, Why it Matters*. Brighton, MA: Harvard Business Press.

Kerr, S. and Jermier, J. M. (1978), 'Substitutes for Leadership: Their Meaning and Measurement'. *Organizational Behavior and Human Performance*, 22(3): 375–403.

Kerrissey, M. J. and Edmondson, A. C. (2020), 'What Good Leadership Looks Like During This Pandemic'. *Harvard Business Review*. April 13. https://hbr.org/2020/04/what-good-leadership-looks-like-during-this-pandemic (accessed 19 April 2025).

Kotter, J. P. (2001), 'What Leaders Really Do'. *Harvard Business Review*, 79(11): 85–96.

Kuchler, H. (2023), 'FT Person of the Year: Lars Fruergaard Jørgensen of Novo Nordisk'. *Financial Times*. December 19. https://www.ft.com/content/d4d289a7-e1a5-4848-8e7e-b592f7018722 (accessed 19 April 2025).

Learmonth, M. and Morrell, K. (2019), *Critical Perspectives on Leadership: The Language of Corporate Power*. London: Routledge.

Leitch, J., Lancefield, D. and Dawson, M. (2016), '10 Principles of Strategic Leadership'. *Strategy + business*. May 18. https://www.strategy-business.com/article/10-Principles-of-Strategic-Leadership (accessed 19 April 2025).

Liu, H. (2021), *Redeeming Leadership: An Anti-racist Feminist Intervention*. Bristol: Bristol University Press.

McClure, T. (2023), 'From Stardust to an Empty Tank: One-of-a-kind Leader Jacinda Ardern Knew Her Time Was Up'. *The Guardian*. January 19. https://www.theguardian.com/world/2023/jan/19/from-stardust-to-an-empty-tank-one-of-a-kind-leader-jacinda-ardern-knew-her-time-was-up (accessed 19 April 2025).

McHale, S. (2020), *The Insider's Guide to Culture Change: Creating a Workplace That Delivers, Grows, and Adapts*. London: HarperCollins Leadership.

Meindl, J. R., Ehrlich, S. B. and Dukerich, J. M. (1985), 'The Romance of Leadership'. *Administrative Science Quarterly*, 30(1): 78–102.

Moore, J., Elliott, I. C. and Hesselgreaves, H. (2023), 'Collaborative Leadership in Integrated Care Systems; Creating Leadership for the Common Good'. *Journal of Change Management*, 23(4): 358–73.

Narayen, S. (2023), 'Adobe's CEO on Making Big Bets on Innovation'. *Harvard Business Review*. November–December. https://hbr.org/2023/11/adobes-ceo-on-making-big-bets-on-innovation (accessed 19 April 2025).

Pfeffer, J. (2016), 'Getting Beyond the BS of Leadership Literature'. McKinsey. January 1. https://www.mckinsey.com/featured-insights/leadership/getting-beyond-the-bs-of-leadership-literature (accessed 19 April 2025).

PwC (2020), 'Six Paradoxes of Leadership'. April. https://www.pwc.com/gx/en/issues/assets/pdf/six-paradoxes_brochure.pdf (accessed 19 April 2025).

Ramachandran, S., Balasubramanian, S., James, W. F. and Al Masaeid, T. (2023), 'Whither Compassionate Leadership? A Systematic Review'. *Management Review Quarterly*, 74: 1473–557. https://link.springer.com/article/10.1007/s11301-023-00340-w (accessed 19 April 2025).

Raven, B. H. (1993), 'The Bases of Power: Origins and Recent Developments'. *Journal of Social Issues*, 49(4): 227–51.

Schneider, D. M. and Goldwasser, C. (1998), 'Be a Model Leader of Change'. *Management Review*, 87(3): 41–6.

Siren, P. M. A., Anthony, S. D. and Bhatt, U. (2022), 'Persuade Your Company to Change Before it's too Late'. *Harvard Business Review*. January–February. https://hbr.org/2022/01/persuade-your-company-to-change-before-its-too-late (accessed 19 April 2025).

Snowden, D. J. and Boone, M. E. (2007), 'A Leader's Framework for Decision Making'. *Harvard Business Review*, 85(11): 68–76.

*The Economist* (2021), 'How Adobe Became Silicon Valley's Quiet Reinventor'. October 16. https://www.economist.com/business/2021/10/16/how-adobe-became-silicon-valleys-quiet-reinventor (accessed 19 April 2025).

*The Economist* (2023), 'Jacinda Ardern Resigns as New Zealand's Prime Minister'. January 19. https://www.economist.com/asia/2023/01/19/jacinda-ardern-resigns-as-new-zealands-prime-minister (accessed 19 April 2025).

Tourish, D. and Pinnington, A. (2002), 'Transformational Leadership, Corporate Cultism and the Spirituality Paradigm: An Unholy Trinity in the Workplace?' *Human Relations*, 55(2): 147–72.

Unwin, W. (December 2024), 'How Nuno Transformed Nottingham Forest From Circus to Contenders'. https://www.theguardian.com/football/2024/dec/28/nottingham-forest-nuno-espirito-santo-transfers-tactics (accessed 19 April 2025).

Waters, R. (2015), 'Monday Interview: Shantanu Narayen, Adobe CEO'. *Financial Times*. February 22. https://www.ft.com/content/4178b02c-b758-11e4-981d-00144feab7de (accessed 19 April 2025).

Wilson, S. (2023), 'Jacinda Ardern's Resignation: Gender and the Toll of Strong, Compassionate Leadership'. *The Conversation*. January 20. https://theconversation.com/jacinda-arderns-resignation-gender-and-the-toll-of-strong-compassionate-leadership-198152 (accessed 19 April 2025).

Woodward, S. and Hendry, C. (2004), 'Leading and Coping with Change'. *Journal of Change Management*, 4(2): 155–83.

Yakola, D. (2014), 'Ten Tips for Leading Companies Out of Crisis'. *McKinsey*. March 1. https://www.mckinsey.com/capabilities/strategy-and-corporate-finance/our-insights/ten-tips-for-leading-companies-out-of-crisis (accessed 19 April 2025).

Zaar, S., Van den Bossche, P. and Gijselaers, W. (2020), 'How Business Students Think About Leadership: A Qualitative Study on Leader Identity and Meaning-making'. *Academy of Management Learning & Education*, 19(2): 168–91.

Zaccaro, S. J. and Banks, D. (2004), 'Leader Visioning and Adaptability: Bridging the Gap Between Research and Practice on Developing the Ability to Manage Change'. *Human Resource Management*, 43(4): 367–80.

# The Role of Human Resource Management

## Good Practices for Effective Organizational Change

### Learning Outcomes

At the end of this chapter you will be able to:

1. Understand HR's role as a change agent in the organization.
2. List the knowledge, skills and competences needed to be an effective 'change agent'.
3. Describe different categories of organizational change and the contribution HR makes to each.
4. Distinguish between how support is given to change projects in the organization and HR's own role in initiating changes.
5. Evaluate the methodology for determining the success of change projects.
6. Understand the value of communication for facilitating effective change.

## Introduction

The overall aim of this chapter is to explore and understand the important role of HR professionals in initiating and facilitating organizational change and good practices. Whilst this chapter refers specifically to HR, we are conscious that some individuals have significant people responsibilities, yet may not necessarily be recognized formally by an HR title. As we have seen throughout this text, a key factor for managing significant change effectively, whether at the macro, micro or meso unit of analysis, is **people**. Whatever the driver, change is always initiated and managed by people with varying effectiveness. As we have discussed in previous chapters, change impacts individuals and groups of people differently. Some managers and leaders are naturally systematic planners, have emotional intelligence, are culturally intelligent (Chapter 5) and understand power and politics (Chapter 6). They are therefore better equipped to manage change effectively. However, this is not guaranteed. One of the core functions in facilitating the effective management of change is Human Resources (HR), which in contemporary organizations takes a strategic role in an organization's ongoing development. In this respect HR is viewed as making a significant contribution to employees' wellbeing and constitutes a key driver of organizational effectiveness (Nielson et al., 2017). HR professionals are thus influencers and facilitators of organizational strategy (Higgins, Roper and Gamwell, 2016), as well as being gatekeepers and custodians of both the employees' and the organizations' welfare (Parkes and Davis, 2013). It is inevitable, therefore, that HR, as the 'people function', is drawn into change in various ways.

This chapter evaluates the professional support and facilitatory role that HR should provide in the change process, in particular to those accountable for initiating and coordinating change. It also analyses different types of organizational change projects alongside the role HR can play in each. As part of this we consider the support required from HR in terms of knowledge, skills and competencies across the function.

## Is Organizational Change the Business of the HR Function?

In his seminal work *HR Champions*, Ulrich (1997) saw four key roles for HR. One of these was the 'Management of Transformation and Change' (see Figure 8.1). He included this role based on the reality that a high proportion of organizational change is actually about new or changed systems and processes, new ways of working or new restructuring efforts. These all require a degree of people skills.

He described the role as a 'change agent' role. What did he mean by this?

He meant that every organization needs professionals who know how to convert strategy and ideas into reality, with minimum pain and disruption. This is what we might call *proactive* change. However, all organizations have problems to which they must *react*, which 'the change agent' must see, analyse and propose solutions to.

Some organizations may have a separate 'change' department, but Ulrich believed the expertise should sit within HR.

## ACTIVITY 8.1

1. Given what you have learnt throughout this book, would you agree with Ulrich's view that the expertise for organizational change should sit within HR? If yes, please explain. If not, then with whom or which department do you think the expertise should sit and why?

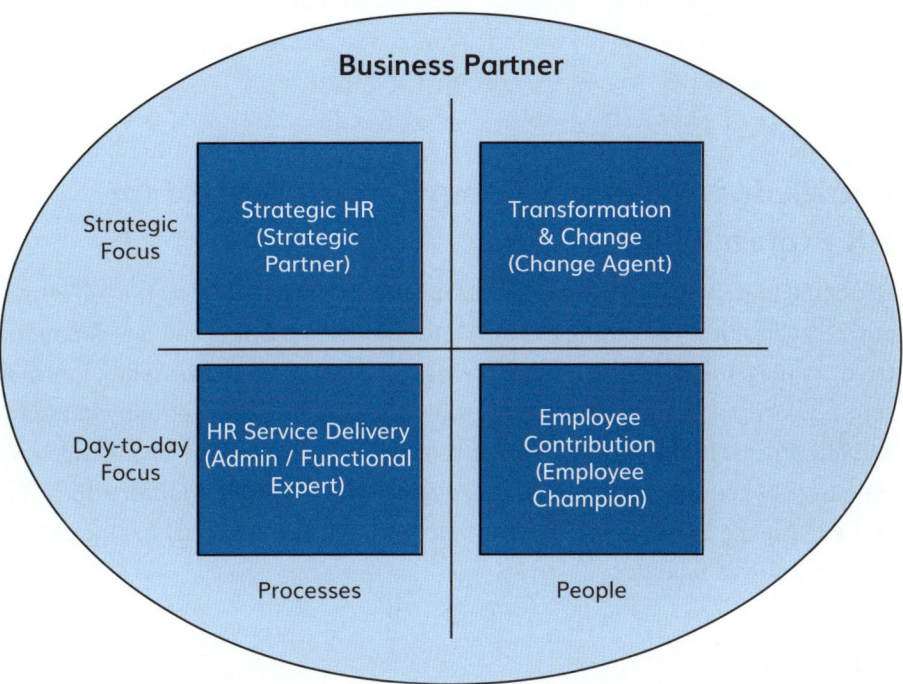

**Figure 8.1** Ulrich's roles of HR in business partnership (Ulrich, 1997).

# Dedicated 'Change Agent' Professionals in HR

Today's HR professionals are expected to have had some training in 'Organizational Development (OD)' which, as we saw in Chapter 4, is about organizational change and transformation. As a consequence, organizations with, say, 3,000 employees or more, will commonly have fulltime HR professionals focused on 'OD'. However, what they actually do may vary considerably.

OD has its origins in the 1970s and the study of 'organizational behaviour'. It drifted away from its original remit of organizational change as many professionals and consultants involved became consumed with psychological and behavioural processes, and losing sight of the 'business benefit'. However, whichever terminology is used, all change should be directed towards some form of business improvement (which may or may not be immediately financial). The credibility of any HR professional depends on the extent to which they recognize this. In this respect 'organizational effectiveness' (OE) may be a better description, as it focuses on the potential definable benefits to the organization from change that is managed well. One way or another, it is the individual and team that need to be dedicated to contributing towards a well-performing organization, which is often achieved through change. This includes making improvements to the organization – improving the way an organization is structured, the way it works together and its effectiveness at individual and team level.

## Knowledge, Skills and Competencies Needed for HR Professionals

HR's contribution in positively contributing to change may draw on the full gamut of HR capabilities – including recruitment, selection, training and development, talent management, health and wellbeing, remuneration and benefits, internal communications, employee relations, diversity and inclusion, employment law and HR processes and procedures. For those directly involved as 'change agents', the range of requirements is broad and deep, and a combination of education and experience is required. The knowledge, skills and personal competencies necessary are as follows:

### Knowledge

- Being able to choose and apply effective models of systematic change management.
- Managing transitions resulting from change.
- Organizational culture – its evolution and limitations for change.
- The psychology of self, self-management and interpersonal interactions.
- The many aspects of emotional intelligence.
- Power and politics in organizations.
- Leadership and motivation theories and models.
- The processes and modes of learning and knowledge management, particularly in and beyond teams.

- Basics of commercial understanding and 'business models'; cost benefit analysis.
- Data management, presentation and interpretation.

Team dynamics.

- Models of organizational design and structure.
- Survey design and management.

Process re-engineering.

## Skills

- Basic project management skills and tools.
- Helping managers define end states.
- Analysis and diagnosis of both 'hard' and 'soft' data, particularly the latter.
- Consulting, questioning and listening.
- Problem analysis.
- Group facilitation – for discussions, decision-making and focus groups.
- Coaching and giving feedback.
- Political and influencing skills.
- Conflict management.

## Personal attributes

- Ability to remain objective and neutral at all times.
- Empathy for others and their positions and motivations.
- Discernment of what is significant and important.
- Ability to build relationships and trust.
- Openness and curiosity.
- Ability to tolerate ambiguity.
- A systems thinker – able to see the big picture and interconnections.

The knowledge can be acquired through formal learning, but the skills need practice, experience and feedback. In terms of personal attributes, we need to recognize that some are innate abilities that are hard to learn if not there already.

### ACTIVITY 8.2

1. In view of your learning throughout the book, if you were asked to build a course for change agents, what would be your top three picks from the knowledge category, the skills category, and the personal competencies category, and why?

## A Note on Using External Consultants

All the major consultancies – and many small niche firms – will say they can help with significant change management and will have their own models of change management that they follow. Some of these are excellent. However, many consultants tend to over-engineer a change project, because it takes them more time (and hence yields more revenue for them), rather than designing a simpler and likely more effective process. Whilst there may be good reason to seek external help, the internal expertise, commitment and knowledge of internal players are invaluable. Of course, some transformational projects may just be too large for the internal capability. Nevertheless, external help needs to be kept firmly under control by a project steering group, and is best used for specifically identified niche contributions.

## The Leadership of Change – Two Scenarios

In Chapter 7 we considered the role of leadership in organizational change. There are two demands on the role of leadership, based on who 'owns' the project. This includes:

→ The 'orchestration' of a change project that a leader has *initiated*, within their own department or across several departments.

→ The team leader making change happen, as required and instigated *by someone else*.

Of course, a team leader may have their own localized change projects, which may run parallel with implementing other people's projects. They will be simpler to manage, have fewer stakeholders and probably involve the whole team. However, they also often have change projects coming at them from many directions, which they are expected to implement, which can distract from daily tasks. There will often be one or more that they see little benefit from in their own context.

## Towards Better Managing Change

One of the general contributions of HR is the encouragement of better change management practice(s) generally. Everyone manages change in some way – in their work and home life. Few feel the need to have a systematic approach – they just get on with it. Organizations are, as we have seen, much more complex and change may affect multiple stakeholders. In view of this, three key areas for HR are:

→ Initiating and seeking agreement to a systematic methodology of change management (such as Kotter's Eight Steps) or, preferably, a holistic joined-up model that recognizes change as a dynamic multi-faced phenomenon.

→ Training managers in the effective management of change.

→ Training their own HR professionals to be able to empathetically help individuals through change.

# The Contribution of HR Professionals in Different Change Categories

We have previously discussed *'transformational change'*, which affects the whole of the organization, as opposed to *incremental* change. Substantive change is frequently initiated by the senior management team and is likely to be led by a multidisciplinary steering group. Substantive change proceeds in phases over a longer period of time. It is also typically disruptive. For these reasons, whilst the macro environment is dynamic, organizations may not engage in substantive change frequently. *'Incremental change'* however, goes on all the time – or should do, to avoid complacency and stagnation. One of the 'mantras' of the global company Procter and Gamble is *'if we don't manage change, it will manage us'*. They constantly look for changes which would benefit stakeholders, with team meetings at every level exploring and discussing possibilities.

To help us understand different types of change project and HR's role and contribution, see Table 8.1. This shows a typology of five categories of HR contributions to organizational change, which are referenced A–E.

| Typology | Description | Initiated By | Examples |
|---|---|---|---|
| **Initiation of Change Outside of HR** | | | |
| A | Organization-wide | CEO/Executive Team | • An organizational restructuring, changing the vertical and horizontal boundaries, creating new departments and abandoning others<br>• An organization-wide cultural change programme – new values and principles of management requiring changes in attitude and behaviour<br>• Adapting to a major shift in technology requiring a different business model<br>• Integrating an acquisition or managing a merger |
| B | Operational change – within a specific department or operational process | Business Leader | • The manufacturing director may want to change the manufacturing process, by introducing new machinery or changing the quality standards<br>• The customer service director may want to outsource certain kinds of customer calls<br>• The marketing director may want to have some special promotions or introduce some new products<br>• The estates manager may want to change the layout of the retail outlets<br>• A department wishes to reorganize itself / change its job structures |
| C | 'Support Department' (see explanation below) – change in systems and processes, affecting all departments | 'Support Department' Leader | • New versions of software initiated by the IT department<br>• A new cybersecurity requirement initiated by the IT department<br>• A new process for capital investment control from the finance department<br>• An office move or restructuring |

| Typology | Description | Initiated By | Examples |
|---|---|---|---|
| **Initiation of Change From Within HR** | | | |
| D | HR changes in systems and processes, affecting all departments | Chief HR Officer | • A new performance management process<br>• Introduction of 'self-service' intranet-based HR<br>• The introduction of regular pulse engagement surveys |
| E | HR recognizes the need for a change in categories A/B/C above and influences the appropriate leader to initiate it | One of the above | • A change in an external 'PESTLE' factor – such as the legal employment framework<br>• Keeping professionally up to date, looking for improvements to organizational effectiveness that could be made<br>• Observations from interactions with managers<br>• Trends and issues derived from HR analytics, from opinion surveys or exit interviews |

**Table 8.1** Categories of Change and HR's Role

Note – by '*support departments*', we mean a department in the 'back office'. These departments span across the organization, but are not involved front-line operations. Examples of such departments are:

→ Human resources.
→ Finance.
→ IT.
→ Quality assurance.
→ Strategy and planning.
→ Communications and PR.
→ Property and security.

These departments (and those similar) are the drivers of many changes to an organization's systems and processes.

## ACTIVITY 8.3

1. Can you think of two additional examples for each of the five categories listed above?

We will now explore the five change categories and the contribution that HR can (and often *must*) make in its 'change agent' capacity.

## HR's Role in Supporting Category A and B Change Projects

For major projects it is likely there will be a 'change steering group'. A member of HR will be a member of that team, led by the project 'owner' or their designated deputy. That person will probably be senior – but it is worth remembering that a 'change leader' role can be valuable career development and experience for a person with high potential, and HR (talent management) may advise on that.

There should always be an initial *diagnostic phase* before a change project is planned, which HR may help with. It is too easy for a busy senior management team to rush into a solution that appears 'right' to them without considering alternatives. That process has the following steps:

1. Often major change is driven by a CEO or next level 'C' leader who wants to create a different organization that they believe will be more effective, and conforms to their own values and experience – for example, a different structure or culture. It can also be driven by a new business strategy, or by an external 'PESTLE' factor through horizon scanning. For example, competition and technology frequently force change. Depending on the degree of trust between the senior leader concerned and HR, HR can take a unique role in understanding the underlying *motivation* for the change. There may be a personal agenda at work, lying behind the espoused reason for the change.

2. A general vision of where the organization should move to must be backed up by a clear understanding of the 'end state' that should exist at the end of the change. The 'desired end state' can be described and confirmed in a way that enables progress to be measured. It will probably have several components and the gap between the desired and current components of each can be defined.

3. A lot of change is driven by the need to respond to organizational dysfunction or problems. Here it is important to guard against senior management jumping to conclusions about the cause(s) and defining solutions. A thorough cause and effect analysis is needed, which may involve collecting a lot of 'data' or evidence through surveys and interviews. This is the classic work of an 'OD' professional.

HR brings a unique organization-wide perspective through its overview of all departments and their interaction, and the 'talent(s)' the organization has available. It can also be seen as 'neutral' with (usually) no gains or losses at the end of most changes.

HR has an important role in challenging changes proposed by line managers that it believes will *have unintended consequences*, such as negative effects on other parts of the organization, or where cost–benefit analysis is incomplete.

### ACTIVITY 8.4

1. Consider the following scenario: a manager decides to relocate one of their units to a site that is five miles away. They have planned the move carefully and fixed a weekend when it will take place. What kind of 'unintended consequences' might they not have thought of? Please explain.

When a project is underway, the change project leader may look to HR to:

→ Secure resources for the change 'steering group'.

→ Advise as to the most appropriate systematic change management process, before working with the project owner to follow it.

→ Provide expert advice on the communications strategy for different stakeholder groups, especially internally, which is vital for successful change management.

→ As part of communications, design and conduct consultation sessions, particularly with employees and/or their representatives, which may lead to negotiations.

→ Predict likely resistance through stakeholder analysis and techniques such as Force Field Analysis (Lewin), and develop strategies for managing this resistance.

→ Design and conduct team workshops, which explore the application of the change at a local level.

→ Provide counselling support to individuals as needed, harnessing Bridges' Transitions work.

→ Facilitating individual change as needed – job changes, redundancies, promotions, career counselling and changes to terms and conditions.

→ There may be a need to design new jobs, evaluate and grade them, design new incentive schemes and reposition salaries.

- The recruitment department may need to look for new staff and new skills, which requires job descriptions and person specifications to be written.
- The Learning and Development department may be required to design and deliver training in new skills and areas of knowledge.
- Design appropriate surveys to check the effectiveness and reactions to the change – during the process if it is a long one, or at the end.

HR may also make other contributions depending on the nature of the project. In category B projects a 'local' HR representative should be involved, one who knows the business and its people well. That person can call on other parts of HR for help if needed.

## Category C Projects – HR's Role in Supporting Them

These projects, owned by other support departments, will frequently be organization-wide and therefore close to category A. It would not be uncommon, however, for such a department to feel they have no need of HR, or not properly consider the added value they could be responsible for. This can be a big mistake, as all the problems of people grappling with change are the same. Many a new system from the IT department has run into trouble through due to a lack of understanding of the fears and insecurities of subordinates that can arise from such changes. Plus, many of the contributions outlined in the previous section may be needed.

## Category D projects – What Kind of Changes Does HR Initiate and Own?

HR is a department in its own right and may have its own localized 'B' projects. Examples would be internal reorganization and job design, setting up a new department (such as HR Analytics), bringing in new specialized software, outsourcing a function or new internal processes. They will not be looking for someone else to help them – although if they have an OD department, they will certainly draw on that.

Some initiatives will apply to all in the organization; others may only apply for some job families or at some levels. The following summarizes some of the typical areas in this category:

→ *New or changed policies and procedures*

A few examples might include the promotion of diversity, working from home, legal compliance changes or support for additional qualifications.

→ *New or changed processes*

HR owns a multitude of processes for people management, but often rely on line management to carry them out. This requires careful briefing and may require training. HR may also need to monitor a shared partnership, to ensure it is effective. For example, when introducing a new performance management process, conducting surveys and responding to them, using mobile apps and self-service procedures, and changing recruitment processes by deploying by AI.

→ *New salary grading, recognition schemes, benefits or incentive schemes*

This can be a very controversial area, where change may need an additional dimension of negotiation with employee groups and individuals.

→ *New company-wide learning and development opportunities; talent management*

This goes beyond new training courses. It could include coaching and mentoring schemes, trainee programmes, company level onboarding and secondment opportunities.

Talent management may involve cultural changes, new processes for assessing potential, competency frameworks for assessment, coaching and mentoring and retention incentives. These company-wide programmes would require line management buy-in.

→ *Internal communication strategies*

HR is usually the originator of new channels of communication within the organization, and some may be significant interventions involving senior and line management.

→ *New community/corporate responsibility/internal communications/ diversity and inclusion initiatives*

Ideas for these may come from many sources, but generally it is HR that makes them into a reality. Examples can include volunteering opportunities, charitable 'doubling', work with schools, celebrating diversity, or organizing 'speak-up' sessions.

→ *Health, Safety and Wellbeing Programmes*

This is a growing area in HR, stimulated by the COVID epidemic, and can involve the provision of a variety of services and facilities.

In all of these, the organization should expect HR to role model professional and exemplary change management processes. This will include:

→ Identification of all stakeholders involved in the change.

→ Change implementation planning.

→ Consultation where appropriate.

→ Clear and inclusive communications material.

→ Anticipation of reasons for resistance and preparing appropriate rationales.

→ Establishing and empowering 'agents' for the change across the organization.

→ Explanation and training workshops as needed.

→ Evaluating the effectiveness and perceived value of the change.

### ACTIVITY 8.5

1. As part of a new flexible working policy, people will be permitted to work from home three days a week. However, they must install an app that tells HR when they are doing company work. What kind of resistance might you anticipate? How might you, as a HR professional, counter this resistance in order to make the change successful?

## Category E Projects

Arguably, this is not a separate category of projects as they eventually become category A, B or C projects. But returning to Table 8.1 and Ulrich's quadrant of HR roles, the role he defined as 'change agent' includes proactive *change stimulation* as well as giving reactive support to others.

The HR Director/CHRO will be part of the senior management team and, depending on the HR structure, it is common for 'HR business partners' around the organization to belong to local management teams. This provides a twofold opportunity. The first is that of involvement in the issues across the business, listening to and witnessing challenges and problems as they arise. The second opportunity is that of proposing, describing and sometimes presenting a case for change that will meet those issues. Particularly, of course, with a 'people perspective'.

This role is one of *leading* in its own right – leading the organization towards being more effective in some way, stimulated by views into both the internal and external environments of the organization and the 'labour market'. Proposals should not be put forward because the senior HR person wishes to be a 'follower of fashion', although this can frequently happen and is largely for the sole benefit of some HR individuals.

Finding ideas that are attractive and can appeal to the rest of the business team is not so difficult – but it is the *specific*, preferably quantified, benefit to the organization that needs to be articulated.

CEOs always have their own focus of interests. Some CEOs are technical and are inspired by product ideas. Others are financially orientated and focused exclusively on the bottom line. A few are so interested in people and organization that they drive the HR function personally. As we can imagine, this can be both a blessing and a curse. But without such a CEO (which is the 'norm'), if the HR Director does not lead in the areas of organizational change and people management processes, *no one else will*. They are the ones who have the whole picture and all of the detail.

HR needs some influencing skills to make many of these proposals for change. One aspect of that skill would be lining up 'champions' (managers who share the needs for change), before any general discussion takes place.

In what areas might this be? There is no perfect organization – there may be many problems to solve and many candidates for change – so there are a multitude of potential areas for change; HR needs to be able to prioritize and rationalize the conclusions with the executive team; always bearing in mind that there are limits to how much change an organization can handle while still functioning effectively in its core business. Here are some possibilities for change initiatives:

→ *Identifying cultural dysfunction, enabling the defining of a cultural vision and leading cultural change*

Often it is a CEO that recognizes and initiates a culture change, but there are a number of situations where HR might propose it. The first might be that the organization has no coherent cultural framework for people to assimilate to. It may have been shaped by multiple acquisitions, or allowed dominant leaders in different parts to instil their own, differing values. Does it matter? Sometimes the strategy of the centre is that of being no more than a holding company for different businesses with their own brands. In this case, a shared culture is not important. But usually there is one overriding company brand (usually its name), and it is confusing for all stakeholders if it operates in widely inconsistent ways.

### ACTIVITY 8.6

1. Imagine your company has a set of statements in a document called 'The Way We Do Business'. This is intended to clarify to the ethics and values of the company to staff and customers. You run a graduate training scheme across all locations and, when you bring them together (as you do every two months), new graduates report very varying adherence to this document in their everyday experiences. Some are embarrassed to be associated with behaviours alien to the document. You know this is not good for the company brand. As an HR professional, what kind of cultural change intervention would you suggest to senior management?

A second reason a company would lack a universal culture is due to a merger. In fact, it is cultural clashes that are the largest causes of failure in mergers. It would not be done immediately, but there comes a time when the best of each partner in the merger should be welded into a new culture (see the case study at the end of this chapter).

A third reason might be that a culture is unethical, or exclusive or is clearly operating in a manner that is contrary to the espoused values. The senior management team may not be conscious of this, or if they are, may not consider it important. HR might need to make the case as to why change is needed. We often read of organizations with 'toxic' cultures – we are entitled to ask 'where is HR in this?'

➔ *Organizational change – structure and ways of working*

HR constantly deals with different layers and units in the organization. It is able to see conflicts of accountability, or inefficient and cumbersome structures and processes, which hinder the organization in its mission. It can take an independent, objective and professional view of how this might be changed.

➔ *Executive and management development*

It is usually HR that makes proposals for development programmes for leadership, executives and management in general. *Individual* programmes can be proposed and designed, but whenever there is a new business strategy or an industry disruption, there is benefit in *collective* learning. There should be clarity about the objectives that are to be achieved. 'Everyone else has one' is not a good reason for a leadership development programme.

→ *Resource planning and strategies*

If HR is doing strategic workforce planning – as it should be – it will have advance warning of predicted resource and skills gaps. It will evaluate possible strategies to close those gaps. This could involve new trainee programmes, job redesign, new approaches to career movement, flexible working and so on.

## Evaluating the Success of Change Management

Many changes in organizations drift into the future, once the main plan of communication and implementation has taken place and imperceptibly merged into everyday life. Yet they may have been costly to implement and we should know whether the money was spent wisely in terms of the benefits.

The problem with many 'impact' studies is that they are only ever conducted after the intervention or change has happened. We argued at the beginning of this chapter for precision in the definition of the 'desired end state'. This provides clarity as to the 'size of the gap' we are trying to close. We can then evaluate the costs and merits of different ways to close that gap. We should not be going ahead with any change project where the balance of benefits vs. costs is inadequate.

However, this is not easy to evaluate. Costs can all be described financially, but most benefits cannot – they are 'soft'. They may have long-term financial implications, but the links are often not direct. But they can all be measured and we can specify a percentage improvement in that measure as a goal. Without such (and it is rarely done), we are left with only anecdotal descriptions of success.

Some organization-wide projects take a long time to complete, even years, for major culture change. En route they become 'contaminated' with additional change interventions. Their completion is thus rarely visible or celebrated, as in a 'tomorrow we go live' project. This requires continual periodic evaluation of the effectiveness of the change against the end state. Other projects fail to anticipate all the consequences of making the change due to a lack of 'systems thinking' at the beginning, and consequently incur unforeseen costs.

One of HR's significant contributions should be in the measurement of change success through its expertise in analytics, especially in 'soft areas'. Wherever it is involved with a project, be it someone else's or its own, one of the first tasks is to help define specifically what will be different at the end of the change, using quantitative targets wherever possible. It can then design instruments, where needed, that will enable measurement along the journey, and particularly at the end.

> ### ACTIVITY 8.7
>
> 1. Your division has recently combined four separate departments in different locations, all providing different aspects of customer service, into one central call centre. The locations were all in the same city, but the change did involve some redundancies. The programme did have three key 'end state' objectives. What might they have been? And how would you go about evaluating the success of this change?
>
> 2. In another scenario, the IT Director of the organization in which you work as a HR professional is concerned about recent cybersecurity scares. They are worried about the extensive customer database that the organization has, through which they provide information on offers, etc. Therefore, the IT Director has decided to institute a new system of two-factor authentication for all customers and staff. Staff working on front-line processes will need to be able to explain to customers who ask them why this is important and, if necessary, show them how to do it. How do you think HR might help the IT department alongside the employees that are working in customer-facing processes?

## Communication for Effective Change

A common theme throughout this book is the interpersonal nature of organizational change in action. This includes verbal and non-verbal interpersonal communication, which is flagged as having a significant impact on the success of organizational change initiatives (Li, Ruoyu, Weiting and Yeunjae, 2021; Kitchen and Daly, 2002) (see Chapter 6 in particular). During substantive change the exchange of ideas and information enables the senior management team to better manage employees' expectations. Juxtaposed against this, poor communication creates uncertainty and a general lack of trust in what is being proposed. It is the responsibility of the senior management team, with the help of HR, to articulate the change narrative, including a coherent vision of the organization's future changed state, in order to encourage employees' proactive engagement with the process. The challenge for HR in both facilitating and leading the change is to create an organizational culture that proactively engages in communication that is both top-down and bottom-up. This type of communication is recognized as a precursor for effective organizational change (Goodman and Truss, 2004). See Figure 8.2 below, which illustrates the appropriateness of top-down and bottom-up communication for successful organizational change (Goodman and Truss, 2004).

At the macro and meso level effective communication influences:

→ Employees' perceptions of the validity of the proposed change.

→ Employee morale and retention rates.

→ The ability to challenge and question organizational norms and conventions.

→ The overall success of the change programme.

Whilst at the individual level, communication is recognized as influencing:

→ Personal acceptance of the need for change.

→ Understanding of how the change will impact each stakeholder.

→ The speed and success with which individuals progress through the coping cycle.

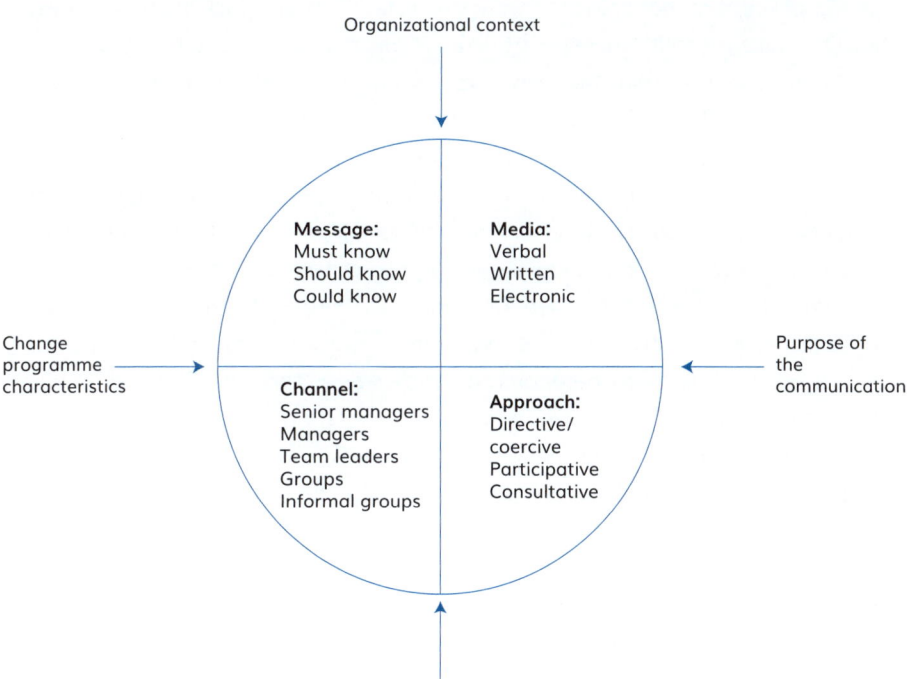

**Figure 8.2** The change communication wheel (Goodman and Truss, 2024).

### ACTIVITY 8.8

1. Please reflect on a recent experience in which poor communication affected a key event, either in your professional or personal life. What were the implications and consequences of this poor communication?

2. What are your recommendations for improving this poor communication?

### CASE STUDY: CULTURAL ADAPTATION THROUGH AN ANGLO-NORDIC MERGER – THE MERGER OF INTERNATIONAL COMPUTERS LTD AND NOKIA DATA

International Computers Ltd (ICL) was once the core of the British computer industry. It operated globally, but was relatively weak in continental Europe at the birth of the common market, strong in 'heavy' mainframe computing and public IT, but weaker in the fast growing PC market. Nokia Data (ND) was HQ'd in Sweden, and was part of the Finnish conglomerate that wanted to divest of all its non-telecomms businesses. It was strong in Europe and in personal computers.

At the beginning of 1991 the management of ICL Europe, which turned over only 15 per cent of that of ICL UK, were frustrated with their lack of growth. It was hard to make a profit. Attempts at acquisitions had so far failed.

At the time, Nokia was the second largest publicly owned company in Finland. It had started ND in 1970. In early 1988 it bought the Swedish Ericsson Data Systems, which extended its technical capability and product range and gave it new operations in Europe. The breakup of the Soviet Union (the major export market) and recession in Finland dictated the need for focus and divestment by the parent company. ND began looking for a partner to merge with.

There were powerful arguments in favour of a merger between ICL Europe and Nokia Data (which would actually be an acquisition by ICL). Adding ND would treble the size of ICL's European operations and give it new strength in PCs and terminals, the biggest product growth area in the IT business.

The style employed in the negotiation meetings was friendly and open. Previous experience had showed that it is easy to antagonize the seller through arrogant or suspicious questioning. HR in ICL had always had a high profile, but this was not the case for ND. From the beginning, the HR Director of ICL Europe (HRD) was fully involved, including in the initial due diligence checks, which went way beyond finance and included assessment of the organization and the key staff. This was all in total secrecy and the Human Resource Department was very involved in the planning of communications to all stakeholder groups, all coordinated for one big announcement day.

The company decided not to bring in outside consultants to aid the integration, instead deciding to use the whole of the ICL Europe HQ top management team. This team would manage the ongoing business with the deputies in department for the first four months. During this time each functional head would work with his or her opposite number, and every Monday a weekly reporting and planning meeting was held. Joint review meetings were held every four weeks.

HR focused on organization and key appointments at this early stage. The earlier assessments enabled the latter to be made speedily; inevitably some country managers could not be retained, but great emphasis was placed on identifying the best choice from both sides. Naturally however, the appointed country manager ran things in the way they were familiar with and inherited managers/employees from the other side who were forced to cope with considerable change. Not all Nokia Data countries had their own HR Manager – but with the exception of the Finland and Sweden appointees, all HR managers originated from ICL. The two HRDs worked together for about a year, focusing on the small number of people processes that needed central oversight. They also needed to reduce the combined HQ from about 400 to 130, a major task.

The 'integration' philosophy adopted was to identify commonalities and differences in all areas before prioritizing them in three categories: (1) must be harmonized quickly or will cause problems, (2) should be harmonized within the next eighteen months for efficient working, and (3) can be decided locally.

In HR, the first category included, for example, expatriate terms and conditions (there was a lot of interchange between the countries), executive bonus schemes, travel policy and graduate training schemes. The major item in the second group was to create one culture for ICL Europe and the integration of a number of operational processes outside of HR.

HR gave a lot of attention to cultural analysis; a comparison was made on twenty-three parameters of both processes and values. The two cultures were very different. They had divergent national approaches, and while the decision-making style of NHD was fast moving and empowered, the ICL decision-making style was controlled and process-heavy. The overriding principle was to mutually learn from 'the way they did things' and pick the best for the management of the 'new' business. Many features were attractive to ICL managers: ND's simplicity of decision-making processes (using telephones and face-to-face contact rather than reports and forms), their dynamism, style and creativity in image building, the business sharpness and independence of several of their country managers. And yet, there were attractive ways ICL did things too, for example, its management training, its reviews of strategy, its processes for talent management, operational control and coordination. As a result of the analysis, a number of decisions were made which changed the established ways of operation on both sides, but they were generally welcomed.

> One year on, all the senior people came together in Switzerland for a team building and consolidation event, organized by HR. The general atmosphere was of being part of a united new business team, and this was justified by the retention of most key players in the following years.

## ACTIVITY 8.9

1. Which category of change, as put forward in Table 8.1, does this case study fall into? Explain your response by finding evidence for your decision in the case study above.

2. Which sorts of roles do you think HR should take in the situation outlined in the case study? Initiator, facilitator or both? Again, use evidence from the case study and your learning in this chapter to illustrate your answers.

3. Thinking about the core capabilities that are required by change agents, including knowledge, skills and personal attributes, which do you think would be absolutely necessary in the case study scenario, and why?

## ACTIVITY 8.10

1. Firstly, reflect on what it is you wish to achieve in either your personal or professional life. This should be a future ambitious state.

2. Having reflected, write down what it is you wish to achieve, then detail which approaches you will use to attain your future ambitious state.

3. List the changes you will need to make in your personal or professional life to attain your future ambitious state.

 **CONSULTANCY IN THE CHAIR**

### Cup of Kindness Activity

One consequence of the takeover is that the new parent company wants to introduce the share buying/share ownership scheme it currently employs in its US operations to Cup of Kindness. This would be partly paid for by a salary sacrifice, and all employees would be asked to participate after two years' service. An HR Director has come to you to express serious concerns about the appropriateness of such a scheme for a coffee retailing business, especially in time of economic hardship and the transient labour force the organization has. What advice would you give to this HR Director? If the ultimate decision goes against the HR Director, who has to implement the scheme, what would your advice be in view of the facilitating and initiating the role of HR?

## Competency-based Interview Questions

1. Have you ever had to go along with a decision that you fundamentally disagreed with? If so, how did you manage this?
2. Can you describe a situation when you had to adapt to the work environment at hand, despite the fact that you didn't agree with the direction the organization was taking?

## Chapter Summary

As seen throughout this book, the effectiveness of organizational change is dependent on many variables. However, a hallmark characteristic of effective change is managing the human aspects well, with empathy and systematically, which is a difficult balancing act. In this respect, HR has a crucial role. This chapter has critically evaluated this role and contribution that HR can make. Particular attention has been given to HR's role in initiating and facilitating different types of organizational change. Emphasis has been given to HR's role as a dedicated change agent in converting organizational change strategies into realities through a combination of knowledge, skills and personal attributes. HR's complex role as both initiator and facilitator is illustrated by way of different change categories. In summary, the HR's role is very complex. It has to negotiate and find a way forwards with both the senior management team and the employees who are involved with day-to-day organizational processes, systems and practices. In doing so effectively, HR can make a major contribution to the success of both incremental and transformative change.

## Useful Resources

- http://www.geert-hofstede.com. This site explains dimensions of national culture and explains how different countries compare.
- https://www.youtube.com/watch?v=EcHpgsTg458 (accessed 21 April 2025). 'Corporate culture Apple example.' An interesting insight into a specific organization culture.
- https://www.youtube.com/watch?v=j518qByx2Ng (accessed 21 April 2025). 'The two different approaches to cultural change.' This video describes 'top-down' and 'middle-out' approaches.
- https://efqm.org/the-efqm-model (accessed 21 April 2025).
- https://mailchi.mp/73aee6f4941d/6fmwnr14te (accessed 21 April 2025).
- www.unglobalcompact.org (accessed 21 April 2025).

## Bibliography

Cameron, K. S. and Quinn, R. E. (2011), *Diagnosing and Changing Organisational Cultures: Based on the Competing Values Framework*, third edition. San Francisco, CA: Jossey-Bass.

Corporate Research Forum (2018), *Designing Adaptable Organisations for Tomorrow's Challenges* Research Report.

Deshler, R. (2016), 'HR's Role as a Transformation Agent'. *Strategic HR Review*, 15(3):141–2.

Galbraith, J. (2002), *Designing Organizations: An Executive Guide to Strategy, Structure and Process*. San Francisco, CA: Jossey-Bass.

Goodman, J. and Truss, C. (2004), 'The Medium and the Message: Communicating Effectively During a Major Change Initiative'. *Journal of Change Management*, 4(3): 217–28.

Higgins, P., Roper, I. and Gamwell, S. (2016), 'HRM as an Emerging New Managerial Profession', in Wilkinson, A., Hislop, D. and Coupland, C. (eds), *Perspectives on Contemporary Professional Work* (pp. 286–312). Cheltenham: Edward Elgar.

Hodges, J. and Crabtree, M. (2000), *Reshaping HR: The Role of HR in Organisational Change*. London: Routledge.

Hofstede, G. H. (2010), *Cultures and Organisations: Software of the Mind*, third edition. London: McGraw-Hill.

Judge, M.-J. and Holbeche L. (2011), *Organisation Development – A Practitioner's Guide*. London: Kogan Page.

Kitchen, P. J. and Daly, F. (2002), 'Internal Communication During Change Management'. *Corporate Communications: An International Journal*, 7(1): 46–53.

Li, J. Y., Ruoyu, S., Weiting, T., and Yeunjae L. (2021), 'Employee Coping With Organizational Change in the Face of a Pandemic: The Role of Transparent Internal Communication'. *Public Relations Review*, 47(1): 1–11.

Mishra, P., Shukla, B. and Sujatha, R. (2021), *Human Resource Management for Organisational Change: Theoretical Formulations*. London: Routledge.

Nielsen, K., Morten, B., Ogbonnaya, C, Känsälä, M., Saari, E. and Isaksson, K. (2017), 'Workplace Resources to Improve Both Employee Well-being and Performance: A Systematic Review and Meta-analysis'. *Work & Stress*, 31(2): 101–20.

Parkes, C. and Davis, A. J. (2013), 'Ethics and Social Responsibility – Do HR Professionals Have the "Courage to Challenge" or are They Set to be Permanent "Bystanders?"' *The International Journal of Human Resource Management*, 24(12): 2411–34.

Schein, H. E. (2004), *Organisational Culture and Leadership*, 3rd edition. San Francisco, CA: Jossey-Bass.

Trompenaars, F. and Prud'homme, P. (2004), *Managing Change Across Corporate Cultures*. Chichester: Capstone Publishing.

Ulrich, D. (1997), *Human Resource Champions: The Next Agenda for Adding Value and Delivering Results*. Boston, MA: Harvard Business School Press.

# Doing Change Ethically    9

## Learning Outcomes

At the end of this chapter you will be able to:

1. Understand and explain the importance of ethics in relation to organizational change, both from a moral and sustainable business perspective.
2. Demonstrate knowledge and understanding of ethical concepts that are relevant in relation to organizational change.
3. Make proposals on how ethics should be considered in relation to specific organizational change initiatives.
4. Identify opportunities for the UN Sustainability Goals to be incorporated in, or become the focus of, organizational change initiatives.

## Introduction

This chapter concludes *Organizational Change in Action*. 'Doing Change Ethically' is not left until the end because it is an afterthought, or secondary to your learning on change. Instead, we believe that doing change ethically, be that at the macro, micro or meso unit of analysis, is imperative for all organizations. This chapter is therefore a highly relevant and appropriate conclusion to *Organizational Change in Action*.

Ethics is about differentiating between right and wrong and good and bad, and about increasing positive consequences and decreasing negative ones (By and Burnes, 2013). Organizational change may, at first, be regarded as a business problem – as something that the organization is required to engage in, in order to ensure its profitability and/or survival. However, it cannot be separated from ethical questions, as decisions and actions related to organizational change 'affect people or relationships between people such that an alternative action or inaction would affect them differently' (Werhane and Freeman, 1999, p. 2). As such, doing change ethically means that organizations need to consider a host of reflective questions to ensure that organizational change initiatives are both successful and ethical. It also requires companies to be mindful of the fact that positive organizational outcomes and ethics are strongly intertwined.

Reflective considerations in organizational change pertain to the *process* of change – that is, *how* the change is enacted within the organization and in relation to relevant stakeholders. But they will go deeper, probing into the *objectives* of change initiatives, asking questions such as why has this change been enacted, for what purpose, and who benefits from the change (and who might lose out). Processes and objectives are deeply interlinked. For example, those affected by the proposed change action, such as employees, are more likely to support it if they recognize a good purpose behind it, even if the change presents a challenging and emotionally charged situation for them. At the same time, this goodwill can be quickly undermined if those charged with implementing the organizational change make 'bad choices' in their interactions with those affected by the change, leading to a depletion of trust and confidence (Stokes and Harris 2012). Going beyond ethical considerations that purely focus on *how* organizational change is enacted is also important. There is a growing interest in the wider societal purpose of business and organizations, particularly in terms of environmental, social and economic sustainability concerns.

The perceived need for organizational change opens up unique opportunities to create organizations that pursue a good purpose, are sustainable and help address – rather than exacerbate – societal challenges. And, indeed, the perceived need to move the organization to *a more ethical position*, for example, when organizations and their members have been engaged in ethical misconduct or irresponsible practice, may even be the main instigating force for organizational change initiatives. In turn, the creation of an ethically and socially responsible organization as part of, or a main focus of, organizational change efforts is likely to make the organization a more attractive employer to motivated employees, be more appealing to customers and, more generally, help the organization maintain or improve societal approval (Suchman, 1995). All of this will help to make the organization more sustainable in the long run.

This chapter will therefore focus on both the ethics of the *process* of organizational change, as well as the ethics around the *purpose* of organizational change. It will first introduce ethical lenses through which we find points for analytical reflection and guidance to address both aspects of 'doing change ethically'. It will then discuss the ethical qualities that should underpin the *process* of organizational change, before offering some reflections as to how organizational change may be utilized to incorporate wider goals into the organization.

## Ethical Lenses for Organizational Change

Normative ethical theories, or moral philosophies, offer guiding principles, norms or rules for people to follow, enabling them to make ethical decisions in organizations. From the various ethical perspectives or 'lenses' (cf. Crane, Matten, Glozer and Spence, 2019; see Chapter 3 for an overview) we propose *virtue ethics* as a primary lens through which to approach organizational change. As opposed to theories that solely focus on the moral rightness or wrongness of an individual action (for example, does this action produce good consequences? Or does this action adhere to a specific moral principle?), virtue ethics offers a more comprehensive way of thinking about ethics by considering the idea of the 'good life' or 'human flourishing' (*eudaimonia*) (Crane, Matten, Glozer and Spence, 2019: 115; Griseri and Seppala, 2010: 53). It is concerned with the development of the virtues, which include human qualities or habits of character, such as integrity, kindness and fairness, which help people to achieve the good life and help guide their ethical decision-making (Hartmann, 2017). The section below will set out a range of virtues relevant to organizational change contexts. Ultimately, virtue ethics is about desiring and finding satisfaction in the elements of a life worthy of a human being (Hartmann, 2017); of things that are decent, honourable, meaningful and worthwhile (Stokes and Harris, 2012). Ideas of virtue ethics have been widely adopted in management scholarship. For example, Jane Collier (1995) sets out the vision of a 'virtuous organization', which she defines as an organization that discerns its purpose as carrying meaning beyond profitability and survival, and in being concerned about the welfare or 'flourishing' of its stakeholders. This may be expressed, for example, in the provision of an excellent product and service that truly meets the need of its customers/clients, in ensuring that employees find satisfaction, meaning and pride in their work, and in seeking harmonious relations with stakeholders (Crane, Matten, Glozer and Spence, 2019: 116). These ideas are also reflected in Freeman's stakeholder approach, which holds that in order to create value in business, the focus must be on how value is created for each legitimate stakeholder, with customers, employees, communities, financiers and suppliers constituting important groups. Freeman further proposes that the conceptualization of 'stakeholder value' ought to be a broad one (Freeman, Harrison, Wicks, Parmar and De Colle, 2010: 283), going beyond financial value, or narrow notions of utility, and taking the complexity of humans and what they need and value into account. The ideas of a 'virtuous organization' or of 'stakeholder value creation' might indeed provide an important North Star when initiating and implementing organizational change initiatives.

In addition to using virtue ethics as an overarching ethical framework, we also propose *discourse ethics* and *justice* as complementary ethical lenses for evaluating organizational change. *Discourse ethics* is about seeking to generate ethical solutions through open communication and dialogue (Crane, Matten, Glozer and Spence, 2019: 122). Rather than imposing preconceived ideas, followers of discourse ethics should involve those affected by organizational decisions to seek solutions to which everyone can agree. Such 'stakeholder dialogue' should be based on the principles of an ideal 'speech situation', which include, among other things, that dialogue will be based on equal participation, without domination or coercion by any party, and that only rational/reasoned arguments be put forward (Crane, Matten, Glozer and Spence, 2019). The open-endedness of discourse ethics and its 'ideal speech' requirements may make it seem like a rather idealistic ethical perspective, but it nevertheless presents an important challenge to those engaged in organizational change initiatives, as we shall see in the next section.

The second additional lens, *justice*, is concerned with how resources, benefits and burdens are allocated, emphasizing the importance of these being allocated in a fair manner. There is a broad distinction between *distributive* justice, which focuses on *outcomes*, and *procedural* justice, which focuses on the *processes* by which outcomes are arrived at (Crane, Matten, Glozer and Spence, 2019: 108). Added to this is *interactional justice*, which focuses on perceptions of fairness in relation to the actions of leaders and their treatment of their followers (Cobb, Folger and Wooten, 1995). Justice is a complex concept as there are many different criteria by which just outcomes can be assessed (Cobb, Folger and Wooten, 1995): equity (related to the notion of 'merit' and reflecting a person's contribution), equality (where everyone receives the same) and individual needs. However, all three aspects of justice – outcomes, processes and enactment – are important in organizational change, as we shall see in the next section. They all also interlink with the other ethical perspectives of virtue and discourse.

## The Ethical Change Process

Depending on its scale and scope, organizational change can be a rather unsettling experience for those affected. Organizational change typically affects employees, but, depending on their depth and length of relationship with the organization, other stakeholders such as suppliers, customers/clients, and community can also be affected. For employees organizational change might be particularly unsettling, as both their ability to earn a livelihood from their job *and* the meaning and satisfaction they derive from their work may be affected by the change.

More important is that organizational change is seen by organizational members and stakeholders to be conducted in an ethical and fair manner. Newton (2013) speaks of the need for leaders/managers enacting change to be 'virtuous agents'. The following will set out some of the virtues regarded as crucial for the sustainable success of a change initiative.

## Crucial Virtues for Sustainable Change

The first set of virtues revolve around *communication* with those affected by the change. In particular, *honesty, transparency and openness* are key here (Newton, 2013). Those implementing change should be *honest* about the current reality, which includes being honest about any difficult choices the organization might have to make. Those affected by change should be told openly *why* the change has to happen, ensuring that everyone understands its objectives and reasons. The organization should also be transparent as to how changes are going to be enacted. If those charged with implementing change fail to be honest, transparent and open, instead engaging in secrecy and/or failing to provide relevant information, this is likely to affect the trust and collaboration efforts of the organizational members and stakeholders, and may be perceived by insiders, as well as outsiders, as unethical (Newton, 2013). An example of how *not* to enact organizational change is provided in Case 1. Whilst this might be an extreme example, it shows that any organizational change without communication and transparency is likely to end in undesirable consequences.

### CASE STUDY 1: P&O FERRIES NO-NOTICE SACKING OF 800 CREW MEMBERS

On 17 March 2022, after cancelling a number of services that day, P&O Ferries, one of the major ferry operators in the UK, announced via a video recording sent to approximately 800 seafaring employees, that they were to be dismissed with immediate effect by reason of redundancy. The employees were told in the video that the P&O Ferries business had lost £100 million for each of the last two years, that P&O Ferries had considered a wide range of options, but that it had decided it had to restructure. This restructure would result in crewing being undertaken by a third-party crewing agency at far lower rates of pay, something that was possible because P&O vessels were flagged (i.e. registered) outside of the UK, which meant that the company did not have to observe UK minimum wage laws.

On the day, security staff were prepared to remove crew from ships, after unions instructed crew not to leave vessels. Coaches carrying replacement agency staff were reported to be standing by. Union representatives said that guards with handcuffs were seeking to board ships to remove crew so that they could be replaced with cheaper labour.

A spokesperson for P&O Ferries said the company had to take a 'very difficult but necessary decision' to 'secure the future viability of our business, which employs an additional 2,200 people, and supports billions in trade in and out of the UK'. They added that the million-pound losses the company incurred over the past few years – due to the disruption from COVID and post-Brexit paperwork in cross-Channel traffic, in addition to the rising cost of diesel – had been covered by their Dubai-based parent company DP World, and that this was not sustainable. They emphatically stated: 'Our survival is dependent on making swift and significant changes now'. Following the announcement, P&O ferry services were halted for a number of days, which caused severe disruption to freight services and passengers, and left many customers stranded.

The effect of P&O Ferries' actions brought instant and universal condemnation from employees, trade unions, politicians and the general public, with unions calling P&O actions a 'scandalous betrayal' and appealing to the government to halt the mass sacking. P&O's move was seen in a particularly critical light as the company had received £33 million in emergency funding during the COVID-19 pandemic.

At the time of P&O's announcement the company was thought to have broken employment law, which would have required the company to observe legally mandated dismissal periods and engage with their staff in consultations. In a hearing on 24 March, P&O's CEO admitted that the company had chosen not to consult with the unions, as the company believe that 'the change was of such magnitude that no union could accept our proposals'. The UK business secretary, Kwasi Kwarteng, asked the Insolvency Service, a government agency, to investigate whether any criminal or civil offences had been committed by the company. But in August 2022 the Insolvency Service determined there was 'no realistic prospect of a conviction', thought to be based on the fact that the vessels were not registered in the UK. The Insolvency Service's decision sparked calls for changes in the law. The Service's decision came one day after DP World announced record profits, making the company's claims on operational sustainability questionable.

## Sources:

Agencies (2022), 'P&O Ferries Will Not Face Criminal Proceedings for Mass Sacking of Staff'. *The Guardian*. 20 August. https://www.theguardian.com/business/2022/aug/20/po-wont-face-criminal-proceedings-for-mass-sacking (accessed 21 April 2025).

Humphreys, N. (2022). 'A Case Study on How Not to Dismiss 800 Employees'. Pennington, Manches, Cooper, 21 March. https://www.penningtonslaw.com/news-publications/latest-news/2022/a-case-study-on-how-not-to-dismiss-800-employees (accessed 21 April 2025).

O'Dwyer, M. (2022), 'P&O Ferries Escapes Criminal Prosecution Over Mass Sackings'. *Financial Times*, 19 August. https://www.ft.com/content/8c7ed91d-d74e-4175-b7da-7c54de92bdaa (accessed 21 April 2025).

Topham, G. (2022a), 'P&O Ferries Sacks all 800 Crew Members Across Entire Fleet'. *The Guardian*, 17 March. https://www.theguardian.com/uk-news/2022/mar/17/po-ferries-halts-sailings-before-major-announcement (accessed 21 April 2025).

Topham, G. (2022b), 'P&O Ferries Boss Admits Firm Broke Law by Sacking Staff Without Consultation'. *The Guardian*, 24 March. https://www.theguardian.com/business/2022/mar/24/po-ferries-boss-says-800-staff-were-sacked-because-no-union-would-accepts-its-plans (accessed 21 April 2025).

### ACTIVITY 9.1

1. What are the ethical issues arising in the P&O case study, and why would they be considered ethically objectionable?
2. What may have been alternative courses of action for P&O?

The virtue of *openness* also asks those enacting change to go further than just honesty, giving those both directly and indirectly affected by the change a say in the direction of the change (Nielsen, Nykodym and Brown, 1991) and the organization's vision for the future, thereby touching on the ideals of discourse ethics. Giving everyone an extensive say is likely to be too challenging for time and resource reasons. But, to involve a broader range of people rather than just top management, ensuring a good representation of all affected groups, who in turn can consult with and effectively represent the members of their group, is likely to put the organizational change initiative on a surer footing. Such involvement and dialogue involves ascertaining perceptions of what needs to change, eliciting ideas of what change objectives the organization should set itself, and sourcing input into how changes can best be enacted (Newton, 2013; Nielsen Nykodym and Brown, 1991). A genuine engagement with organizational stakeholders about change requires the organization to relinquish at least some degree of control. Case 2 shows an interesting example of how involving employees in the search to find a way out of a company crisis can lead to successful outcomes for all involved.

### CASE STUDY 2: DAN PRICE VS. ELON MUSK – A TALE OF TWO COMPANIES, OR HOW TO TREAT EMPLOYEES IN CHALLENGING TIMES

In November 2022 billionaire entrepreneur Elon Musk made headlines for slashing half of the Twitter workforce on the day of his takeover. He claimed that the financial situation of the company left him 'no choice' but to do as he did.

A few weeks later, Elon Musk appeared on a Roundtable Show panel with Dan Price – founder of Gravity Payments – who made headlines years earlier over his decision to pay all of his 250 staff a minimum annual salary of $70,000. Mr Price took this opportunity to challenge Mr Musk over the Twitter layoffs. He said that many of the daily losses in revenue were caused by interest payments due to the debt financing Musk engaged in to acquire Twitter, and asked Mr Musk: 'What was it like, as a visionary billionaire entrepreneur, to do the same old thing by financing your acquisition debts with savings from layoffs?' Musk replied that Twitter had 'tripled headcount' in two years while revenue was 'flat to negative'. He argued that if he hadn't enacted layoffs then, they would have needed to be done later. Musk also added that the Federal Reserve was unwise to raise interest rates, making the situation worse. After the interview, Mr Price was challenged by people who said that objectively Twitter was 'bloated' and needed drastic cuts. However, while Mr Price acknowledged that Twitter had massive problems that needed addressing, he put forward an alternative course of action to 'Wall Street's favourite combination of debt/layoffs'. An alternative course of action that he pursued, at his own company, Gravity Payments, when it faced a massive drop in revenue.

Mr Price argues that a better option is for businesses to share full details with employees, give them time to process and to give feedback, listen to their ideas and create with them a shared vision for the company.

> Employees know how to help. In 2020, I was stressed to be CEO when, [during the pandemic] revenue halved. We were losing $2 million per month with only a handful of months left before we lost it all. I told my employees. I gave them time. They were self-sacrificing, and came up with a solution.

> But it overwhelmed me when I saw it. The employees set up anonymous, voluntary and temporary pay decreases.
>
> In doing so the employees also rejected the idea to jack up payments to the company's 20,000 customers by $100 a month. That would have given the company an extra $2 million a month, and would have solved our financial crisis. But the employees said they'd rather take the pain themselves in a pandemic rather than enact 'any kind of insult or injury to the small businesses that rely on our services'.
>
> Mr Price says that in all the years Gravity Payments has been in business, it has never laid off any employees. He didn't want to do that this time, either. And it paid off. He said that the company later 'had record sales and we paid "the employees" back. We then reinstituted small raises at the end of the year plus record raises the next year, including increasing our minimum wage to $80,000'. He asks, 'could Musk have temporarily kept expenses flat while fixing product and growing revenue? He wouldn't have been the first to grow and thrive with that strategy. Employees would engage to save jobs and [the company]'.

## Sources:

Rushe, D., Oladipo, G, Bhuiyan, J., Milmo, D. and Middleton, J. (2022), 'Twitter Slashes Nearly Half its Workforce as Musk Admits "Massive Drop" in Revenue. *The Guardian*, 5 November 2022. https://www.theguardian.com/technology/2022/nov/04/twitter-layoffs-elon-musk-revenue-drop</URI> (accessed 21 April 2025); @DanPriceSeattle tweets 5 December 2022, https://twitter.com/DanPriceSeattle/status/1599648642226610176 (accessed 21 April 2025).

Sowell, J. (2020), 'He Employs 50 Boise Workers. They Took Pay Cuts to Avoid Layoffs. The Choice Paid Off'. *Idaho Statesman*. https://www.idahostatesman.com/news/business/article244968805.html (accessed 21 April 2025).

### ACTIVITY 9.2

1. How, in ethical terms, would you describe the contrast between Musk's and Price's approach to dealing with company crises?

2. To what extent can Price's approach act as a model to be followed by other organizations? What might the barriers be for organizations who wish to act with their employees in a similar way?

Another important virtue in organizational change is *fairness*. To establish what *fairness* means we draw on the features of justice theory set out above (see Cobb, Folger and Wooten, 1995). Openness, honesty and transparency in communicating with organizational stakeholders may already fulfil the requirements of interactional justice. But distributive and procedural aspects of justice also require fair outcomes, and a fair process by which those outcomes are arrived at.

This may mean, for example, that any additional efforts that are required of organizational members and stakeholders as part of the change process will, following the principle of 'equity', be adequately and appropriately compensated for. It may also mean that any losses arising from organizational change are fairly distributed, using 'equality' as a guiding principle to avoid an unequal allocation of burdens and benefits across the organization. In practical terms this could mean, for instance, that rather than laying organizational members off, any loss arising from organizational change is distributed more evenly, by having everyone across the organization work fewer hours or have an equal reduction in pay (Cobb, Folger and Wooten, 1995). What might particularly endanger the success of organizational change is if lower paid workers are forced to take on all of the loss, while top management receive substantial rewards. Fairness also means looking after those hit by the loss, using the principle of 'need' and, for example, ensuring that any laid off employees receive adequate compensation and assistance in finding a new job. Cobb, Folger and Wooten (1995) argue that the behaviour and attitudes of those not experiencing such loss, and thus the maintenance and success of the organizational change, is a function of how fairly the remaining staff believe that those who have been adversely affected are treated. This points to the fact that a fair treatment of those experiencing 'loss' is in the enlightened self-interest of the organization.

Procedural justice, of course, demands that those affected by change are given a voice in relation to distributive justice, but also in the change process and its outcomes as a whole, which links fairness back to ideas of discourse ethics. An important aspect of procedural justice, as Cobb, Folger and Wooten (1995) highlight, is the establishment of new channels of communication to resolve any issues that might cause conflict and grievances as a result of the organizational change.

Newton (2013) points out that change in itself does not necessarily generate resistance. In fact, organizational members might be aware that the organization needs to change, and might even welcome change efforts. What is important however, is how these changes are implemented; resistance, after all, is often about how the change is managed, rather than the change content itself. It is therefore imperative that the virtues of honesty, transparency, openness and fairness are observed, to ensure organizational members and stakeholders are taken along in the change process, ensuring their collaboration and trust.

### ACTIVITY 9.3

Consider an organizational change initiative with which you are familiar.

1. List all stakeholder groups that are likely to be affected by the change and consider *how* they will be affected.
2. List any ethical concerns that might arise in relation to each stakeholder group.
3. Drawing on the ethical concepts introduced in this section, set out what it might mean to engage with each stakeholder group in an ethical and fair manner.

## The Purpose of Organizational Change or Change to Incorporate Wider Goals

As stated earlier, 'doing change ethically' also involves considering the purpose of the change initiative, which, in turn, is linked to questions about the purpose and goals of the organization. According to modern stakeholder value creation thinking, and in line with the teleological orientation of virtue ethics, efforts to engage in change to improve the organization's performance should look beyond concerns for survival and competitiveness to ensure that a whole range of stakeholders can flourish. As such, the perceived need for organizational change opens up opportunities to incorporate wider goals related to stakeholder welfare.

Case 3 provides an example of how this was done within the context of a medium-sized manufacturing company. It will be of note that the organization did not just have an honourable end goal in mind – that is the commitment to paying their workers a Living Wage – but that they also felt the process of getting there had to be ethical, following some of the virtues set out in the previous section.

### CASE STUDY 3: HOW A COMPANY BECAME AN ACCREDITED LIVING WAGE EMPLOYER AS PART OF ORGANIZATIONAL CHANGE

Good Foods is a medium-sized food manufacturing firm, a family business employing about one hundred staff. Over the years the business has grown in size and the company decided to invest several million pounds into a new factory with state-of-the-art machinery. The company's managers knew that the transition period of moving between the old and new company premises would require lots of hard work and commitment on part of the employees, as the company had to juggle the requirement to fulfil all their orders to keep money coming into the business, while getting everything ready to move into the new premises. This meant that employees worked lots of overtime during this period. To reward their employees for their hard work during the transition period, the managers decided that they would receive a pay rise once they had moved into the new building, and that they would be paid the real Living Wage. The real Living Wage is a wage rate that is calculated to cover the cost of living. It is higher than the legal minimum wage and in the United Kingdom, for example, employers can choose to pay this rate voluntarily and receive accreditation for it. The managers felt this decision was aligned with their company values, as they believed that their staff was crucial to the company's success. They therefore felt they had to care about their staff's wellbeing. The company's HRM director emphatically stated that 'instead of giving directors big dividends we would rather re-invest that into the staff'.

The introduction of the Living Wage required the company to uplift the wages of about a third of their existing staff, but they also looked to maintain pay differentials, which was another addition to the wage bill. As part of the company's investment strategy, they had set aside money to meet their initial Living Wage commitment. However, in order to meet their Living Wage commitment in the long-term, they also decided to cut overtime rates to the normal hourly rate. This required management to engage in extensive consultations with their employees, as they were used to overtime and had come to rely on the additional income they amassed from it. This included presenting calculations to the workers that showed that their overall income (normal hours and overtime) on the new Living Wage rate was better than their income on the old wage rates, supplemented by the higher overtime rates. Management wanted to reduce overtime anyway as they felt that this was better for their employees' work-life balance. The reduction of overtime was only one part of a culture change that managers sought to implement as part of the transition. They also placed more emphasis on health and safety training, appointing a full-time health and safety officer and having a dedicated training room available in the new premises.

As a result of their change, the company experiences an extremely good retention record, and is renowned in the local area as a company that does look after people. The company also receives better quality applications for job vacancies and productivity has increased, too.

Source: Anonymized case study from the author's Living Wage project.

## ACTIVITY 9.4

1. What would you admire, and what would you critique, about the company's efforts to implement the Living Wage as part of organizational change?
2. What lessons can be drawn from this example that could help other organizations?

The need to (re-)consider organizational purpose and priorities has taken on a new urgency as societies have shifted their expectations, demanding ethical, socially and environmentally responsible behaviour from organizations. At its most basic, organizations should pursue their activities in a way that does not harm others. Should this not be the case, organizational change needs to focus on addressing these issues of misconduct and irresponsible behaviour. An instructive example here is BP. Following the Deepwater Horizon explosion in 2010, in which eleven people lost their lives and which led to severe environmental pollution in the Gulf of Mexico, BP instigated a range of change initiatives to improve their health and safety culture. They began by introducing an improved and independent Safety and Operating Risk function, before introducing a new performance management system, which explicitly linked safety and reward (BP, 2011).

## Global Challenges

Beyond this, however, organizations are increasingly expected to make a *positive*, proactive contribution to help address global challenges. The 2023 Edelman Global Trust Barometer (Edelman, 2023), conducted in twenty-eight countries, found that people around the world expect businesses to show more engagement in regards to challenges such as climate change and economic inequality.

An important reference point in this regard are the seventeen Sustainable Development Goals (SDGs), which were adopted by all United Nations member states in 2015 as part of the 2030 Agenda for Sustainable Development Goals, an agenda about 'people, planet and prosperity' (see InfoBox 1). Engaging with the SDGs as part of organizational change efforts – or indeed as the sole or main focus of organizational change initiatives – should move organizations to provide new and better value propositions, able to meet the challenges of our times. Case 3 provides an interesting example here, as the organization's drive to improve the financial position of its workers as part of its expansion strategy links to a range of SDGs: the promotion of inclusive economic growth

(SDG8), the reducing of inequalities (SDG10) and the eradication of poverty (SDG1). Similarly, many cold meat producers, such as the German company Rügenwalder Mühle (Vegconomist, 2022), have increasingly focused their development of new recipes on 'animal free' alternative meat products to help meet SDG12 (responsible consumption and production) and SDG15 (sustainable use of terrestrial ecosystems), whilst at the same time making their companies future-proof in a changing marketplace. In addition, a growing number of companies seek to meet SDG12 by improving the recyclability of their materials and packaging. A leading example is the UK's Co-op supermarket chain, which increased the recyclability of their own-brand packaging from 46 per cent to 78 per cent in five years. The Co-op are working towards specific actions/goals on plastics, which has so far led to changes in their packaging designs and new plastics recycling bins in their stores, as well as efforts to educate customers about good recycling practices (Co-op, n.d).

### INFO BOX: THE SUSTAINABLE DEVELOPMENT GOALS

Goal 1: End poverty in all its forms everywhere.
Goal 2: End hunger, achieve food security and improved nutrition and promote sustainable agriculture.
Goal 3: Ensure healthy lives and promote wellbeing for all at all ages.
Goal 4: Ensure inclusive and equitable quality education and promote lifelong learning opportunities for all.
Goal 5: Achieve gender equality and empower all women and girls.
Goal 6: Ensure availability and sustainable management of water and sanitation for all.
Goal 7: Ensure access to affordable, reliable, sustainable and modern energy for all.
Goal 8: Promote sustained, inclusive and sustainable economic growth, full and productive employment and decent work for all.
Goal 9: Build resilient infrastructure, promote inclusive and sustainable industrialization, and foster innovation.
Goal 10: Reduce inequality within and among countries.
Goal 11: Make cities and human settlements inclusive, safe, resilient and sustainable.
Goal 12: Ensure sustainable consumption and production patterns.
Goal 13: Take urgent action to combat climate change and its impacts.
Goal 14: Conserve and sustainably use the oceans, seas and marine resources for sustainable development.

Goal 15: Protect, restore and promote sustainable use of terrestrial ecosystems, sustainably manage forests, combat desertification and halt and reverse land degradation and halt biodiversity loss.

Goal 16: Promote peaceful and inclusive societies for sustainable development, provide access to justice for all and build effective, accountable and inclusive institutions at all levels.

Goal 17: Strengthen the means of implementation and revitalize the global partnership for sustainable development.

Source: https://sdgs.un.org/goals

### ACTIVITY 9.5

1. Which of the SDGs might be particularly relevant for (business) organizations, as they have the capabilities to help work towards these goals? You might want to look up more detailed descriptions of the goals online to inform your answer.

### ACTIVITY 9.6

1. Pick a change initiative with which you are familiar. How would you link one or several SDGs to that change initiative? Set out the opportunities and the barriers for incorporating the SDGs you have chosen into the organization as part of the change effort.

2. Pick an organization with which you are familiar. What SDGs ought they focus on and why? How can these SDGs be made a focus of a change initiative? What would the organization need to put in place to succeed with this?

Requiring organizations to make a positive contribution towards a more sustainable future will add to the complexity of any change efforts. This is because a multiplicity of goals, including any potential tensions between them, will need to be considered. Considerations regarding the short-term and long-term bottom line will need to be finely balanced against the achievement of social and ecological goals (Dunphy and Benn, 2013). Expectations regarding social and environmental performance are increasingly voiced by a range of 'new' external stakeholders – encompassing a diversity of actors from environmental NGOs to ESG investors (Benn, Dunphy and Griffiths, 2014: 186). This will require organizations to balance between being open with, and genuinely listening to, these stakeholders' voices on the one hand, and working out which sustainability efforts have the best fit with the internal purpose and mission of the organization on the other.

All sustainability initiatives will require organizations to make at least some initial investments, although many of these investments might result in win/win scenarios in the long-term (Dunphy and Benn, 2013). There will also need to be careful consideration as to what pace such initiatives should take. Benn, Dunphy and Griffiths (2014) compare and contrast an *incremental* sustainability change approach to a *transformational* one. They argue that incremental changes, which are changes that are planned, emergent, continuous and ongoing, and mainly have an impact on the organization's day-to-day operational processes, have a range of organizational benefits. They lead to the development of small wins (e.g. efficiency improvements), they allow for capability development (e.g. the introduction of new technologies and the upskilling of employees), and they might enable positive culture change, as it can modify values and build commitment through employee involvement and participation. At the same time, incremental changes might lack clear vision and could lead to regression and abandonment in addition to employee cynicism over the latest 'management fad'. The *transformational change approach*, by contrast, will embed sustainability change initiatives in a radical new vision of organizational purpose, creating a compelling new image of a desirable future organization. This will go hand in hand with very pronounced changes in organizational strategy and structure, making it less easy to abandon the new 'sustainability path', but also requiring a deeper, much more costly commitment in the short term. One organization that exemplifies the transformational approach is Interface Inc., which, following a radical re-visioning of the company by its CEO, changed from being a conventional carpet manufacturer to a company that offered a sustainability-focused carpet product-service system with the aim of becoming a carbon-negative company (Mainwaring, 2020).

Whatever path organizations choose, it is important that all efforts are *credible* to both its internal and external stakeholders. Stokes and Harrison (2012) point out that managers need to display consistent 'good character' and 'good behaviour', even in micro-interactions with their employees, in order to make any wider sustainability efforts credible. They argue that 'bad' character and behaviours have a propensity to engender ambivalent unsustainable and irresponsible environments, running counter to any sustainability efforts. In relation to external stakeholders in particular, organizations need to be careful not to overclaim on their sustainability achievements, engaging in 'greenwashing' or 'social washing'. It is much better to display *openness* and *transparency* – the virtues we identified earlier as being crucial for conducting change ethically. This includes *being honest* about the fact that sustainability is a journey (Dunphy and Benn, 2013), and that although some achievements may be celebrated, there should be open acknowledgement of the challenges organizations will face.

## Summary

In this chapter we have discussed the need for organizations to do organizational change ethically in order to achieve sustainable results. Taking a virtue ethics approach we have highlighted a range of virtues that organizations and their leaders ought to observe if they wish to see their change initiatives succeed. This includes honesty, transparency, openness (including giving organizational members and stakeholders a say in the direction and enactment of change), and fairness. This chapter also highlighted that the perceived need for organizational change invites deeper questions regarding organizational *purpose* and the ethical position the organization wishes to move to. This might be partially driven by changing societal expectations towards organizations, often voiced by civil society actors but also, increasingly, by institutional investors. This chapter suggests that, in order to meet these expectations, organizational change should be utilized to incorporate wider social and environmental goals, in particular those articulated by the UN SDGs. It provides some proposals as to how this might be achieved, highlighting in particular the need to be genuine and credible when engaging in sustainability-focused change action.

## Useful Resources

Corporate Ethics – YouTube channel featuring academic thought leaders in the field of business ethics about a range of ethics topics, https://www.youtube.com/@corporateethics/featured</URI> (accessed 21 April 2025).

Crane, A., Matten, D., Glozer, S. and Spence, L. (2019), *Business Ethics: Managing Corporate Citizenship and Sustainability in the Age of Globalization*, fifth edition. Oxford: Oxford University Press – an accessible and comprehensive introduction to the topic of Business Ethics.

Institute of Business Ethics – a non-profit professional organization, that encourages high standards of business behaviour based on ethical values, ibe.org.uk (accessed 21 April 2025).

Living Wage Foundation (UK) – a guide for employers setting out the business case for the real Living Wage and steps to be taken towards Living Wage accreditation, livingwage.org.uk (accessed 21 April 2025).

UN Sustainable Development Goals – the United Nation's call for action to promote to promote prosperity while protecting the planet, sdgs.un.org (accessed 21 April 2025).

## Bibliography

BP (2011), 'Sustainability Review 2010'. https://www.bp.com/content/dam/bp/business-sites/en/global/corporate/pdfs/sustainability/archive/archived-reports-and-translations/2010/bp_sustainability_review_2010.pdf (accessed 21 April 2025).

Benn, S., Dunphy, D., Griffiths, A. (2014), *Organizational Change for Corporate Sustainability*, third edition. London: Routledge.

By, R. and Burnes, B. (2013), 'Introduction: Ethical Change Leadership', in R. By and B. Burnes (eds), *Organizational Change, Leadership and Ethics* (pp. 1–5). London: Routledge.

Collier, J. (1995), 'The Virtuous Organization'. *Business Ethics: A European Review*, 4(3): 143–9.

Cobb, A. T., Folger, R. and Wooten, K. (1995), 'The Role Justice Plays in Organizational Change'. *Public Administration Quarterly*, 19(2): 135–51.

Co-op (n.d.), 'Packaging and Recycling'. https://www.coop.co.uk/environment/packaging-recycling (accessed 21 April 2025).

Crane, A., Matten, D., Glozer, S. and Spence, L. (2019), *Business Ethics: Managing Corporate Citizenship and Sustainability in the Age of Globalization*, fifth edition. Oxford: Oxford University Press.

Dunphy, D. and Benn, S. (2013), 'Leadership for Sustainable Futures', in R. By and B. Burnes (eds), *Organizational Change, Leadership and Ethics* (pp. 195–215). London: Routledge.

Edelman (2023), 'Edelman Trust Barometer – Global Report'. https://edl.mn/3X0QXQE (accessed 21 April 2025).

Freeman, R. E., Harrison, J. S., Wicks, A. C., Parmar, B. L. and De Colle, S. (2010), *Stakeholder Theory: The State of the Art*. Cambridge: Cambridge University Press.

Griseri, P. and Seppala, N. (2010), *Business Ethics and Corporate Social Responsibility*. London: Cengage Learning.

Hartman, E. (2017), 'Aristotle's Virtue Ethics and Virtuous Business', in A. J. G. Sison, G. R. Beabout and I. Ferrero (eds), *Handbook of Virtue Ethics in Business and Management* (pp. 3–13). Dordrecht: Springer.

Mainwaring, S. (2020), 'Purpose at Work: How Interface Transforms Sustainability to Rewrite Our Future'. Forbes. https://www.forbes.com/sites/simonmainwaring/2020/12/08/purpose-at-work-how-interface-transforms-sustainability-to-rewrite-our-future/?sh=56ddce8f2673 (accessed 21 April 2025).

Newton, R. (2013), 'Perceptions and Development of Ethical Change Leadership', in R. By and B. Burnes (eds), *Organizational Change, Leadership and* Ethics (pp. 35–54). London: Routledge.

Nielsen, W. R., Nykodym, N. and Brown, D. J. (1991), 'Ethics and Organizational Change'. *Asia Pacific Journal of Human Resources*, 29(1): 82–93.

Personnel Today (2022), 'Unions Call P&O Ferries Mass Sackings a "Scandalous Betrayal". 22 March. https://www.personneltoday.com/hr/po-ferries-sack-800-crew-with-no-notice (accessed 21 April 2025).

Stokes, P. and Harris, P. (2012), 'Micro-moments, Choice and Responsibility in Sustainable Organizational Change and Transformation: The Janus Dialectic'. *Journal of Organizational Change Management*, 25(4): 595–611.

Suchman, M. C. (1995), 'Managing Legitimacy: Strategic and Institutional Approaches'. *Academy of Management Review*, 20(3): 571–610.

Vegconomist (2022), 'Germany's Rügenwalder Mühle Sold More Meat-Free Than Meat Products in 2021', 2 May. https://vegconomist.com/company-news/facts-figures/germanys-rugenwalder-muhle-sold-more-meat-free-than-meat-products-in-2021 (accessed 21 April 2025).

Werhane, P. H. and Freeman, R. E. (1999), 'Business Ethics: The State of the Art'. *International Journal of Management Reviews*, 1(1): 1–16.

# Index

## A

Abu Dhabi police force 52
action learning 137
Adidas 73, 102
ADKAR model 112, 142, 145
Adobe 229, 230, 245, 246
Adrià, Ferran 120
adult development 118
Affective Events Theory (AET) 197–8, 210
Africa 47, 152
agility 40, 76, 128. *See also* groups and teams
Alibaba 63
Alpenresort Schwarz 52
Amazon 59
ambidextrous organization 67, 68, 72, 103, 104
Amway 96, 103
Apple 59, 73, 102, 270
Ardern, Jacinda 239, 240, 245, 246
Artificial intelligence (AI) 9, 25, 30, 57, 186
Asda 220
Australia 96
authenticity 44, 73, 84, 139, 224

## B

balanced scorecard 32, 33, 47, 54, 62, 100
Barrowford Primary School 5–6
BBC Worldwide 76
behavioural and brain sciences 120
Belbin, Meredith 125, 143
Big Five personality traits 113
Blue ocean strategy 160
BMW 52
board of directors 9, 74
Boulter, Louise 29, 39, 47, 48, 49, 53
brand 27, 72, 81, 82, 83, 84, 94, 95, 262, 286
Bridges transition model 199, 201, 202, 208, 257
British Airways (BA) 189, 190
British Petroleum (BP) 19, 20, 285, 290
Burke-Litwin model 62, 138
Burning platform 12, 20, 23
business model 59, 64, 71, 120, 147, 230, 251, 254
buy-in 93, 180, 221

## C

change
  classic change curve 111
  change curve 111, 200, 206
  content of change 4
  context of change 8
  cultural change 55, 93, 95, 96, 151, 156, 156, 157, 158, 175, 176, 254, 259, 261, 262, 270
  different levels of analysis, 1, 16, 18
  emotions and change 8, 106, 116, 119, 130, 134, 142, 161, 163, 196, 197, 198, 199, 203, 210, 220
  ethics and change 18, 47, 84, 96, 108, 135, 180, 215, 234, 243, 262, 271, 273, 274, 275, 276, 279, 282, 283, 289, 290
  external environment and change 7, 25, 56, 58, 59
  first-order 4, 5, 6, 21
  group/meso 2, 8, 11, 14, 15, 16, 17, 18, 20, 23, 29, 30, 34, 38, 47, 51, 61, 74, 76, 79, 85, 86, 87, 96, 102, 105, 106, 107, 109, 110, 111, 123, 124, 126, 127, 129, 130, 134, 135, 138, 139, 142, 146, 150, 151, 167, 169, 170, 180, 181, 182, 183, 184, 194, 195, 196, 197, 198, 199, 200, 218, 219, 221, 225, 226, 226, 228, 229, 236, 237, 239, 251, 259, 265
  human aspects 8, 9, 105, 106, 108, 131, 133, 138, 142
  HRM 18, 138, 147, 270, 284
  incremental change 5, 8, 19, 25, 26, 30, 53, 68, 71, 253, 269, 288
  individual/micro 1, 2, 7, 8, 14, 15, 16, 17, 18, 26, 29, 30, 32, 33, 34, 35, 36, 37, 38, 44, 46, 47, 51, 61, 85, 87, 105, 106, 109, 110, 111, 112, 113, 114, 115, 116, 120, 123, 124, 125, 131, 132, 133, 138, 139, 142, 151, 152, 160, 161, 162, 180, 181, 184, 188, 191, 194, 198, 199, 200, 201, 204, 208, 212, 213, 226, 228, 234, 257, 239, 248, 250, 253, 259, 265, 276
  intercultural management 149
  leadership 211, 12, 18, 29, 48, 50, 58, 63, 64, 68, 71, 87, 93, 97, 122, 125, 125, 129, 134, 167, 192, 211–46
  lean management 40, 41, 42, 53, 54
  measurement 25, 28, 31, 32, 39, 61, 147, 230, 244, 263, 264
  nature of change 1, 2, 4, 22, 55–103
  organizational/macro 2, 3, 8, 9, 10, 17, 18, 21, 25, 51, 79, 106, 180, 186, 188, 194, 218, 248, 253, 265, 273
  organizational culture 3, 12, 17, 18, 56, 58, 65, 83, 84, 85, 86, 86, 87, 89, 93, 94, 96, 100, 102, 107, 125, 166, 167, 196, 250, 264
  outcomes 3, 16, 33, 35, 36, 81, 112, 123, 124, 129, 133, 175, 180, 182, 191, 195, 30, 199, 213, 237, 274, 276, 280, 282
  power and politics 14, 179–210
  process of change 117, 127
  second-order 4, 6, 7, 8, 9, 12, 21, 56
  substantive change 16, 22, 26, 150, 167, 168, 190, 253, 264, 25
  transform 2, 6, 20, 56, 68, 108, 114, 211, 219, 220, 223, 241
  transformative 2, 9, 17, 18, 19, 53, 182, 269
  transition 7, 8, 11, 18, 22, 79, 80, 105, 111, 135, 136, 199, 199, 201, 202, 206, 208, 283, 284, 202
Chatbot 30, 31
China 152, 157
Ciba Vision 68
classic change curve 111
climate change 8, 63, 234, 240, 243, 285, 286
coaching 109, 112, 117, 118, 122, 136, 251, 259

# Index

COM-B system of behaviour change 121
communication 3, 11, 12, 13, 15, 29, 34, 76, 78, 87, 108, 122, 124, 136, 162, 164, 165, 167, 171, 176, 186, 199, 200, 212, 215, 240, 247, 259, 263, 264, 265, 266, 271, 276, 277, 282
Competing Values Framework (CVF) 81, 88, 89
competition 25, 60, 89, 141, 154, 189, 231, 256
consultants 79, 80, 107, 108, 112, 137, 249, 252, 267
continuous improvement activities 5, 26, 53
Co-op supermarket chain 286
coping 8, 111, 114, 115, 116, 117, 197, 216, 218, 246, 265, 271
counselling 43, 44, 45, 46, 117, 118, 257
covert dimensions of change 133
COVID-19 pandemic 82, 135, 140, 145 160, 175, 215, 237, 239, 243, 260, 278
Crisis 10, 15, 64, 69, 72, 118, 134, 214, 215, 222, 227, 232, 233, 237, 240, 243, 246, 280
critical success factors (CSFs) 32
culture. *See* intercultural management, culture, organizational culture
cybersecurity 254, 264

## D

daily hassles 115, 145
Dan Price 280
Death valley 111, 144
Deepwater Horizon 285
Deming, Edwards 29, 53
dialogue 75, 108, 138, 276, 279
DICE framework 80, 81
Disney 84, 95, 99
downsizing 71, 72, 73, 94, 100, 134, 135, 143
Drucker, Peter 57
due diligence 77, 82, 266

## E

eBay 229
Edelman Global Trust Barometer 285, 290
Elon Musk 280, 281
Emergent 9, 288
Emotional intelligence (EI) 130, 144, 148, 163, 179, 203, 204, 208, 209, 248, 250
emotions 8, 103, 106, 116, 119, 130, 134, 142, 161, 163, 196, 197, 197, 198, 199, 203, 204, 210, 230. *See* Affective Events Theory (AET)
empathy 13, 136, 164, 165, 203, 204, 251, 269
entrepreneurial 68, 81, 82, 120, 140
equality, diversity and inclusion (EDI) 134
equity 19, 51, 237, 276, 282
Ericsson 266
Erikson, Erik 118, 144
ethics 273–91
  Dan Price 280
  discourse 282
  Elon Musk 280
  ethical change process 276
  ethical lenses 274, 275, 276
  fairness 136, 275, 276, 281, 282, 283, 289
  global challenges 237, 285
  Good Foods 283
  honesty 216, 277, 279, 282, 289
  justice 160, 276, 281, 282, 287, 290
  lenses for organizational change 275
  openness 113, 139, 165, 216, 251, 277, 279, 282, 288, 289
  P&O Ferries 277–91
  purpose 283, 285, 287, 288, 289, 290
  Sustainable Development Goals 51, 237, 285, 286–7, 289
  virtue ethics 275
ethnicity 163, 275
European Values Studies (EVS) 158
evaluating change 117
evidence-based 109, 132
excellence models/frameworks 47, 51
  European Foundation for Quality Management (EFQM) 270, 48, 52, 54
  excellence frameworks for change 51
  fundamental concepts 29, 50
  joined-up approach for managing change 47
  RADAR 51, 52

## F

Facebook 129, 143, 144
Finland 266, 267
first-order change 4, 5, 6, 21
foresight 2, 3
founder 28, 73, 83, 112, 280
Frontier Airlines 30
frontline workers 106, 128
Fujifilm 63

## G

gender(s) 151, 154, 246, 286
generations 76, 150
glass cliff 235, 244
*Good to Great* (Jim Collins) 215
Good Foods 283
Google 85, 157
Gravity Payments 280, 281
Greenpeace 85
groups and teams
  agile teams 128
  high-performing teams 124, 144
  input-process-output (IPO) models 72, 125
  international teams 130
  large-group interaction methods 129
  limitations and challenges 105, 106, 131
  meso/group 2, 17, 18, 21, 22, 248, 265, 273
  role inventories 125
  team-building 129, 130
  team types 127, 145
  Tuckman's stages of development 126, 147

## H

Handy, Charles 85, 101
health care 43
Hershey 81, 82, 83, 100
HM Revenue and Customs (HMRC) 76
Hofstede, Geert 150, 151, 152, 153, 154, 155, 156, 157, 158, 167, 168, 174, 175, 176, 177, 270
holacracy 69, 101
human aspects of change 8, 9, 105–48
  good practice 199, 247
  organization development and soft systems 106, 137, 144, 247
Human Resources (HR). *See* Human Resource Management (HRM)
Human Resource Development (HRD) 138, 210
Human Resource Management (HRM) 138, 147, 270, 284
  business partnership 249
  change agent 11, 12, 247, 248, 249, 256, 260, 269
  competencies 250, 252
  role in categories of change project 253, 255, 256, 267, 269

## I

IBM 68, 72 101, 152
implementing strategic change 78, 79

# Index

inclusion 84, 97, 134, 167, 215, 237, 240, 250, 259
individual differences 105, 112, 113, 144
 adjusting to change 110, 114
 individual transition 8, 111, 208
inequality 153, 236, 285, 286
influence. *See* power
*In Search of Excellence* (Peters and Waterman) 83, 103
intercultural management 149–77
 cultural competence 149, 162, 163, 167
 cultural humility 166
 cultural intelligence (CQ) 150, 162, 166, 167, 174, 175
 cultural theories 167, 168
 Gelfand, Michele 159, 160, 175
 Hofstede's cultural dimensions 150, 151, 152, 153, 154, 155, 156, 157, 158, 167, 168, 174, 175, 176, 177, 270
 intercultural intelligence 164, impact on individual behaviour 160
 independent and interdependent 151, 152
 Inglehart's theory 156, 157, 174, 175, 176
 intercultural competence 163, 164
 language and worldview 162
 Lewis, Richard 161, 176
 national culture 149, 150, 151, 155, 157, 162, 166, 174, 175, 270
 socialization 150, 158, 161
 tight and loose 151, 158, 159, 160, 161, 175
International Computers Ltd (ICL) 266
iterative approach 16

## J

Johnson & Johnson 68
Jørgensen, Lars 230

## K

Kaplan and Norton, Robert and David 32, 33, 62
Key Performance Indicators (KPIs) 32, 62
Kindler, Jeff 239
King & Wood Mallesons 231
Klopp, Jürgen 239
Kodak 67, 223
Kotter, John 12, 23, 205, 206, 209, 216, 221, 243, 244, 253
Kübler-Ross, Elisabeth 8, 111, 145, 199, 200, 206, 209

## L

leadership 211–46
 bad leadership 234
 bottom-up forms 211, 227, 241, 242
 *cynefin* framework 227
 future of change leadership 236
 humble leadership 218, 219
 leading and managing change 216
 limits of change leadership 230
 responsible leadership 238, 239
 styles 213, 214, 215, 218, 220, 230, 240, 242
lean management 42, 40, 41, 42, 43, 53, 54
 process wastes 42,
 lean principles 41
Learning and development (L&D) 76, 122, 225, 258, 259
legitimacy 84, 290
LEGO 72, 73, 109
levels of analysis 1, 2, 16, 18, 159
Lewin, Kurt 107, 110, 111, 144
 field theory 23, 144, 257
 force field analysis 257
 life space 110
 National Training Laboratories (NTL) 107
 three-step approach 10
life events 114, 115, 145
living wage 283, 284, 285, 289

## M

McKinsey influence model 109
McKinsey 7-S framework 60, 62
Maslow, Abraham 156, 176
measurement 25, 28, 31, 32, 39, 61, 147, 230, 244, 263, 264
mental health 115, 198, 43, 44, 46
mergers and acquisitions (M&As) 56, 82, 98, 141
Microsoft 63, 229
middle managers 79, 80, 106, 228, 244
mindfulness 122, 164, 165
minority employees 96
modernization 156, 176
Musk, Elon 280, 281
multinational 72, 81, 96, 129, 135, 153, 156, 221, 225, 229
Myers-Briggs Type Indicator (MBTI) 113, 114, 144, 145

## N

Narayen, Shantanu 229, 230, 245, 246
National Health Service (NHS) 42, 43, 45,
Netflix 63
neuroscience 122, 123, 144
News UK 76
New Zealand 115, 146, 239, 240
Nike 73, 128
Nokia 64, 99, 135, 136, 147, 266, 267
Nortel 73
Nottingham Counselling Services (NCS) 43
Nottingham Forest Football Club (NFFC) 218, 219, 242, 243, 246
Novo Nordisk 230

## O

Ohno, Taiichi 42, 54
open systems perspective 25
operating model 59, 82
organization design (and redesign) 55, 64, 65, 66, 67, 68, 69, 70, 73, 76, 79, 98, 100, 101
organizational behaviour (OB) 107, 123, 145, 210, 244
organizational culture
 critical perspectives 94
 cultural end-states 94
 cultural web 89, 90
 culture surveys 87
 defining and classifying 83, 85, 89
 models/tools for diagnosing 85
 organizational climate 103
 subcultures 85, 92, 93
 strong or weak 84
 toxic 95, 96, 97, 103, 104, 180, 182, 188, 191, 192, 194, 262
 tribes 87, 128, 147 170, 172
 value statements 84
organizational development (OD) 9, 54, 107, 142, 249
 soft systems approaches to change 105, 106, 137, 144
organizational politics (OP) 179–210
 cost of dark side 192
 dark side 191, 192
 emotional intelligence 203, 204
 internal organizational politics 192
 Kubler-Ross change curve 200, 201
 negative emotions 196, 197, 198
 resistance 194, 195, 196, 199, 205, 206
 resistors 204, 205
 social skill 191, 193
 transformational change and organizational politics 191, 193
Orsted 63

outcomes 3, 16, 33, 35, 36, 81, 112, 124, 129, 133, 180, 182, 191, 195, 197, 199, 213, 237, 274, 276, 280, 282
ownership 9, 72, 230, 233, 268

## P

P&O Ferries 277, 278, 279, 291
Papua New Guinea (PNG) 168
paradoxes 134, 144, 231 232, 242, 245
Parker-Follett, Mary 186
participation 91, 206, 219, 239, 276, 288
people management. *See* Human Resource Management (HRM)
personality traits 112, 113, 114
personal transformation 119, 142
PESTEL/PESTLE analysis 255, 256, 59
Ping, Ho Kwon 230
planned change 9, 11, 15, 23, 133, 244
politics. *See* organizational politics
Porter, Michael 59
  five forces model 59, 101
Post-merger integration (PMI) 77
power 179–210
  bases 186, 187, 22
  British Airways (BA) 95, 101, 189, 190
  coercive power 183, 187, 188
  compliance theory 183, 185
  cooperation 41, 84, 85, 106, 116, 124, 126, 130
  definitions, approaches 180–3
  French and Raven, John and Bertram 182, 183, 187, 189
  influence 181, 182
  power of lower subordinates 189, 190
  power relationships 185
  sources of influence 187
Price, Dan 280
processes
  characteristics of 36, 37
  diagnostic tools 37–40
  different types 34–5
  importance of processes for change 33–4
  measuring processes to drive change 39–40
  process improvement 40–1
  process mapping 37, 38, 41
  process outcomes 35
  process wastes 42–3
  role of perception 35
  transformational change and processes 40–1
project teams 70, 79, 106, 127
psychology 64, 107, 108, 113, 116, 120, 123, 144, 145,

146, 148, 150, 155, 157, 162, 174, 175, 176, 177, 203, 209, 210, 243, 250
COM-B system of behaviour change 121
psychodynamic perspectives on change 117
Public sector 35, 43, 53, 71, 72, 115, 228,

## Q

quality
  quality as a strategic approach 26–8
  quality and getting ready for change 29–30
  total quality management (TQM) 54, 28, 29

## R

rebranding 71, 72, 73, 122
recruitment 78, 250, 258, 259
redundancies 78, 95, 257, 264
remote working 140, 141, 144, 145
reputation 43, 78, 96, 182, 190, 192, 193, 223
resistance to change 15, 167, 168, 180, 194, 195, 208, 209, 226
  Affective Events Theory (AET) 197, 198, 209
  Bridges, William 199, 201, 202, 208, 257
  classic change curve 111
  emotional intelligence 148, 179, 203, 204, 205, 208, 209, 248, 250
  Kubler-Ross change curve 200, 206, 211
  Kubler-Ross, Elizabeth 8, 23, 111, 145, 199, 200, 206, 209
  individual cognitive processes 199–202
  managing resistance effectively 199–203
  negative emotions 198, 203, 210
rhetoric 77, 95
Rio Tinto 96
Ritz London 37
role model 84, 109, 110, 112, 125, 143, 167, 204, 218, 221, 260
Rolls-Royce plc, 19–23

## S

Schein, Edgar 86, 89, 103, 271
schemas 131, 132
second-order change 4, 6, 7, 8, 9, 12, 21, 56
Seiko 68
self-awareness 113, 118, 162, 163, 165, 203, 215, 225

shareholders 62, 74, 212
Shigeo Shingo 41, 54
Shell 128
Siemens 63
simple rules 70, 101
Singapore International Airlines 230
social change 23, 87, 145, 229, 240
Social Readjustment Rating Scale (SRRS) 114, 145, 147
sociotechnical systems approaches 138
soft systems approaches 105, 106, 137, 144
Southwest Airlines 60
sponsors 79
Spotify 128
stage models of change 126, 221, 222
steering group 252, 253, 256, 257
storytelling 99, 118
strategic leadership
strategy 55–104
  behaviours and leadership 80, 81
  diagnostic tools 59
  DICE, a strategic implementation system
  implementing strategic change 78
  organization design and redesign 64
  top-down and bottom-up influences 74
  transformational strategic change 75
stress 114, 115, 116, 117, 143, 145, 146, 173, 197, 198, 271
strikes 95, 195
supply chain 29, 32, 50, 51, 64, 66, 73, 149
surveys 87, 96, 153, 158, 255, 256, 258
Sustainable Development Goals (SDGs) 51, 237, 285, 286, 289
Sweden 266, 267
SWOT analysis 59

## T

task and general environment 59
Tavistock Institute of Human Relations 107
teams. *See* groups and teams
Tencent 63
top-down and bottom-up influences 74
top management team (TMT) 56, 74, 267
total quality management (TQM) 54, 28, 29
Toyota Production System (TPS) 41, 54

trade union 195, 212, 278
transparency 3, 77, 79, 84, 96, 192, 199, 205, 224, 238, 277, 282, 288, 289
transformational change 40–1, 75 191, 193
transition 7, 8, 11, 18, 22, 79, 80, 105, 111, 135, 136, 199, 199, 201, 202, 206, 208, 283, 284, 202
Travelodge 37
triggers of change 8, 56, 57
Tulsa Remote work program 140
turnarounds 223

Twitter 280, 281
types of strategic transformation 71

## U

Ubuntu 152
UJET 30, 31
Ulrich, David 248, 249, 271
unintended consequences 64, 78, 102, 257
United Nations (UN) 51, 287

## V

Virgin 84
Vodafone 84

## W

Weber, Max 181, 210
Weiss and Cropanzano, Howard and Russell 197, 210
whistleblowing 97
Womack and Jones, James and Daniel 41
WorldCom 73
World Values Survey (WVS) 158, 174, 175

## Z

Zappos 69, 101
Zurich UK Life 76